The Innateness of Myth

Continuum Advances in Religious Studies
Series Editors: James Cox, Peggy Morgan

Conceptions of the Afterlife in Early Civilizations, Gregory Shushan
Contemporary Western Ethnography and the Definition of Religion, M. D. Stringer
A New Paradigm of Spirituality and Religion, MaryCatherine Burgess
The Appropriation of Native American Spirituality, Suzanne Owen
Religion and the Discourse on Modernity, Paul François-Tremlett
Theology and Religious Studies in Higher Education, D. L. Bird and Simon G. Smith

The Innateness of Myth

A New Interpretation of Joseph Campbell's Reception of C. G. Jung

Ritske Rensma

continuum

NEW YORK • LONDON

Continuum International Publishing Group
The Tower Building, 11 York Road, London SE1 7NX
80 Maiden Lane, Suite 704, New York NY 10038

www.continuumbooks.com

British Library Cataloguing-in-Publication Data
A catalogue record for this book is available from the British Library.

ISBN-10: HB: 1-4411-5112-5
ISBN-13: HB: 978-1-4411-5112-4

Library of Congress Cataloging-in-Publication Data
Rensma, Ritske. The innateness of myth : a new interpretation of Joseph Campbell's reception of C.G. Jung / Ritske Rensma.
p. cm.
Includes bibliographical references (p.).
ISBN 978-1-4411-5112-4
1. Campbell, Joseph, 1904-1987. 2. Myth. 3. Jung, C. G. (Carl Gustav), 1875-1961–Influence. 4. Jungian psychology–Religious aspects. I. Title.

BL303.6.C35R46 2009
200.92–dc22 2009010752

Typeset by Newgen Imaging Systems Pvt Ltd, Chennai, India
Printed and bound in Great Britain by

Contents

Abbreviations

Books by Jung

Collected works: *CW* followed by volume number.

Memories, dreams, reflections: *MDF*.

Wandlungen und symbole der libido: *Wandlungen*.

Books by Campbell

The flight of the wild gander: *Gander*.

The hero with a thousand faces: *Hero*.

The historical atlas of world mythology: *Atlas* followed by volume and part number.

The masks of God – primitive mythology: *Masks: primitive*.

The masks of God – oriental mythology: *Masks: oriental*.

The masks of God – occidental mythology: *Masks: occidental*.

The masks of God – creative mythology: *Masks: creative*.

Other

Robert Segal, *Joseph Campbell – an introduction*: *Introduction*.[1]

Anthony Stevens, *Archetype revisited – an updated natural history of the self*: *Archetype*.

Note

1 I refer throughout the book to the revised paperback edition: Robert A. Segal, *Joseph Campbell – an introduction* (New York: Penguin Books [Mentor imprint], 1990).

Preface

When Joseph Campbell died after a brief struggle with cancer in the autumn of 1987, *Newsweek magazine* wrote in his obituary:

> [Campbell] has become one of the rarest of intellectuals in American life: a serious thinker who has been embraced by the popular culture.[1]

There can be no doubt as to the truth of these words. Although in many ways a serious and often difficult thinker, Joseph Campbell's work has mostly found its audience outside the world of academia up until now. One of the most important reasons for this has probably been the series of interviews with Campbell that the American television channel PBS broadcasted under the name 'The power of myth'. The show – which consisted of six one-hour interviews with Campbell by TV journalist Bill Moyers – is one of PBS' most popular broadcasts to date. When the interviews were aired in 1988 each episode drew about 2.5 million viewers,[2] and a book based on the series[3] stayed on the *New York Times* best-seller list for over six months after it was published.[4] As Robert Walter, president of the Joseph Campbell Foundation, has put it: '[Campbell] was already on his ascendancy, but Moyers blew the lid off it.'[5]

Another factor that has been an important driving force behind the association of Campbell with popular culture is his surprisingly large influence on the world of Hollywood screenwriting. The most well-known example of this connection is his influence on George Lucas, the billionaire writer and director of the *Star Wars* films (which are often reported to be among the highest grossing films of all time). Ever since the first movie came out in 1977 Lucas has claimed in interviews that he used Campbell's *The hero with a thousand faces* to help structure the screenplays for the movies. When Campbell was awarded the 'Medal of Honor' for literature by the National Arts Club in New York in 1985, Lucas was one of the guests, and on this occasion he had the following to say about Campbell's work:

> [While working on the first Star Wars script] I went around in circles for a long time trying to come up with stories, and the script rambled

all over and I ended up with hundreds of pages. It was *The Hero with a Thousand Faces* that just took what was about 500 pages and said, Here is the story. Here's the end; here's the focus; here's the way it's all laid out. It was all right there and had been there for thousands and thousands of years, as Dr. Campbell pointed out. And I said, 'This is it.' . . . It's possible that if I had not run across him I would still be writing Star Wars today.[6]

Campbell's influence on movie making doesn't stop with Lucas, however. Other Hollywood 'insiders' who have acknowledged Campbell's influence are the director Stephen Spielberg (*E.T.*, *Schindler's list*), the screenwriter and director George Miller (*Babe, Mad Max*) and the script consultant Christopher Vogler (whose best-selling book *The writer's journey*[7] is based for a large part on the 'hero's journey' model from *The hero with a thousand faces*). Like Lucas, most of them have frequently mentioned Campbell's name in interviews, which has probably done just as much – if not more – to increase Campbell's popularity with a non-academic audience than the Moyers interviews have done.

While it is certainly true, then, that Campbell has been embraced by the popular culture, the academic community has never really caught on to the Joseph Campbell 'phenomenon'. This was already the case in 1987, when Robert Segal wrote the following in the first edition of his *Joseph Campbell – an introduction* (from hereon abbreviated as *Introduction*):

> [Joseph Campbell] is certainly the most famous and in some circles the most esteemed living writer on myth. Yet surprisingly little has been written about him. There have been no books and only a few articles.[8]

More than twenty years later, these words still ring true. Apart from Segal's book there remains no other book written solely about Campbell, and even though two collections of articles about his ideas have been published (*Paths to the power of myth*[9] and *Uses of comparative mythology*[10]), the total number of articles written with the sole purpose of analysing Campbell's key ideas or assessing his influence is still extremely limited. Yet there are many reasons why Campbell's work would make an excellent subject for academic research. Given his popularity, one of the most important reasons to justify studying his ideas is a sociological one: just why exactly are so many people drawn to his work? What kind of 'spiritual hunger' lies at the root of the 'Joseph Campbell phenomenon'? Bill Barry, who oversaw the publishing of the book *The power of myth* for the publishing house Doubleday, said the following about this topic right after the book crash-landed onto the *New York times* best-seller list in 1988:

> I was talking to Bill Moyers two weeks ago about the success [of *The power of myth*]. We agreed this book just spoke to a yearning of a spiritual nature on the part of a large number of Americans.[11]

Scholars interested in mapping contemporary trends relating to the search for 'spirituality' or the 'turn to the self', then, would surely find many relevant issues when studying Campbell's ideas and influence. But there are other reasons apart from sociological ones that make studying Campbell's ideas relevant. Campbell's ideas are not only interesting from a sociological perspective, but have had a profound theoretical impact as well. Some of his ideas, for example, have hugely influenced scholars working in what has become known as transpersonal psychology, the most well-known ones being Stanislav Grof (whom Campbell was friends with during the last decade or so of his life) and Ken Wilber. Although his influence outside the field of transpersonal psychology seems to have been smaller, he has certainly had an impact on thinkers in other fields as well. Several well-respected scholars within Religious Studies have written extensively about his work (the most important ones being Robert Segal, David Miller and William Doty), *The hero with a thousand faces* remains a favourite with scholars in Literature and Film Studies departments, and his ideas have even influenced thinkers working in the field of neurobiology (Andrew Newberg and Eugene D'Aquili[12]). Campbell's work, then, has influenced many scholars of significance, and for that reason alone research into his work is relevant.

On top of all this, a large number of primary sources related to his life and ideas exist, which to date go largely unexplored. These sources have been collected together by the Opus Archive and Research Centre.[13] They are known as the *Joseph Campbell collection*,[14] and are stored on the two campuses of the Pacifica Graduate Institute[15] in California. Among other things, the Joseph Campbell Collection includes all of the books Campbell owned, most of his personal documents, an overwhelming collection of audiotapes of lectures, as well as transcripts of almost every single interview with him (many of which are impossible to find elsewhere). Yet I'm aware of only a handful of scholars who have used this 'treasure trove' for serious academic research. Campbell's work, then, is a topic about which some truly innovative research can still be done, with most of the sources collected together in an easily accessible location (if one is willing to travel to California, that is, which may not be possible for all, but is by no means impossible).

It was for these reasons (to which personal interest may be added) that I began the research project which resulted in the writing of this book. Even though Campbell's popular influence would have made a fascinating subject as well, I decided in the end to keep my approach strictly theoretical, choosing as my topic a subject matter about which there is much confusion: the relationship between Campbell's ideas and those of Carl Gustav Jung. I will devote the next chapter to further clarifying the approach I have taken to studying this topic. For now, I would like to state that it is my strong conviction that having an understanding of Jung's influence on Campbell is not just interesting in its own right, but also represents a subject matter which is crucially important if one wants to grasp the *essence* of Campbell's ideas. In this book I will argue that Campbell's career can be divided into three phases, and that it was in the last of these phases that Campbell made Jung's ideas – particularly his concept of the archetype – part of the very backbone of his theoretical framework. With this model of the three phases of Campbell's career I am offering the reader a 'roadmap' which serves both to clarify how Campbell's core ideas changed over time, and what the exact nature is of the final theoretical position Campbell arrived at towards the end of his life. As such, my hope for this book is that it will not only find an audience among those with an interest in Jung's influence on Campbell, but also among those seeking to 'fine-tune' their understanding of Campbell's overall theory of myth and religion.

For their input and support, I would like to thank Prof. James Cox, Prof. Robert Segal, Dr Christian Lange, Dr Elise Collins-Shields (director of Opus Archive, which in collaboration with the Joseph Campbell Foundation gave me a travel grant which allowed me to visit the *Joseph Campbell collection* in 2006), Richard Buchen (librarian *extraordinaire* of the *Joseph Campbell collection*) and my wife, Mariëlle van Velzen-Rensma. I would also like to thank the following institutions for their financial aid:

Joseph Campbell Foundation (U.S.A.)
New College, University of Edinburgh (Scotland)
Prins Bernhard Culture Foundation (The Netherlands)
Nuffic Talent Scholarship (The Netherlands)
Radboud Foundation (The Netherlands)
Vrijvrouwe van Renswoude Foundation (The Netherlands)

Notes

[1] K. C. Cole, 'Master of the myth,' *Newsweek*, 14 November 1988 (Campbell Archive: box 113, folder A92).
[2] Ibid.
[3] Joseph Campbell, *The power of myth*, ed. Betty Sue Flowers (New York: Doubleday, 1988).
[4] Linda Moss, 'Myth to the money at doubleday,' *Crain's New York business*, 16 January 1989 (Campbell Archive: box 106, folder AA70).
[5] Ibid.
[6] Quoted in Joseph Campbell, *The hero's journey: Joseph Campbell on his life and work*, ed. Phil Cousineau (San Francisco/London: Harper & Row, 1990), p. 180.
[7] Christopher Vogler, *The writer's journey* (London: Pan Macmillan, 1999).
[8] Robert Segal, *Joseph Campbell – an introduction* (New York/London: Garland Publishing, 1987).
[9] D. C. Noel, ed., *Paths to the power of myth: Joseph Campbell and the study of religion* (New York: Crossroad, 1990).
[10] Kenneth L. Golden, ed., *Uses of comparative mythology: essays on the work of Joseph Campbell* (New York/London: Garland Publishing, 1992).
[11] Moss, 'Myth to the money at doubleday.'
[12] Andrew Newberg et al., *Why God won't go away: brain science and the biology of belief* (New York: Ballantine Books, 2001).
[13] http://www.opusarchives.org/
[14] http://www.online.pacifica.edu/cgl/Campbell
[15] http://www.pacifica.edu/index.html

Chapter 1

Points of departure

1.1 Jung's influence on Joseph Campbell

That there is a connection between the ideas of Jung and Joseph Campbell is something that has always been acknowledged in some form or other, both throughout Campbell's life and after his death. Most of the time that acknowledgement has taken the form of the perception that Campbell's ideas are not just influenced by Jung but are actually 'Jungian' in nature. Eric Sharpe, in his well-known and influential *Comparative religion – a history*, wrote the following about Jung's influence on Campbell:

> The American scholar Joseph Campbell (b.1907 [*sic* – 1904]) has for many years been the major representative among students of comparative religion of the heritage of Jung. His industry has been remarkable, and he has in fact attempted a total Jungian interpretation of world mythology.[1]

Another example is the *Macmillan encyclopaedia of religion* (edited by Mircea Eliade), which contains the following description of Campbell's work:

> Many excellent and widely acclaimed studies of religious myths have been created that utilize Jung's psychology. Of these, the best known are the works of Joseph Campbell, in particular *The hero with a thousand faces.*[2]

For some scholars the notion that Campbell's ideas are completely compatible with Jung's is so obvious that they combine the work of both men and treat it as a single approach to the study of myth and religion. John Tigue, for example, uses the ideas of Campbell and Jung interchangeably to interpret myths in his book *The transformation of consciousness in myth,*[3] without ever reflecting on the question as to whether this approach is actually justified. Other scholars who have taken this approach are Mary Henderson[4] and Stephen Rauch.[5]

Even though the perception that Campbell is a Jungian has certainly been held by scholars, as the above examples show, the perception that Campbell is a Jungian seems mostly to be held by non-academics. Especially on the internet the confident claim that Campbell is a Jungian is rife, and I have even come across websites which claim that Campbell personally studied under Jung (Jung and Campbell met only once, in 1954, and on that occasion appear to have done nothing more than exchange formalities[6]). A recent development I have also come across is for people to attribute some of Jung's ideas directly to Campbell, with no mention of Jung himself. Here, for example, is the actor Will Smith, talking about his personal philosophy about film-making:

> I think with movies I am really connecting to the Joseph Campbell idea of the collective unconscious. There are things that we all dream. There are things that each one of us has thought, that connect to life, death, and sex. There are things that are beyond language. To me, this is one of those concepts.[7]

Both scholars and non-scholars alike, then, readily assert that Campbell's ideas are Jungian in nature, most of them without offering reasons as to *why* this is the case. Very few people actually state the opposite: that Campbell was *not* a Jungian. In the scholarly world I have only come across two authors who hold this position: Robert Segal and David Miller, both Religious Studies scholars. That so few people put emphasis on the differences between Jung and Campbell is surprising, as at first glance it is far from obvious that Campbell's work is Jungian in nature. To be sure, there are a lot of similarities: both put far more emphasis on the similarities between myths than the differences; both focus on biological 'mechanisms' to explain these similarities; both see myth and religion as ultimately positive phenomena, which have the power to heal as well as transform the psyche. If one looks more closely, however, these similarities soon vanish into the background. Campbell, for example, relied heavily on the notion of the 'open innate releasing mechanism' (open IRM for short) to explain the similarities found in myths. This is a concept which he borrowed from the ethologists Niko Tinbergen and Konrad Lorenz, and which cannot be found in Jung's work at all. To further complicate matters, Campbell also frequently spoke about what he came to call 'the transcendent', a mystical ground of being that he believed was the ultimate reference point of all myths and rituals. At first glance, it may seem that such a metaphysical dimension cannot be found in Jung's theories either, which so heavily emphasize the psychological structures of the mind as the origins, as well as the ultimate reference point, of myth and religion.

Miller, however, does not really deal with these complexities at all. The only difference between Jung and Campbell that he acknowledges is one of attitude, not of theoretical disposition. In his article 'The flight of the wild gander: the post-modern meaning of "meaning"'[8] Miller argues that Campbell is not a Jungian because the latter had a different attitude to mysticism: rather than wanting to do away with the ego – which Miller claims is Campbell's position – Jung argued for strengthening the ego, which we need to hang on to in order to keep the unconscious in check. This approach on Miller's part seems to me to be a highly unsatisfactory one. This is not because I don't think that the difference between Jung and Campbell that he mentions doesn't exist – I do – but because he completely fails to look at any of the apparent differences that I mentioned above, all of which I consider to be of much more significance than the one he mentions.

Here I must give praise to Robert Segal, who offers a much more complete analysis of the differences between Jung and Campbell in his *Introduction*. In a very concise and lucid chapter titled 'Campbell as a Jungian' Segal does indeed reflect on what I believe are some of the most important areas where Campbell's work appears to be different from Jung's. The final conclusion that Segal draws in this chapter is that Campbell is not a Jungian: according to him, Campbell and Jung differ radically regarding their ideas about both the functions and origins of myth. As far as the origins of myth are concerned, Segal claims that Campbell and Jung are different because the latter wrote about psychological structures that are wholly innate (the concept of the archetype), whereas Campbell wrote about psychological structures that are open to 'imprinting' by the environment (the so-called open IRM mentioned above). As far as the functions of myth are concerned, Segal argues that Jung would have seen the four functions of mythology that Campbell often mentioned 'as a whole askew to his own'.[9] Although he frequently mentions Campbell's 'metaphysical' bent elsewhere in his book, Segal does not reflect on whether this is something that separates Jung from Campbell in his 'Campbell as a Jungian' chapter. Given what he has to say about this topic in other writings, however, I get the impression that he does see this as an important difference between Campbell and Jung. In a book review of John Tigues' above-mentioned *The transformation of consciousness in myth*, for example, he has this to say:

> The author takes for granted that Jung and Campbell espouse a common view of myth. . . . Tigue thereby presupposes the very 'integration' of Jung with Campbell that his book is supposed to forge. In fact, Jung and Campbell held contrary views of myth, and Campbell regarded himself as an original theorist rather than a disciple of Jung's. For example, Jung interprets myth almost wholly psychologically. By contrast, Campbell interprets myth metaphysically as well: myth refers to the universe as well as the unconscious.[10]

After having examined all the writings about the relationship between Jung's ideas and Campbell's that I am aware of, I have come to the conclusion that Segal's *Introduction* is the only work that does a satisfactory amount of justice to this important topic (even though I do not agree with most of his conclusions, about which more below). For this reason I will be referring to his book throughout this book (for which end I have made use of the second, revised edition from 1990[11]). The reader may think of this book as a kind of 'companion' volume to Segal's book, as it has very much been written in dialogue with the ideas which are propagated in it.

If we examine the reasons for separating Jung from Campbell that Segal offers, it may seem at first glance that these are indeed valid. Campbell does appear to go down a decidedly different road than Jung with his 'open IRM', and his four functions aren't necessarily Jungian through-and-through either (a topic which I will deal with in depth in Chapter 6). Finally, Segal's assertion that '[in contrast to Jung], Campbell interprets myth metaphysically as well'[12] may seem to hold water too. In this book, however, I will be contradicting Segal's conclusions in several ways. As I will be arguing, Campbell's ideas underwent what I am calling a 'Jungian turn' around 1968. After this date Campbell suddenly became highly positive about Jung, and consistently started to associate him with all of his own key ideas; before this date, however, he was often vague and sometimes even dismissive about Jung. Take for example the following quote, from the first volume of the *Masks of God* series (*Primitive mythology*, 1959), in which Campbell stresses that Jung's theories are not a viable approach to explaining the origins of myth.

> Therefore, though respecting the possibility . . . of such a psychologically inspired parallel development of mythological imagery as that suggested by . . . C. G. Jung's theory of the collective unconscious, we cannot [in

this book] attempt to interpret in such terms any of the remarkable correspondences that will everywhere confront us.[13]

Compare this passage with the following one, taken from an interview from 1971:

Interviewer: In other words, a journey into the unconscious is now necessary to find the meanings and comforts that myths once gave us?

Campbell: Yes. After all, the myths originally came out of the individual's own dream consciousness. *Within each person there is what Jung called a collective unconscious* [my italics]. We are not only individuals with our unconscious intentions related to a specific social environment. We are also representatives of the species homo sapiens. And that universality is in us whether we know it or not. We penetrate to this level by getting in touch with dreams, fantasies and traditional myths; by using active imagination.[14]

If we compare these two quotes it becomes immediately obvious that a change has taken place. Whereas Campbell dismisses Jung's approach in the first quote, he suddenly says that he thinks the collective unconscious exists in the second quote, even claiming that it is the source out of which the myths once arose. In Chapter 6 I will offer many more passages from interviews, books and lectures in which Campbell makes similar highly positive comments about Jung. After having examined a great deal of sources, I have established that all of these comments were uttered after 1968; I have come across none from before this date. The reason that this shift in Campbell's attitude to Jung took place around this time, as I will be arguing, is the fact that Campbell's *interpretation* of Jung also changed in 1968. As I will show in Chapters 3 and 6, an interpretation of Jung is possible which, in contrast to Segal's interpretation of Jung, does lead to the conclusion that Campbell's most important ideas are highly similar to Jung's.

It is this interpretation of Jung that I believe Campbell came to adopt in the final phase of his career, and which led him to suddenly become so positive about Jung after 1968. This, in a nutshell, is the position that I am defending in this book. I will now give a brief overview of its structure in the next section.

1.2 Overview of book structure

I have divided this book into two sections. The first section is devoted to analysing Jung's ideas (with a special focus on the concept of the archetype);

the second section is devoted to analysing Campbell's reception of Jung. I will give a short summary of both of these parts.

Part one: Jung

As the concept of the archetype is what Campbell's reception of Jung revolves around, it is this aspect of Jung's theoretical framework that I will be focusing on in this part of the book. I will begin by giving an overview of the *development* of Jung's ideas about archetypes (Chapter 2). Sketching this development is important, as Jung frequently readjusted his ideas and rewrote the key texts which deal with the concept of the archetype incessantly, sometimes up to six or seven times. If one wants to use Jung's concept of the archetype for a certain end (in our case, a comparison with the ideas of Campbell), a question which will therefore inevitably come up is this: '*Which* Jung are you talking about?' What Jung wrote about archetypes in the period right after the breakup with Freud isn't necessarily the same as what he had to say towards the end of his life, and for this reason it is highly important that we establish exactly which changes took place in Jung's thinking as his career progressed. This, then, is what I will be doing in Chapter 2. Just mapping these changes, however, is not enough to make interpreting Jung's work a completely straightforward endeavour. Having an understanding of the development of Jung's ideas is certainly important to understand why there is conflict between statements made in texts from different time periods; what makes interpreting Jung's work problematic even *after* one has mapped the changes of mind he went through, however, is that there is also a high degree of ambiguity within the key texts themselves. When one writes about Jung, therefore, a second question that will inevitably come up is this: '*Whose* Jung are you talking about?' Two scholars who have both invested an equal amount of time in reading Jung's work might still arrive at two different, incommensurable conclusions about what he meant. In Chapter 3 I will therefore give an overview of the interpretation that I am using in this book: that of the scholar Anthony Stevens. As I mentioned above, an interpretation of Jung is possible which, when compared with the ideas of Campbell, does lead to the conclusion that Campbell's ideas can be thought of as highly similar to Jung's ideas (as opposed to Segal's interpretation of Jung, which leads to the exact opposite conclusion). As will become obvious in Part two of the book, Stevens' interpretation of Jung is exactly such an interpretation.

Part two: Campbell

The key point I will be making in this part of the book is that Campbell's reception of Jung changed significantly over time. A close analysis of the most important changes has led me to divide his career in three phases. As these three phases form the backbone of the structure of this part of the book, I will give a short overview of them here.

Phase one: 1943–1959

In this phase of his career Freud and Jung were both of equal importance to Campbell, and his theoretical position is an amalgamation of both Jungian and Freudian ideas. This phase contains all of Campbell's early works, and ends with the publication of the first volume of the *Masks of God* series, which marked a change of direction for Campbell. The most important work written in this phase is *The hero with a thousand faces* (from hereon abbreviated as *Hero*).

Phase two: 1959–1968

In this phase Campbell dismissed Jung's concept of the archetype as irreconcilable with his own ideas. The most important works written during this phase are the first three volumes in the *Masks of God* series. This phase ends with the publication of *Creative mythology* (volume 4 in the series, published in 1968), in which Campbell suddenly claims that his ideas and Jung's concept of the archetype are compatible after all. It is with the publication of this book that the 'Jungian turn' that I have identified above begins.

Phase three: 1968–1988

From 1968 onwards Campbell became highly positive about Jung. He also arrived at an interpretation of Jung which is different from the one he had in phase two, and which is almost completely identical to Anthony Stevens' interpretation of Jung. In this phase (which, as I will argue, lasts until his death in 1988) Campbell consistently associated Jung with all of his key ideas.

After first giving a brief overview of the most important events in Campbell's life in Chapter 4, I will deal with the ideas of phases one and two in Chapter 5. Because of the fact that phase three is the most important phase as far as the arguments I am making in this book are concerned,

I will devote an entire chapter to it (Chapter 6). In this chapter I will also make some suggestions as to what may have caused this change in Campbell's thinking about Jung. One of the most important suggestions I will make is the fact that Campbell edited *The portable Jung*, which was published in 1971. It seems highly likely to me that this was a big job, and that Campbell would therefore have been actively re-reading Jung's key texts around 1968 in order to prepare. This process of refamiliarizing himself with Jung's work may have been one of the factors which led him to change his interpretation of Jung, although I will also suggest some other factors which may have been involved as well.

Conclusion: Chapter 7

In this chapter I will further clarify the most important arguments I am making in this book. They can be summarized as follows:

1. *Campbell's attitude to Jung became highly positive around 1968.*
2. *Campbell's interpretation of Jung changed around 1968.*

This new interpretation of Jung (which is virtually identical to Anthony Stevens' interpretation of Jung) led Campbell to conclude that his own ideas were much more compatible with Jung than he had previously thought, thus altering his evaluation of Jung's significance.

3. *Campbell's theoretical framework from 1968 onwards is the same as Anthony Stevens' interpretation of Jung.*

If one compares Stevens' interpretation of Jung with Campbell's theoretical framework in this final phase of his career, it becomes obvious that Campbell's most important ideas can be thought of as highly similar to Jung. When using Stevens' work as a lens to study Campbell's ideas the logical conclusion is indeed that the very backbone of Campbell's theoretical framework in phase three can be seen as Jungian in nature. Campbell himself was aware of this, despite often denying that he was a Jungian.

I would like to make it clear that I am not arguing that Campbell's work is Jungian on every single count. I am not so naïve as to claim that there are *no* differences between Jung and Campbell. There certainly are differences, and I am well aware of them (I will give an overview of some of the most important ones in Chapter 7 as well). Because of the reasons outlined above, however, the continuity between Campbell's work and Jung's work is much greater than is immediately obvious. I am therefore arguing at the end of Chapter 7 that we should think of Campbell's work not as Jungian but as post-Jungian, which is the Jung scholar Andrew Samuel's term for a thinker who does not agree with Jung about every single issue but whose ideas are still firmly rooted in Jung's core ideas. At the end of Chapter 7 I will also offer some suggestions as to how my conclusions may be useful for other scholars.

1.3 Methodological reflection

I will now offer a short reflection on the following methodological issues:

- The sources I have used
- The audience which my work is aimed at
- The terminology I have used.

Sources

As this book is first and foremost theoretical in nature, books and articles – not fieldwork – will be its primary sources. Needless to say, I will make heavy use of Campbell's published body of work, which amounts to roughly 20 books. Of these books, 11 books deal with a single, homogeneous topic;[15] the other books are either collections of essays, collections of lectures, or transcriptions of interviews. I would like to stress again that few secondary sources exist; Robert Segal's *Introduction* is the only book I have come across that deals solely with Campbell's ideas, and the number of articles about Campbell is limited as well. For reasons clarified above I will refer primarily to Segal's work throughout this book, although I will make mention of some articles by other scholars as this becomes relevant in the discussion.

Although I will draw primarily on sources that are widely available, I have also made use of material that can only be found in the afore-mentioned *Joseph Campbell collection*, managed by Opus Archive and Research Centre and stored on the campuses of the Pacifica Graduate Institute. Truth be told, Opus really is in charge of two collections, not one. First there is the Campbell Library [my term], which consists of all the books Campbell owned at the end of his life (many of which are heavily underlined and contain marginal notes). This collection is based on Pacifica's Lambert campus (which falls under the Santa Barbara area code). Then there is also the Campbell Archive [my term], which consists of – among other things – Campbell's lecture notes, many unpublished or hard to find interviews, his letters, as well as an overwhelming amount of audiotapes. This collection is based on Pacifica's Ladera campus (which falls under the Carpinteria area code). Although Pacifica refers to both of them as The *Joseph Campbell collection*,[16] I have chosen to refer to them from hereon as the Campbell Archive and Library, which means it is easier to refer to a specific collection (i.e. just the archive or just the library) without causing undue confusion. I had the good fortune of obtaining a grant (funded by the Joseph Campbell Foundation, in collaboration with Opus) to undertake research in both collections in the spring of 2007. This has proven to be an invaluable aid to the writing of this book. Especially the many, many interviews that can be found in the Campbell Archive were of tremendous use, as many of them contained passages in which Campbell reveals things about his thoughts on Jung's theories that cannot be found in any of the published interviews. When I am referring to a source found in the Campbell Archive that is hard to find elsewhere (or impossible to find, as is sometimes the case) I will always make specific mention of both the box and folder number in which it can be found in the Campbell Archive. I realize that not many of my readers will have the willingness or ability to travel to Pacifica to check these sources, but I mention them anyway for consistency's sake. I will also refer frequently to books found in the Campbell Library, but will use no specific reference system here: it will be obvious from the context in which they are mentioned that a volume from the Campbell Library is concerned.

As far as my evaluation of Jung's ideas in Part one of the book is concerned, I am aiming for a much less 'all-encompassing' approach than I am in the part which deals with Campbell. Because Jung wrote so much, I have chosen a selection of texts on which to base my overview of the development of his ideas (Chapter 2). For reasons clarified above, I have also decided to focus on a single concept: the concept of the archetype. Finally, for reasons also mentioned above, I have chosen to focus on a single interpreter of Jung's work: Anthony Stevens (Chapter 3). I would like to make it clear that in this part of the book my goal is not to put forward an interpretation of Jung which is 'right'. I do not think that Stevens' work represents the be-all and end-all of Jungian scholarship; I am merely focusing on his work because of the similarities his interpretation of Jung has to the one that Campbell arrived at in phase three of his career.

Audience

I have made certain presumptions about the background knowledge that my reader will have. First of all, I am assuming that the reader will have some prior knowledge about Jung's main theories. I did not think it necessary to start with the usual summary of all of Jung's core ideas; instead, I have chosen to give an in-depth analysis of the development of one of Jung's core ideas, followed by an overview of one scholars' individual interpretation of this idea. I expect that someone with little or no background knowledge of Jung's ideas will still be able to read both chapters and understand them; however, I do suggest that such a reader makes an effort beforehand to read up on Jung's most important findings. Many excellent summaries of Jung's work exist, but to ensure consistency with the interpretation used in this book it is perhaps a good idea to start with Anthony Stevens' *Jung – a very short introduction*.[17] As far as Campbell's work is concerned, I have made far less assumptions about the reader's prior knowledge. Because his core ideas aren't as well known as Jung's, I have decided to include much more background information (including a chapter with biographical information). That said, I am nevertheless presuming that the reader will have some idea of who Campbell is and what kind of ideas he defended, if only because I do not think it is very likely that anyone would read a book that attempts to clarify his core ideas without at least a passing interest.

Terminology used in this book

In this book I will frequently speak of the three 'phases' of Campbell's career. I would like to make it clear that I am not implying that *all* of Campbell's ideas remained fixed within each phase: the phases, as I have identified them, relate only to Campbell's reception of Jung, and it is my opinion that his attitude to (and interpretation of) Jung remained constant in each of these three phases. This may not necessarily be the case, however, for his other ideas. Although I consider it likely that Campbell changed his mind about a host of other topics that are not related to Jung's ideas at all, the current book does not attempt to map such changes. It is concerned solely with shedding light on Campbell's reception of Jung, and it is my conviction that my model of the three phases adequately represents the changes he made in this regard. Needless to say, one of the most important issues that needs to be dealt with when one attempts divide a thinker's career into separate phases is the question of where to draw the dividing lines between the phases. Where does one phase begin and the other end? This is a topic that I will deal with for each of the phases separately, and which I will reflect upon in the introductions to the respective sections dedicated to them.

Campbell made no clear-cut separation between mythology and religion. 'Myth is other people's religion' is what he jokingly used to say, and that – for him – was the end of the matter. In this book I have decided to follow Campbell's usage of these two terms, which means that I will use the terms mythology, myth and religion relatively interchangeably. I have also decided to follow Campbell's lead as far as the connotation of these three terms is concerned. As such, I am taking the same approach as Robert Segal, who writes in the opening chapter to his *Introduction*: 'Throughout the book I use Campbell's own, exceedingly broad definition of myth, which includes rituals and beliefs as well as stories of all kinds.'[18]

1.4 My hopes for this book

My first hope for this book is that it will help people with a general interest in Campbell's work to understand his core ideas better. Campbell's books deal mostly with the myths themselves, not with the putting forward a theory of myth, and for that reason one has to 'read between the lines' to a large extent if one wants to understand the exact nature of his theoretical framework. Add to this the fact that Campbell changed his mind about certain important issues as time went on, and it becomes clear why so many people find it hard to pinpoint exactly what he was trying to say (the discussion forums hosted by the Joseph Campbell Foundation at www.jcf.org bear witness to this). Although Segal's *Introduction* is certainly a good place to start for those wanting a clear picture of the exact nature of Campbell's theoretical framework, I believe that my book could also be used for such a purpose. Understanding Campbell's reception of Jung is essential if one wants to understand the exact nature of his theoretical framework, as Campbell made Jung part of the very backbone of his theoretical framework in the final phase of his career. Failing to see the exact relationship between Jung's ideas and Campbell's, therefore, means that it is impossible to fully assess the status and nature of this framework.

My second hope for this book is that it will find an audience among readers with an interest in psychological approaches to the study of religions.

Both Jung and Campbell propagated ideas related to this field that are only now being taken seriously by the academic community. The fact that the mind bears the imprints of humankind's evolutionary history, for example (as both Jung and Campbell held), is now commonplace among scholars working in fields like evolutionary psychology and neurobiology. In Religious Studies, a cognitive approach to the study of religions is drawing much interest; here, too, the idea that the mind is not a 'blank slate' but a complex and highly structured mental mechanism with a clear evolutionary history is becoming commonplace. Even though Jung and Campbell advocated highly similar ideas many years before they became the current norm, their contributions have been largely overlooked. Now that the 'blank slate' model is rapidly losing ground I believe that it is only fair that we recognize that Jung and Campbell were important pioneers in this field, and do not deserve to be the outcasts which they are at the present moment. If my book can contribute to correcting this imbalance then it will, to my mind, have been a success.

Notes

1 E. J. Sharpe, *Comparative religion: a history* (London: Duckworth, 1975), p. 212.
2 Peter Homans, 'C.G. Jung', in *The encyclopaedia of religion*, ed. Mircea Eliade (editor-in-chief) (New York: Macmillan, 1987).
3 John W. Tigue, *The transformation of consciousness in myth: integrating the thought of Jung and Campbell*, The reshaping of psychoanalysis series, vol. 4. (New York: Peter Lang, 1994).
4 Mary Henderson, *Star wars: the magic of myth* (New York: Bantam, 1997).
5 Stephen Rauch, *Neil Gaiman's the Sandman and Joseph Campbell: in search of the modern myth* (Holicong: Wildside Press, 2003).
6 Joseph Campbell, *The hero's journey: Joseph Campbell on his life and work*, ed. Phil Cousineau (San Francisco/London: Harper & Row, 1990), p. 47.
7 Will Smith, *Press conference about the movie I am Legend* [online] (2007, accessed 12 June 2008); available from http://tinyurl.com/594gg2
8 D. C. Noel, ed., *Paths to the power of myth: Joseph Campbell and the study of religion* (New York: Crossroad, 1990), pp. 108–117.
9 Robert Segal, *Introduction*, p. 259.
10 Robert Segal, 'Book review: "The transformation of consciousness in myth" by John W. Tigue', *Zygon* 32.3 (1997), pp. 436–437.
11 Robert Segal, *Joseph Campbell – an introduction.* (New York: Penguin Books, 1990).
12 Segal, 'Book review', pp. 436–437.
13 Joseph Campbell, *Masks: primitive*, p. 48.
14 Sam Keen, 'Man and myth: a conversation with Joseph Campbell', *Psychology today*, July 1971 (Campbell Archive: box 107, folder I11), p. 35.

[15] *Hero*, the four volumes of the *Masks of God* series, *The mythic image*, and the five volumes of the *Historical atlas of world mythology* series.

[16] http://www.online.pacifica.edu/cgl/Campbell

[17] Anthony Stevens, *Jung – a very short introduction* (Oxford: Oxford University Press, 2001).

[18] Segal, *Introduction*, p. 11.

Part One

Jung

Chapter 2

The development of Jung's ideas

In 1909 Jung and Freud embarked on a trip to the United States together after having accepted an invitation to lecture at Clark University. Jung, although he was by that time already quite a successful figure in his own right (he had published a short book about his word-association experiments, which had been well-received), still felt himself very much to be standing in Freud's shadow. As Jung put it himself in an interview long after the split from Freud had taken place:

> He was an old man, and he was way ahead of me. And so I settled down to learn something first.[1]

Their trip to the United States lasted a total of seven weeks. The two men were together almost all the time, spending much time analysing each other's dreams. Much of what happened later – the end of their friendship, and Jung's founding of what he would call 'analytical psychology' (to distinguish it from Freud's term 'psychoanalysis') was already foreshadowed in the way the two men responded to each other's dreams. Freud, Jung tells us in his semi-autobiography[2] *Memories, dreams, reflections* (from now on abbreviated as *MDF*), had a dream that was obviously related to personal details Freud hadn't told Jung about. When Jung pressed his older mentor to give him more details, the latter responded by saying: 'But I cannot risk my authority!'[3] Jung was highly disappointed by this reaction:

> That sentence burned itself into my memory. . . . Freud was placing personal authority above truth.[4]

Jung, too, had dreams that proved difficult to interpret for Freud, if for completely different reasons. The most important one of these dreams has become quite famous, as Jung came to see it as the first inkling that led him to develop his theory of the collective unconscious. In the dream Jung found himself in a house with two storeys. He was on the second floor, which was 'a kind of salon furnished with fine old pieces in rococo style'.[5] Jung descended, and discovered that everything on the first floor was much older than on the second floor: it looked as if it belonged in the fifteenth or sixteenth century. Jung explored the house further, and came upon a heavy door, which he opened. Behind it he discovered a stone stairway. He went down the stairway, and after some time arrived in a room that had been completely furnished as if it belonged in Roman times. One of the stone slabs on the floor had a ring in it. Jung pulled it and went through the hole in the floor it had covered. He then arrived in a cave that looked like it belonged in prehistory. There were two skulls on the floor, which looked incredibly old and were severely disintegrated. At that moment the dream ended.

Freud, as Jung reports in *MDF*, had significant trouble interpreting the dream. He focused primarily on the two skulls at the end of the dream, and wanted to know with whom Jung associated these skulls. Jung continues:

> I knew perfectly well, of course, what he was driving at: that secret death-wishes were concealed in the dream. 'But what does he really expect of me?' I thought to myself. Toward whom would I have death-wishes? I felt violent resistance to any such interpretation. I also had some intimation of what the dream might really mean. But I did not then trust my own judgment, and wanted to hear Freud's opinion. I wanted to learn from him. Therefore I submitted to his intention and said, 'My wife and my sister-in-law' – after all I had to name someone whose death was worth the wishing![6]

Even though Jung did not protest against Freud's interpretation of the dream, he was deeply dissatisfied with what he saw as a rather narrow-minded approach to dream analysis on Freud's part. He spent a long time pondering the dream on his own, and eventually arrived at an interpretation very different from Freud's: he saw the house in the dream – which had so many levels, all of them belonging to different phases of history – as a kind of image of the psyche. Again, from *MDF*:

> Consciousness was represented by the salon. It had an inhabited atmosphere, in spite of its antiquated style. The ground floor stood for the first level of the unconscious. The deeper I went, the more alien and the darker the scene became. In the cave, I discovered remains of a primitive culture, that is, the world of the primitive man within myself – a world which can scarcely be reached or illuminated by consciousness. The primitive psyche of man borders on the life of the animal soul, just

as the caves of prehistoric times were usually inhabited by animals before men laid claim to them.[7]

The lower realms in this description correspond, of course, to what Jung would later call the collective unconscious. All the key themes which Jung would come to associate with this theory can be found in Jung's interpretation of the dream: the idea that the residues of humankind's evolutionary history are ingrained in our psyche ('the world of primitive man within myself'); the idea that these 'archaic' levels of the unconscious should be distinguished from repressed personal memories (which is made apparent by Jung's refusal to associate the skulls to anything in his personal life); the idea that these levels of the psyche are related to instincts and are comparable to animal behaviour ('the primitive psyche of man borders on the animal soul'). Jung, therefore, had as early as 1909 the first intimation of what would become the most important aspect of his theoretical framework: the collective unconscious. According to Anthony Stevens, this view of the psyche put Jung at odds with almost every one else writing about similar topics, not only at that point history but with nearly everyone in the entire twentieth century:

Apart from Jung, nearly all other twentieth-century psychologists and psychoanalysts, as well as sociologists and anthropologists, focused on the myriad ways that individuals differed from one another and attempted to account for these differences in terms of the cultural and social influences they had been subjected to in the course of growing up. In opposition to this view, Jung held that a truly scientific psychology must start from what human beings had in common before the study of individual differences could proceed with any hope of reaching meaningful or valid conclusions.[8]

It should come as no surprise, then, that the book that was the end-result of the ideas Jung developed after he had had his dream about the house with the many storeys (*Wandlungen und symbole der libido*, translated as *Psychology of the unconscious*[9]) – didn't win him many friends. The second part of the book (published in 1912; the first part was published in 1911) cost him his friendship with Freud, and as Jung writes in *MDF*, it also cost him a lot of other friendships:

After the break with Freud, all my friends and acquaintances dropped away. My book was declared to be rubbish; I was a mystic, and that settled the matter.[10]

What I feel is the most important lesson we can learn from the process described above – Jung's dream, and the subsequent split from Freud – is that it illustrates quite clearly what I already pointed out in the introduction to this book: that Jung's ideas changed significantly over time. Jung, throughout his career, always remained highly critical of his own theories, and never stopped fine-tuning and sometimes significantly altering them. At the time he had the dream about the house with the many storeys he had already developed a host of ideas about the nature of the psyche; nevertheless, he was willing to throw a lot of those ideas out of the window on the basis of the intuitions which he began to develop as a result of it. This development of his ideas, however, didn't stop after he had written those intuitions down in *Psychology of the unconscious.* In a way, it was just beginning. According to Peter Homans, Jung had already gone through four distinct phases in his development as early as 1918.[11] In my opinion, the most important alteration Jung made to his ideas (the distinction between the archetype-as-such and the 'archetypal image', which plays an important role in this chapter and the next one) was only developed by him as late as 1946. Analysing Jung's ideas non-chronologically, then, is a luxury one cannot allow oneself when studying Jung. According to Peter Homans, however, much of the secondary literature about Jung does fall victim to this mistake:

> [Most of the secondary literature about Jung] assumes – and communicates to readers – that his thought is a static array of isolated ideas about the origins and nature of the psyche.[12]

For this reason, a chronological approach to the study of Jung's ideas such as the one Homans advocates is exactly what I will take in this chapter. In it, I will be laying the foundations for the chapters to come by giving an overview of the way Jung's ideas developed over time. Only after this development has been sketched will I be able to deal with the question as to how these ideas should be interpreted in the next chapter (Chapter 3, in which I will focus specifically on Anthony Stevens' interpretation of Jung). In these two chapters I will focus primarily on the image of the psyche Jung saw validated in his dream of 1909: the theory of the collective unconscious, and the concept of the archetype which lies at the root of it. The idea that there is a phylogenetic layer in the psyche of man which consists of archetypes is perhaps what Jung is most well known for. As Anthony Stevens claims, this idea should be seen as the theoretical 'essence' of Jung's body of work:

> The archetype . . . is thus Jung's basic concept, in that its significance for analytical psychology is comparable to that of gravity for Newtonian

physics, relativity for Einsteinian physics, or natural selection for Darwinian biology.[13]

The concept of the archetype is also what Campbell's reception of Jung's ideas revolves around, and for this reason it is this aspect of Jung's theoretical framework that I will focus on in this chapter and the next one. It is by no means my intention, however, to offer a discussion of Jung's ideas about archetypes that is complete or all-encompassing. Jung's *Collected works* consists of 20 volumes, and the current amount of secondary literature about his ideas is enough to fill a small warehouse. To think that I can cover all there is to say in just two chapters would therefore be seriously misguided (or, in Jungian terms, a sure sign of an 'ego inflation'). The primary goal of this chapter and the next one is to enable a comparison with Campbell in the chapters to come. For that reason, only those aspects of Jung's ideas about the concept of the archetype that are relevant for the comparison with Campbell have been included.

I have set up the following structure for this chapter.

In section 2.1, I will discuss Jung's development up until the point where he put forward the distinction between the archetype-as-such and the archetypal images and ideas that the archetype gives rise to (a distinction which I have already alluded to briefly above). In section 2.2, I will discuss the paper in which Jung put forward this distinction, 'On the nature of the psyche' (1946). This will be followed by a discussion of a late development in Jung's intellectual history in section 2.3: his ideas about synchronicity.

2.1 Early developments

In the comic movie *Ghostbusters* (1984), three unemployed professors who specialize in parapsychological phenomena set up a business to help people plagued by poltergeists to get rid of their tormenters. In one particularly funny scene, all of the men are gathered around a client, who is telling them that when she came home from work that day and opened the refrigerator, she found a monster where previously her food had been. The professors try to come up with an explanation for this strange discovery. After one of them has said that this could be a past life experience, intruding on the present, the professor called Spengler jokingly says: 'Or even a race memory, stored in the collective unconscious – and I wouldn't rule out clairvoyance or telepathic contact either!'[14]

As this scene rather pointedly illustrates, Jung's collective unconscious hypothesis is for many people still something that belongs in the category of 'wacky' science. The character Spengler mentions it alongside a whole host of other theories which generally aren't taken serious by the scientific establishment, among them reincarnation and telepathy. Although Jung would certainly have objected to the accusation that his theory of the collective unconscious represented an example of bad or 'wacky' science (an accusation which dogged him his entire life, and to which we will return later on in this section), it should be noted nonetheless that Jung developed his first ideas about a collective layer in the human subconscious in response to his experience of exactly such a 'parapsychological' phenomenon as the movie *Ghostbusters* makes fun of. As Christopher Hauke argues in his article 'The unconscious: personal and collective',[15] Jung developed his first ideas about the collective unconscious when working with his cousin Heléne Preiswerk, whose apparent ability to function as a medium for the spirit world was the topic for Jung's Ph.D. thesis. Jung ultimately concluded that his cousin wasn't a medium at all. However, since he had to admit that much of the things she said while in trance were things that she could have no knowledge of, and which could therefore not be attributed to repressed contents of her personal unconscious, he speculated that they might come from a deeper layer of her unconscious, which contained contents that had not been collected there during her lifetime. Jung himself writes the following in *MDF* about these experiences:

> All in all, this was the one great experience which wiped out all my earlier philosophy and made it possible for me to achieve a psychological point of view. I had discovered some objective facts about the human psyche. Yet the nature of the experience was such that once again I was unable to speak of it. I knew no one to whom I could have told the whole story. Once more I had to lay aside an unfinished problem. It was not until two years later that my dissertation appeared.[16]

As he makes clear in the quote above, Jung did not feel ready to share his ideas about this collective layer in the human psyche with other people at that point in time (Jung did his work with Helene Preiswerk in 1900; his doctoral thesis which was the end-result of it was published in 1902[17]). As I already indicated in the introduction, that only happened when he wrote *Wandlungen und symbole der libido* (from now on abbreviated as *Wandlungen*), the first part of which was published in 1911.

There are many misconceptions about *Wandlungen*. One misconception often encountered is that the book immediately cost Jung his friendship with

Freud. It did not. As I already mentioned in the introduction, *Wandlungen* was published in two parts. The first part (published in 1911) still has a distinctly Freudian ring to it, and seems to have been written in such a way so as to not offend the master. Freud, as a matter of fact, approved of the first part of the book, as can be concluded from the following quote, taken from a letter Freud wrote to Jung on 12 November 1911:

> It is the best thing this promising author has written up to now, though he will do better.[18]

It was only with the publication of the second part (in which Jung dismisses Freud's sexual theory of the libido) that the split with Freud become a reality. It was published in 1912, and it soon became obvious that Freud could not accept the ideas Jung expressed in it. Even though Jung had hoped that he could remain friends with Freud (as he writes in *MDF*) a 'parting of the ways' soon became a necessity.

Another common misconception about *Wandlungen* is the notion that Jung used the word 'primordial image' (a synonym for the term archetype) for the first time in *Wandlungen*.[19] This is simply not true. The first edition of the book contains not a single usage of the term, or anything even closely resembling it. This perception probably came about because Jung rewrote the book considerably in 1952. In this new version (which is the one published as part of the *Collected works*[20]) the term primordial image is used frequently by Jung. Many scholars, therefore, seem to have mistakenly concluded that the term was also part of Jung's vocabulary when he wrote the first version in 1911 and 1912.

The word archetype is not used in the first version of *Wandlungen* either: Jung had not yet coined the term at that point in time. What the book does contain, however, is one of the first attempts to put the ideas Jung developed after his dream from 1909 into language that is, at best, vague and tentative. Jung, in the first part of the book, makes the distinction between two modes of thinking: what he calls directed-thinking (the cognitive processes of our normal 'daylight' consciousness) and phantasy-thinking (the cognitive processes going on in the unconscious). According to Jung, the latter mode of thought was once the dominant way of thinking of mankind in the past. It has been 'overgrown' by a more rational, modern way of thinking, but it is nonetheless still a part of our psychological make-up. We relive it in our dreams, and in childhood we go through a phase in which we also make use of this archaic way of thinking. He quotes a passage from Nietzsche's *Human, all too human* to illustrate his point, in which the philosopher says something remarkably similar:

> In our sleep and in our dreams we pass through the whole thought of earlier humanity. I mean, in the same way that man reasons in his dreams he reasoned when in the waking state many thousands of years.[21]

The phylogenetic layer that Jung first conceived of after his dream of 1909, then, has now finally found a place in his writings. 'Just as our bodies still keep the reminders of old functions and conditions in many old-fashioned organs', Jung writes in the first part of the book, 'so our minds, too, which apparently have outgrown those archaic phantasies'.[22]

Reading *Wandlungen* now, in full knowledge of everything that happened between Jung and Freud as a result of it, it almost seems as if Jung was building up his confidence for the confrontation with Freud as he was writing it, reserving the ideas which he knew Freud would not approve of for the second part of the book. The first part, as I already mentioned, is still remarkably Freudian in tone. Jung seems to be pretending that he still endorses Freud's 'dogma' of the sexual nature of the libido, and does not yet put forward his own ideas about the libido as 'psychic energy'. Instead, he says things like this:

> As is easily understood, an innate tendency, an acknowledgment of which one refuses to make, and which one treats as non-existent, can hardly contain a thing that may be in accord with our conscious character. It concerns the tendencies which are considered immoral and as generally impossible, and the strongest resentment is felt towards bringing them into the consciousness. . . . And what in ourselves do we consider immoral and non-existent, or which we at least wish were non-existent? *It is that which in antiquity lay widespread on the surface, viz., sexuality in all its various manifestations* [my italics][23].

Even though Jung keeps his own ideas about the nature of libido firmly in the closet in the first part of *Wandlungen*, he does feel confident enough to discuss his ideas about what he would later call the collective unconscious. Although it may seem strange that Jung did feel confident enough to write about this topic but not about his ideas about Freud's theory of the libido, it is very likely that Jung knew that Freud would not be insulted by his insistence that there is a phylogenetic layer in the unconscious. In fact, Freud would later adopt a position very similar to Jung's position in

Wandlungen in his later work, most notably in *Totem and Taboo* and *Moses and monotheism*.[24] Jung, in the first part of the book, associates this layer of the unconscious with infantile thought, but he does not yet see it as something humanity should get 'in touch' with, as he would come to conclude later on in his career. Instead, he even uses a slightly derogatory tone of voice when he speaks of what he also calls 'archaic strata'. He even writes that the way of thinking which it represents can be found 'in the lower races, like the negroes' (a phrase which he removed when he rewrote the book in 1952):

> The naïve man of antiquity saw in the sun the great Father of the heaven and the earth, and in the moon the fruitful good Mother. Everything had its demons; they animated equally a human being and his brother, the animal. Everything was considered according to its anthropomorphic or theriomorphic attributes, as human being or animal. Even the disc of the sun was given wings or four feet, in order to illustrate its movement. Thus arose an idea of the universe which was not only very far from reality, but was one which corresponded wholly to subjective phantasies.
>
> . . .
>
> We know, from our-own experience, this state of mind. It is an infantile stage. To a child the moon is a man or a face or a shepherd of the stars. The clouds in the sky seem like little sheep; the dolls drink, eat and sleep; the child places a letter at the window for the Christ-child; he calls to the stork to bring him a little brother or sister; the cow is the wife of the horse, and the dog the husband of the cat. We know, too, that lower races, like the negroes, look upon the locomotive as an animal, and call the drawers of the table the child of the table.[25]

In the second part of the book Jung's tone of voice suddenly changes dramatically. It is as if he now finally felt brave enough to throw down the gauntlet, to express himself in a way which he didn't feel ready for while he was writing the first part of the book. He does this by attacking what he knew Freud held most dear: the sexual theory of the libido. Famously, Jung now puts forward his own theory of the libido as a general 'life force' energy, which he compares to Schopenhauer's philosophy:

> This conception forces us to relate it to every desire, including hunger, for now we can no longer make any essential distinction between the will to build a nest and the will to eat. This view brings us to a conception of libido, which extends over the boundaries of the physical sciences into a philosophical aspect – to a conception of the will in general.

> I must give this bit of psychological 'Voluntarismus' into the hands of the philosophers for them to manage. For the rest I refer to the words of Schopenhauer relating to this.[26]

Jung also refers to the libido as the 'universal creative power existent everywhere',[27] and also as 'the creative strength existent in man'[28] and the 'driving strength of our own soul'.[29] In *MDF* Jung wrote the following about what was going through his mind when he put forward this new theory of the libido:

> My idea was to escape from the then prevailing concretism of the libido theory – in other words, I wished no longer to speak of the instincts of hunger, aggression, and sex, but to regard all these phenomena as expressions of psychic energy. In physics, too, we speak of energy and its various manifestations, such as electricity, light, heat, etc. The situation in psychology is precisely the same. Here, too, we are dealing primarily with energy, that is to say, with measures of intensity, with greater or lesser quantities. It can appear in various guises.[30]

This new position suddenly makes it undeniably obvious how different Jung's view of the unconscious is from Freud's. The unconscious, seen in Jung's way, now becomes much more than just the source of neuroses, which must be brought under the control of the rational ego. 'Where id was, there ego shall be', Freud famously put it; Jung however, is by now using quite different language. According to him, the unconscious is also a source of vitality and inspiration. It is, more than anything else, of a *creative* nature. The following quote makes this very clear.

> When some great work is to be accomplished, before which weak man recoils, doubtful of his strength, his libido returns to [its] source [in the unconscious] – and this is the dangerous moment, in which the decision takes place between annihilation and new life. If the libido remains arrested in the wonder kingdom of the inner world, then the man has become for the world above a phantom, then he is practically dead or desperately ill. But if the libido succeeds in tearing itself loose and pushing up into the world above, then a miracle appears. *This journey to the underworld has been a fountain of youth, and new fertility springs from his apparent death* [my italics].[31]

Even though *Wandlungen* is a strange book, full of contradictions, it still contains a lot of essential ideas that would remain an important part of

Jung's theoretical framework throughout the rest of his career. The unconscious, as Jung states in *Wandlungen*, contains more than just 'personal' contents: it contains 'historical' or 'archaic' strata as well. More importantly, it is not a static 'storeroom' (Jung's term – see quote below), but a layer of the psyche which is of a distinctly creative nature. As Jung himself put it in an interview later on in his life:

> To [Freud] the unconscious was a product of consciousness. I mean, it was a sort of storeroom, where all the discarded things of consciousness were heaped up and left. But to me, the unconscious then [at the time of *Wandlungen*] was already a matrix; a sort of basis of consciousness, of a creative nature, namely, capable of autonomous acts – autonomous intrusions into consciousness.[32]

Jung, after having published the second part of *Wandlungen* (which, as we have seen, cost him his friendship with Freud), continued to develop his ideas about the phylogenetic dimension of the unconscious. Most importantly, he quickly abandoned the idea that the 'archaic strata' were an outgrown mode of functioning or way of thinking, as he had held in *Wandlungen*. As Jung writes in *MDF*:

> [The contents of the collective unconscious] I first took to be the traces of earlier modes of functioning. Later, with increasing experience and on the basis of more reliable knowledge, I recognized them as forms of instinct, that is, as archetypes.[33]

It took some time, however, before Jung finally decided upon the actual word archetype to designate the contents of this 'collective a priori beneath the personal psyche'.[34] At first, he used the word 'primordial image' to describe these contents. As I already indicated above, Jung makes no mention of this term in *Wandlungen*; to the best of my knowledge, he first used it in 1916, in an essay called 'The conception of the unconscious'. In that essay he writes the following:

> The recognition of such primordial images obliges me to differentiate between the contents of the unconscious; a differentiation of another kind than that between the pre conscious and unconscious, or between the sub-conscious and unconscious. The justification for those distinctions cannot be discussed here; they have a value of their own and probably merit to be carried further as affording a point of view.[35]

That is all Jung has to say about the term 'primordial image' in 'The conception of the unconscious'. The first text in which he discusses the term in some detail is from 1917, 'The psychology of the unconscious processes', published as chapter 14 in *Collected papers on analytical psychology.*[36] In this text Jung explains that he has taken the term from the historian Jacob Burckhardt (a figure which he also alludes to when discussing similar ideas in *Wandlungen*), and also uses the term 'collective unconscious' for the first time (even though he also uses the alternative terms suprapersonal, impersonal and absolute unconscious). Instead of saying that these primordial images represent an archaic way of thinking, like he did in *Wandlungen*, he now claims that they are potentialities latent in the structure of the brain:

> In every individual, in addition to the personal memories, there are also, in Jacob Burckhardt's excellent phrase, the great 'primordial images', the inherited potentialities of human imagination. They have always been potentially latent in the structure of the brain. The fact of this inheritance also explains the otherwise incredible phenomenon, that the matter and themes of certain legends are met with all the world over in identical forms. Further, it explains how it is that persons who are mentally deranged are able to produce precisely the same images and associations that are known to us from the study of old manuscripts. I gave some examples of this in my book 'The Psychology of the Unconscious' [*The English translation of Wandlungen*]. I do not hereby assert the transmission of representations, but only of the possibility of such representations, which is a very different thing.[37]

In this phase of his career Jung is still searching, tentatively, for the right way to express what he means. For this reason, his choice of words is sometimes awkward. The term 'primordial image', for one, led many critics to accuse Jung of 'Lamarckism'. Lamarck's theory of evolution is nowadays seen as a discredited theory of evolution (with neo-Darwinism being the accepted paradigm), which has as its most important claim that an organism can pass on characteristics acquired during its lifetime to future generations. It is therefore also sometimes described as the 'inheritance of acquired characteristics' theory of evolution. An example which is often used to explain the way Lamarck thought evolution occurred is of giraffes stretching their necks to reach the higher leaves on a tree. Because the ancestors of giraffes stretched their necks to reach the leaves, their necks may have gradually become longer during their lifetime. According to the Lamarckian theory of evolution, these giraffe ancestors passed on their longer necks to their offspring, with the consequent result of giraffe necks becoming longer and longer as evolution progressed. Although Lamarck's theory of evolution is often contrasted with Darwin's theory of evolution, Darwin himself was quite receptive to the 'inheritance of acquired characteristics' theory, even claiming that 'information flows from the organism to its reproductive cells and from them to the next generation'.[38] The theory was only refuted on a scientific basis when Darwinism was combined with Gregor Mendel's theory of genetics to form what is often called 'the modern synthesis' or 'neo-Darwinism'. Mendel's theory confirmed that what an organism passes on to its offspring is determined only by the information stored in its genes. Because genes remain fixed throughout an organism's lifespan, acquired character traits cannot be passed on. Even though this idea did not become associated with Darwinism until well after Darwin's death (according to Henry Plotkin, the 'modern synthesis' took shape between the years 1918 and 1932[39]), it has become common practice to use the term 'Darwinism' for a theory of evolution which does not subscribe to a theory of 'acquired characteristics' but relies solely on the concept of natural selection to explain evolution. In this book I will use the terms 'Darwinism' and 'neo-Darwinism' interchangeably to refer to such a theory of evolution, glossing over the fact that this may not be an accurate reflection of Darwin's actual ideas. I will use the term 'Lamarckism' to refer to the theory of 'inheritance of acquired characteristics'.

In light of all this, it should not be too hard to see why the term 'primordial image' led Jung's critics to accuse him of Lamarckism. Jung, by insisting that there are primordial images in the psyche, seems to be claiming that we have access to 'images' from days gone by, which can only be explained if one holds that our ancestors have somehow passed on to us what they experienced while they were still alive. In fact, in a very early essay from 1912 called 'New paths in psychology', Jung says something which seems to confirm that he does in fact think this way:

> [T]he material at the disposal of the unconscious consists largely of infantile reminiscences. As the latest researches of the Zurich school have shown [Jung, *Wandlungen und symbole der libido*], besides the infantile reminiscences there are also 'race memories' extending far beyond the limits of the individual.[40]

Jung, then, at first used the very term by which he is ridiculed in the movie *Ghostbusters*. In *Wandlungen* similar passages can be found. Even though Jung doesn't use the term 'race memory', he still comes very close to a 'Lamarckian' position at times, for example, when he writes:

> Our foregoing explanations show wherein the products arising from the unconscious are related to the mythical. From all these signs it may be concluded that the soul possesses in some degree historical strata, the oldest stratum of which would correspond to the unconscious. The result of that must be that an introversion occurring in later life, according to the Freudian teaching, seizes upon regressive infantile reminiscences taken from the individual past. That first points out the way; then, with stronger introversion and regression (strong repressions, introversion psychoses), there come to light pronounced traits of an archaic mental kind which, under certain circumstances, *might go as far as the re-echo of a once manifest, archaic mental product* [my italics].[41]

That said, even in *Wandlungen* Jung already seems to be defending himself against claims that he is being Lamarckian, for example when he writes that the archaic layer of the unconscious 'does not set forth any account of the old events, but rather acts in such a way that it always reveals a thought common to humanity, and once more rejuvenated'.[42] This claim, however, brings forth another set of problems. Now Jung seems to be claiming that he believes in such a thing as an innate *idea*, a position that has always been heavily critiqued in the history of Western philosophy (most famously, perhaps, by John Locke). In one of the essays I alluded to above, 'The psychology of the unconscious processes', Jung says similar things. He first claims that he does not 'assert the transmission of representations, but only of the possibility of such representations, which is a very different thing';[43] however, he then goes on to claim that 'primordial images are quite the most ancient, universal, and deep thoughts of mankind', which comes awfully close to saying that there is such a thing as an innate idea. This position, however, was quickly abandoned by Jung as well. In an important essay for those interested in Jung's intellectual development – 'Instinct and the unconscious',[44] published as part of *CW 8* – Jung is putting things quite differently. In this essay he uses the term 'archetype' for the first time, and he is also beginning to sound more and more like the Jung most people are familiar with:

> [W]e also find in the unconscious qualities that are not individually acquired but are inherited, e.g., instincts as impulses to carry out actions from necessity, without conscious motivation. In this 'deeper'

stratum we also find the *a priori*, inborn forms of 'intuition', namely the archetypes of perception and apprehension, which are the necessary *a priori* determinants of all psychic processes. Just as his instincts compel man to a specifically human mode of existence, so the archetypes force his ways of perception and apprehension into specifically human patterns. The instincts and the archetypes together form the 'collective unconscious'. I call it 'collective' because, unlike the personal unconscious, it is not made up of individual and more or less unique contents but of those which are universal and of regular occurrence. Instinct is an essentially collective, i.e., universal and regularly occurring phenomenon which has nothing to do with individuality. Archetypes have this quality in common with the instincts and are likewise collective phenomena.[45]

Jung here still distinguishes the archetypes from the instincts, by stressing that the former 'compel man to a specifically human mode of existence' and that the latter 'force his ways of perception and apprehension into specifically human patterns'. In his later writings Jung would not make such a sharp distinction between instincts and archetypes, as we shall see below. What is more important to notice at this point in our discussion, however, is that Jung is now no longer speaking in such confusing language as he did in the earlier texts I dealt with above. He is no longer claiming that primordial images represent thoughts or ideas; nor is he using language that might lead people to think that an archetype is a 'race memory'; a recollection of actual events, somehow mysteriously passed down to us through the ages. The primordial images, as Jung now claims, are 'the *a priori*, inborn forms of "intuition", namely the archetypes of perception and apprehension, which are the necessary *a priori* determinants of all psychic processes'.

At this point in our discussion it might be fruitful to reflect on the word 'archetype' itself briefly. The term itself was not invented by Jung: as the physicist Charles R. Card points out (who has written extensively about Jung's collaboration with the quantum physicist Wolfang Pauli), the term goes back to antiquity:

There are numerous instances of the use of the term 'archetype', or its Greek form, archetypos, or the Latin form, archetypus. The term was used in the metaphysical sense of Idea, namely as the original in the Mind of God of which all things are copies, by Philo Judaeus (first century) and in a more or less similar way by Plotinus. Apparently, Jung took the term 'archetype' from two sources, namely the *Corpus Hermeticum* and Dionysius the Areopagite's *De Divinis Nominibus*.[46]

Card also claims that the term 'archetype' can be found in the works of thinkers like Augustine, Descartes, Locke and Kepler. Jolande Jacobi, who trained with Jung and has written extensively about his work, offers the following reflection on the etymology of the term archetype:

> The first element arche signifies beginning, origin, cause, primal source, and principle, but it also signifies position of a leader, supreme rule and government (in other words a kind of 'dominant'); the second element 'type' means blow and what is produced by a blow, the imprint of a coin, form, image, copy, prototype, model, order, and norm; . . . pattern, underlying form, primordial form (the form, for example, underlying a number of similar human, animal, or vegetable specimens).[47]

One is immediately reminded of Plato's 'ideas', which are also abstract prototypes of a higher order than the manifold phenomena that they give rise to and determine the shape of. In fact, Jung frequently acknowledged his debt to Plato when discussing his concept of the archetype, for example, when he wrote that archetypes are 'living dispositions, ideas in the Platonic sense',[48] and also when he wrote that the archetype is 'an explaining paraphrase of the Platonic eidos'.[49] It should be pointed out, though, that the similarity with Plato's ideas is just that: a similarity. The archetype, as Jung says, is a 'living disposition': it is alive and dynamic, whereas Plato's 'ideas' were modelled on the static perfection of the truths of mathematics. It is perhaps more fruitful to compare Jung's archetypes to Kant's 'categories'. Compare, for example, the following line from the *Critique of pure reason* with Jung's statement that the archetypes are 'the *a priori*, inborn forms of "intuition", namely the archetypes of perception and apprehension, which are the necessary a priori determinants of all psychic processes':

> There can be no empirical knowledge that is not already caught and limited by the a priori structure of cognition.[50]

The term 'archetype', then, seems to be a fortunate one. It seems to imply, for one, that Jung is not talking about such a scientifically flawed concept as a 'race memory': rather, it implies that the archetype is something of a higher order, which merely shapes the processes of consciousness. Jung, however, continued to use the term 'primordial image' for a long time after he had coined the term 'archetype'. Furthermore, in the first book he wrote after having come up with the term (*Psychological types*, published in 1921), he also gives what still sounds like a distinctly Lamarckian explanation for the existence of the archetypes in the human unconscious. This becomes obvious, for example, when we examine the following two quotes from *Psychological types*:

> The primordial image is a mnemic deposit, an imprint ('engramm' – Semon), which has arisen through a condensation of innumerable, similar processes. It is primarily a precipitate or deposit, and therefore a typical basic form of a certain ever-recurring psychic experience.[51]

And:

> These archetypes, whose innermost nature is inaccessible to experience, represent the precipitate of psychic functioning of the whole ancestral line, i.e. the heaped-up, or pooled, experiences of organic existence in general, a million times repeated, and condensed into types. Hence, in these archetypes all experiences are represented which since primeval time have happened on this planet. Their archetypal distinctness is the more marked, the more frequently and intensely they have been experienced.[52]

Although Jung never mentions Lamarck's theory of evolution in *Psychological types*, he does sound distinctly Lamarckian. This is primarily because of the concepts and terms he uses. By calling the primordial image an 'imprint', as well as by saying that these images represent experiences which have been 'condensed' into types, he seems to be suggesting that these images have become part of our psyche because they were imprinted on the psyche of our ancestors *during their life*. This, of course, would be in direct contrast to a Darwinian position. According to Darwinism, inherited traits start because of random mutations within the organism in which they first arise; these then get passed on to other members of the species through procreation. Natural selection makes sure that a certain trait becomes dominant: other members of the species which do not have the trait (which should always offer the members who do have the trait an environmental advantage) are rooted out and therefore do not pass on their genes. Jung, with his insistence that a primordial image is an 'imprint', gives the impression that he is thinking of an altogether different mechanism. Jung even refers to Richard Semon's concept of the 'engramm' in one of the quotes from *Psychological types* above. Semon (1859–1918) was a German zoologist and evolutionary biologist who developed a theory of evolution that was distinctly Lamarckian in nature. In his most famous book *The mneme* he wrote that stimuli from the environment can produce in an organism a 'permanent record . . . written or engraved on the irritable substance'.[53] Semon's theory of evolution, therefore, is a classic example of an 'inheritance of acquired characteristics' theory. Jung, by stating that his primordial image was 'a mnemic deposit, an imprint ("engramm" – Semon)', is seemingly aligning himself with a theory of evolution that was soon to be discredited.

As his career progressed, however, Jung did begin to sound less and less Lamarckian. For one, he stopped using terms like 'imprints' and 'deposits'; instead, he began to stress more and more that his concept of the archetype was no more 'unscientific' than claiming that human beings are born with a distinctive set of instincts, just like animals. In an essay from 1936 ('Psychological aspects of the mother archetype'), Jung has this to say on the matter:

> Nowadays we have to start with the hypothesis that, so far as predisposition is concerned, there is no essential difference between man and all other creatures. Like every animal, he possesses a preformed psyche which breeds true to his species and which, on closer examination, reveals distinct features traceable to family antecedents. . . . We are unable to form any idea of what those dispositions or aptitudes are which make instinctive actions in animals possible. And it is just as impossible for us to know the nature of the preconscious psychic disposition that enables a child to react in a human manner. We can only suppose that his behaviour results from patterns of functioning, which I have described as images.
>
> . . .
>
> These images are 'primordial' images in so far as they are peculiar to whole species, and if they ever 'originated' their origin must have coincided at least with the beginning of the species.[54]

Even though Jung definitely began to 'sound' less Lamarckian as his career progressed, then, shedding light on the exact nature of Jung's ideas about the relationship between archetypes and evolution is still a remarkably tricky business. Jung definitely could have done more to clear up the confusion which tends to arise when this issue is discussed. For example, there are only four references to Darwin in the general index to the *Collected works*. Of these four references, two refer only to Darwin's character traits (who Jung mentions in his discussion about the typology of psychological traits in *Psychological types*). The other two passages the index refers to do not shed any light whatsoever on Jung's ideas about the validity of Darwin's theories and their relationship to his own work. Futhermore, the index contains absolutely no reference whatsoever to Lamarck. Given the fact that Jung was accused of Lamarckism so often, this fact is surprising to say the least.

To make matters even worse, it is often highly unclear whether a certain text in the *Collected works* represents the early or late Jung's ideas. Jung was an obsessive rewriter of his essays and books: almost all of the texts which are part of the *Collected works* were rewritten at one point, some of them as many as six or seven times. This makes it incredibly hard to 'map' Jung's changes of opinion, which undoubtedly took place as his career progressed. Although I do get the impression that Jung consciously tried to steer clear of sounding Lamarckian later on in his career, one is still faced with passages like this one when reading the *Collected works*:

> I have often been asked where the archetypes or primordial images come from. It seems to me that their origin can only be explained by assuming them to be *deposits of the constantly repeated experiences of humanity* [my italics]. One of the commonest and at the same time most impressive experiences is the apparent movement of the sun every day. We certainly cannot discover anything of the kind in the unconscious, so far as the known physical process is concerned. What we do find, on the other hand, is the myth of the sun-hero in all its countless variations. It is this myth, and not the physical process, that forms the sun archetype. The same can be said of the phases of the moon. *The archetype is a kind of readiness to produce over and over again the same or similar mythical ideas. Hence it seems as though what is impressed upon the unconscious were exclusively the subjective fantasy-ideas aroused by the physical process. We may therefore assume that the archetypes are recurrent impressions made by subjective reactions* [my italics].[55]

In the same section, Jung even states that a certain idea which he claims can be found in many different cultures (the idea of the conservation of energy) now 'lies ready to hand in the unconscious of every man' because it 'has been stamped on the human brain for aeons'.[56] This is about as Lamarckian as it is possible for an author to sound. Although the original text in which it can be found was written very early on in Jung's career (1917), Jung revised it many times afterwards. The version which is part of the *Collected works* (from which the quote above was taken) was revised by

Jung as late as 1942. *Psychological types* was revised by Jung as well for the *Collected works*; here, too, the Lamarckian-sounding positions have been left intact. It is obvious, then, that pinpointing Jung's exact position regarding evolution is a complex endeavour. Does the fact that Jung revised a certain text mean that he still endorsed the ideas which were expressed in the rewritten version? We can only guess at the answer.

All that said, I still get the impression that Jung seems to have taken the critique of Lamarckism into account when writing about his theories. All the texts in which Jung speaks of the primordial image as a memory 'deposit' or 'imprint' are from the early stages of his career; the fact that Jung left some of the more Lamarckian-sounding passages intact when he rewrote these texts does not change the fact that he stopped using such Lamarckian-sounding words like 'imprints' or 'deposits' in his later works. Apart from using different 'language', Jung also puts forward theoretical ideas that make it obvious that he is moving more towards a position which is compatible with Darwinism in his later works. In my opinion, the most important step he took in this regard is when he put forward a distinction which makes it a lot more obvious that he does not think that the archetype is a Lamarckian 'race memory': the distinction between the archetype-as-such and the archetypal images, ideas and feelings which the archetype gives rise to. He did this in what I believe is a seminal paper in the development of Jung's ideas, 'On the nature of the psyche', first presented at the Eranos conference of 1946 and first published as 'Der geist der psychologie' in 1947.[57] As Anthony Stevens puts it, making this distinction was the most important step Jung took towards a theory that was no longer 'tainted' by Lamarckism:

> [It] was not until the publication of his essay 'The spirit of psychology' . . . that he finally freed himself of the Lamarckian taint, making a distinction between the deeply unconscious and therefore unknowable and irrepresentable archetype-as-such (similar to Kant's *das Ding-an-sich*) and archetypal images, ideas and behaviours that the archetype-as-such gives rise to. It is the archetype-as-such (the predisposition to have a certain experience) that is inherited, not the experience itself. This proposition is fully in accord with modern biological usage and is no more Lamarckian than the statement that children are innately disposed to acquire speech or to run on two legs.[58]

Many other Jung scholars also claim that the distinction between the archetype-as-such and the archetypal image is crucial for a correct understanding of Jung's ideas.[59] Because I believe this paper is highly representative of the 'essence' of the late Jung's ideas about the concept of the archetype, I have decided to discuss it here in some detail. Since Jung puts forward the distinction mentioned above in paragraph 7 of the text (titled 'Patterns of behaviour and archetypes') I will deal here only with that section. I will abbreviate 'On the nature of the psyche' as 'Nature' from hereon.

2.2 'On the nature of the psyche'

Jung begins section 7 of 'Nature' by reflecting on what is an important subject matter if one wants to truly understand the late Jung's ideas: the relationship between the archetypes and the instincts. We have already seen above that Jung related the concept of the archetype to the instincts more often. When discussing the direction Jung took after writing *Wandlungen*, for example, I gave the following quote from *MDF*:

> [The collective unconscious] I first took to be the traces of earlier modes of functioning. Later, with increasing experience and on the basis of more reliable knowledge, I recognized them as forms of instinct, that is, as archetypes.[60]

In this quote, Jung almost seems to be saying that the archetypes are a subcategory of the larger category 'instincts'. In section 7 of 'Nature', however, he makes it obvious that this is not what he means at all. As Jung claims in this section, the two categories are not the same, although they are certainly intricately related. The two categories come together in what is a crucial term if we want to understand the ideas of the late Jung: the notion of the 'pattern of behaviour'. As Jung puts it:

> In view of the structure of the body, it would be astonishing if the psyche were the only biological phenomenon not to show clear traces of its evolutionary history, and it is altogether probable that these marks are closely connected with the instinctual base. Instinct and the archaic mode meet in the biological conception of the 'pattern of behaviour'.[61]

What, then, is a 'pattern of behaviour'? In an introduction to a book by Esther Harding released around the time of 'Nature' (1949), Jung calls it 'an inherited mode of functioning, corresponding to the inborn way in which the chick emerges from the egg, the bird builds its nest, a certain kind of wasp stings the motor ganglion of the caterpillar, and eels find their way to the Bermudas'.[62] In 'Nature', Jung gives another example of a 'pattern of behaviour': the instinct of the leaf-cutting ant.

> There are, in fact, no amorphous instincts, as every instinct bears in itself the pattern of its situation. Always it fulfils an image, and the image has fixed qualities. The instinct of the leaf-cutting ant fulfils the image of ant, tree, leaf, cutting, transport, and the little antgarden of fungi. If any one of these conditions is lacking, the instinct does not function, because it cannot exist without its total pattern, without its image.[63]

The two passages quoted above are still rather confusing if we want to shed light on the distinction between the archetypes and the instincts. The term 'pattern of behaviour', although Jung uses it a lot, doesn't shed much light on the matter either. We could just as easily say that the way eels find their way to the Bermudas is because of instinct – we do not necessarily need the term 'pattern of behaviour' to describe this phenomena. Jung himself certainly could have been clearer regarding this issue. There are many passages in 'Nature', for example, where he seems again to be saying that archetypes are the same as instincts:

> To the extent that the archetypes intervene in the shaping of conscious contents by regulating, modifying, and motivating them, they act like the instincts.[64]

If we analyse the text more closely, however, it soon becomes clear that Jung doesn't think that archetypes and instincts are the same. The following quote makes this obvious:

> They [archetypes] are not just relics or vestiges of earlier modes of functioning; they are the ever-present and biologically necessary *regulators of the instinctual sphere* [my italics], whose range of action covers the whole realm of the psyche and only loses its absoluteness when limited by the relative freedom of the will. We may say that the image represents the meaning of the instinct.[65]

The archetypes, as Jung puts it in this quote, 'are the ever-present and biologically necessary regulators of the instinctual sphere'. In other words: they are inborn patterns, which regulate and modify the basic instinctual drives. Jung distinguished five different groups of instincts: creativity, reflection, activity, sexuality and hunger.[66] The archetype is what links these instincts to the outside world. There is no such thing as an 'amorphous' instinct: the instincts are always activated in relation to specific things in the world, in specific contexts. Humans are born not as creatures who could function in any imaginable world; rather, they are born with innate structures (the archetypes) that prepare them for the regular situations they are likely to encounter in *this* world. As Jung put it in a text from 1935:

> There is no human experience, nor would experience be possible at all, without the intervention of a subjective aptitude. What is this subjective aptitude? Ultimately it consists of an innate psychic structure which allows man to have experiences of this kind. Thus the whole nature of man presupposes woman, both physically and spiritually. His system is tuned in to woman from the start, just as it is prepared for a quite definite world where there is water, light, air, salt, carbohydrates, etc. *The form of the world into which he is born is already inborn in him as a virtual image* [my italics].[67]

Although the archetypes are not identical to the instincts, then, they are nevertheless very close to them – as regulators of the instinctual sphere, they are 'contaminated with instinct',[68] as Jung also puts it in 'Nature'. For this reason, Jung also uses the descriptions 'instinctual image',[69] 'formative principle of instinctual power'[70] and 'a priori instinctive type'[71] for the archetypes. All of these descriptions establish with some clarity what the relationship is between archetypes and instincts: archetypes are not the same as instincts, but they are instinctive in nature.

After explaining how he sees the relationship between archetypes and instincts, Jung then goes on to put forward the distinction which, as I stressed above, is so important if we want to understand the late Jung's ideas: between the archetypes-as-such on the one hand, and the archetypal images and ideas the archetype-as-such gives rise to on the other hand. Up until this point in our discussion we have seen Jung say a lot of things about archetypes: they are innate; they are a collective *a priori*; they are the result of mankind's evolution. To this list Jung now adds a very important extra characterization: the archetypes are *irrepresentable.*

> Whatever we say about the archetypes, they remain visualizations or concretizations which pertain to the field of consciousness. . . . *We must,*

> *however, constantly bear in mind that what we mean by 'archetype' is in itself irrepresentable, but has effects which make visualizations of it possible, namely, the archetypal images and ideas* [my italics]. We meet with a similar situation in physics: there the smallest particles are themselves irrepresentable but have effects from the nature of which we can build up a model. The archetypal image, the motif or mythologem, is a construction of this kind.[72]

The innate component of the archetype (which Jung calls 'the archetype-as-such') is a psychological structure to which we have no direct access – in other words, it is 'irrepresentable'. The only thing we can talk about is the *effects* which the archetype-as-such produces in the conscious mind: the archetypal images and ideas, which are something altogether different than the archetype-as-such.

> The archetypal representations (images and ideas) mediated to us by the unconscious should not be confused with the archetype-as-such. They are very varied structures which all point back to one essentially 'irrepresentable' basic form. The latter is characterized by certain formal elements and by certain fundamental meanings, although these can be grasped only approximately.
>
> . . .
>
> It seems to me probable that the real nature of the archetype is not capable of being made conscious, that it is transcendent, on which account I call it psychoid. Moreover every archetype, when represented to the mind, is already conscious and therefore differs to an indeterminable extent from that which caused the representation.[73]

We can now finally see that Jung does not mean that an archetype is a race memory. It is the archetype-as-such that is inherited – not the archetypal image. This position does not have to be seen as 'wacky science' at all. Saying that the abstract archetype-as-such is the result of evolution is just as scientifically acceptable as saying that the instincts are the result of evolution. What human beings inherit are not the specific images, thoughts and feelings that our forebears once had: what we inherit is the *potential* to have similar thoughts and feelings and to display similar behaviour. As we will see in the next chapter, Anthony Stevens claims that this position is 'biologically unimpeachable': it is, in his words, 'fully in accord with modern biological usage and is no more Lamarckian than the statement that children are innately disposed to acquire speech or to run on two legs'.[74] Before we go on to examine Stevens' ideas in greater detail in the next chapter, however, we must deal with one more subject matter: Jung's ideas about what he called 'synchronicity' (a concept he also referred to as 'meaningful coincidence'). As Stevens' attaches primary importance to some of the ideas Jung put forward when discussing this topic, it is important that we deal briefly with these ideas before we start our discussion of Stevens' work. This, then, is what we will turn to in the next section. Because these ideas are also intimately related to the concept of the archetype, they can be seen as representing the final 'phase' in the development of Jung's thinking about archetypes.

2.3 Synchronicity

Jung primarily put forth his ideas about synchronicity in his short book *Synchronicity – an a-causal connecting principle,*[75] first published in German in 1952. As we will see below, some of the ideas he put forward in that book are distinctly metaphysical in nature. Even though Jung claimed time and time again that he was an empiricist who was not interested in metaphysical speculation, he himself at one point admitted that some of his ideas about synchronicity were metaphysical. In a letter to Fordham (3 January 1957) he first congratulates the latter on having written an essay about the relationship between the concept of the archetype and synchronicity. He then writes the following:

> I well understand that you prefer to emphasize the archetypal implication in synchronicity. This aspect is certainly most important from the psychological angle, but I must say that I am equally interested, at times even I more so, in the metaphysical aspect of the phenomena.[76]

In 'Nature', however, Jung already put forward some distinctly metaphysical ideas as well, albeit tentatively. We have already seen that Jung says in that essay that the archetype is 'irrepresentable': we do not have direct, empirical access to it, and for this reason Jung also calls it 'transcendental'. This transcendental status, Jung claims in 'Nature', is what the archetype has in common with the concepts and models that the scientists operating in the field of microphysics work with. These concepts and models, too, refer to realities that lie 'beyond' what is empirically observable. Jung then adds a very important extra step to this line of reasoning, which shows, in my opinion, that he is now taking his discussion to a metaphysical level:

> We must, however, constantly bear in mind that what we mean by 'archetype' is in itself irrepresentable, but has effects which make visualizations

> of it possible, namely, the archetypal images and ideas. We meet with a similar situation in physics: there the smallest particles are themselves irrepresentable but have effects from the nature of which we can build up a model. The archetypal image, the motif or mythologem, is a construction of this kind. When the existence of two or more irrepresentables is assumed, there is always the possibility – which we tend to overlook – that it may not be a question of two or more factors but of one only.[77]

This is a bold claim indeed. Jung is here claiming that he feels that both the 'irrepresentable' archetype and the models of microphysics could both be reflections of the same underlying reality. The implication of this point of view is that both psyche (the archetypes) and matter (the models of physics) are not as radically opposed to each other as philosophers like Descartes have claimed. Rather then there being two worlds, each with their own laws, psyche and matter are exponents of the same transcendental principle:

> Since psyche and matter are contained in one and the same world, and moreover are in continuous contact with one another and ultimately rest on irrepresentable, transcendental factors, it is not only possible but fairly probable, even, that psyche and matter are two different aspects of one and the same thing. The synchronicity phenomena point, it seems to me, in this direction, for they show that the nonpsychic can behave like the psychic, and vice versa, without there being any causal connection between them. Our present knowledge does not allow us to do much more than compare the relation of the psychic to the material world with two cones, whose apices, meeting in a point without extension – a real zero-point – touch and do not touch.[78]

Jung here even mentions his concept of synchronicity, six years before he published his main work on the subject. In order to make sense of the quote above, I would like to briefly focus on what Jung means by his concept of synchronicity. As the title of Jung's main work about this subject shows, Jung thought of synchronicity as an 'a-causal connecting principle'. He coined the term in order to describe what he also called 'meaningful coincidences': those occasions where things happen in the exterior world that appear to have a meaningful connection to what is going on in the interior world of the psyche. Jung gives an example of such a phenomenon in *MDF*. After the break with Freud, Jung went through a period in which he had intense visions and daydreams, which appeared so real to him that he would often think that he was going crazy. In one such vision, a figure appeared who called himself Philemon. Philemon had large wings, which Jung recognized as being similar to the wings of a kingfisher bird. A few days later, while walking through his garden, Jung found a dead kingfisher. He writes the following about this occasion in *MDF:*

> Since I did not understand this dream-image [of Philemon], I painted it in order to impress it upon my memory. During the days when I was occupied with the painting, I found in my garden, by the lakeshore, a dead kingfisher! I was thunderstruck, for kingfishers are quite rare in the vicinity of Zurich and I have never since found a dead one. The body was recently dead – at the most, two or three days – and showed no external injuries.[79]

Jung ultimately came to view this as an example of synchronicity. Because there could have been no causal explanation between the two events – Jung did not go so far as to claim that his vision about a man with Kingfisher wings somehow caused the dead bird to show up in his garden – Jung describes such an event as the end-result of an *a-causal* process. This a-causal connection between psychic events and events in the material world is what Jung is referring to when he writes in 'Nature' that 'the nonpsychic can behave like the psychic, and vice versa, without there being any causal connection between them.'[80] Marie-Louise von Franz, who worked intensively with Jung and who is one of his foremost interpreters, gives the following description of Jung's concept of synchronicity, which again confirms that we should think of synchronicity as an *a-causal* principle:

> From 1929 on Jung observed a class of events that appear to point to a direct relation between psyche and matter. If one observes a series of dreams and unconscious processes in an individual over a considerable period of time, one sees that with some frequency, but sporadically and irregularly, a dream motif or an unexpected fantasy will appear in the material environment also, as an outer event, either in very similar form (which is recognized by parapsychology and explained as telepathy) or in a symbolical way, for instance if one sees a black-clad person in a dream and the next day receives news of a death.
>
> Jung described such a combination of events as a phenomenon of synchronicity. The connection between the inner event (dream, fantasy, hunch) and the outer event appears not to be a causal one, that of cause

and effect, but rather one of a relative simultaneity and of the same meaning for the individual who has the experience.[81]

As I already stated above, Jung's synchronicity concept led him to speculate that both psyche and matter are probably 'two different aspects of one and the same thing'.[82] Jung ultimately coined the term *unus mundus* to describe this idea. *Unus mundus* is a term that Jung took from the writings of the medieval alchemists he was so familiar with. Literally translated it means 'one world'. Jung probably chose the term because he wanted to express that the psychic and the non-psychic are both reflections of the same underlying, unified reality. According to him, both depth psychology and microphysics were both making breakthroughs which showed that such a dimension exists.

[The] idea of the *unus mundus* is founded on the assumption that the multiplicity of the empirical world rests on an underlying unity, and that not two or more fundamentally different worlds exist side by side or are mingled with one another. Rather, everything divided and different belongs to one and the same world, which is not the world of sense but a postulate whose probability is vouched for by the fact that until now no one has been able to discover a world in which the known laws of nature are invalid. . . .

All that is is not encompassed by our knowledge, so that we are not in a position to make any statements about its total nature. Microphysics is feeling its way into the unknown side of matter, just as complex psychology is pushing forward into the unknown side of the psyche. . . . But this much we do know beyond all doubt, that empirical reality has a transcendental background. The common background of microphysics and depth psychology is as much physical as psychic and therefore neither, but rather a third thing, a neutral nature which can at most be grasped in hints since its essence is transcendental.[83]

The archetype, according to Jung, is what links man to this *unus mundus.* This is because the archetype has a strange, dual nature: it is not only a psychological structure, but because of its inherently biological character it also has a non-psychic, material dimension. 'In its lower reaches, the psyche loses itself in the organic-material substrate',[84] Jung writes in 'Nature'. Elsewhere he makes this point as follows:

The archetypes are as it were the hidden foundations of the conscious mind, or, to use another comparison, the roots which the psyche has sunk not only in the earth in the narrower sense but in the world in general.[85]

Because of this dual nature of the archetype Jung felt that it is the aspect of our being which is ontologically closest to the *unus mundus*. Jung thought of the *unus mundus* as a *coincidentia oppositorum*, to use the medieval philosopher Nicholas of Cusa's famous term. In the *unus mundus* the opposites come together: psyche and non-psyche, spirit and matter. According to Jung, this is also true of the archetype. The archetype is therefore not only a bridge between psyche and matter; it is also what connects man to the underlying, transcendental principle which lies at the root of the entire cosmos.

These ideas about the *unus mundus* also put Jung's ideas about the origins of the archetype in a new perspective. We have seen above that Jung frequently claimed that archetypes are the end-result of evolutionary processes. In this new 'metaphysical' phase of his career, however, Jung also related the origins of the archetypes to synchronicity and the *unus mundus*. This is because he now concluded that synchronicity must have played an important role in the way the evolution of the human species came about. In a letter to Erich Neumann (10 March 1959), Jung says the following about this subject matter:

> It staggers the mind even to begin to imagine the accidents and hazards that, over millions of years, transformed a lemurlike tree-dweller into a man. In this chaos of chance, synchronistic phenomena were probably at work, operating both with and against the known laws of nature to produce, in archetypal moments, syntheses which appear to us miraculous. Causality and teleology fail us here, because synchronistic phenomena manifest themselves as pure chance.[86]

This viewpoint seems to imply that Jung's ideas about evolution are distinctly different from the neo-Darwinian viewpoint that is the current norm. Darwin's theory of evolution is ultimately mechanistic in nature, in that it assumes that the forces that shape evolution are *causal*. According to the Darwinians natural selection has shaped the patterns of order that we see in nature, and it has done so in a way that can be explained in terms of linear cause and effect. Jung's hypothesis of an *a-causal* order having influenced evolution, however, is the product of a world-view that is far from mechanistic. Jung, by positing his synchronicity concept, was actually trying to break free from the causal, mechanistic world-view in which he had grown up. According to Marie-Louise von Franz, Jung's research into the synchronicity phenomena led him to the conclusion that causality was a principle that did not apply to all observable phenomena:

> As he reviewed the facts he came back to a criticism of the absolute validity of causality, which is on very shaky ground in atomic physics in any case, and suggested using as a model, along with causality, a principle which he called that of 'a-causal orderedness'.[87]

Von Franz does not claim in this passage, however, that Jung *refuted* the notion of causality. Instead, she points out that he felt his principle of 'a-causal orderedness' should be used *alongside* a causal point of view. Much like modern physicists hold that Newtonian physics adequately describes phenomena observed in the macrophysical world but not in the microphysical world (which should be studied using the findings of quantum-mechanics), Jung believed that his a-causal approach should be used alongside the generally accepted causal way of thinking. I think the implication of this is that Jung did not refute mechanistic theories of evolution, which would include Darwinism; rather, he felt that his theory of synchronicity could be used alongside such theories. Archetypes, therefore, can be seen as both a reflection of the causal, mechanistic forces described by Darwinism *and* the a-causal orderedness which Jung believed the synchronicity phenomena to be an expression of.

When we go back through Jung's work and look for clues regarding his ideas about the archetypes and their relationship with evolution, this conclusion seems to be confirmed. As early as 1921 (in *Psychological types*) Jung was already stressing that he didn't think archetypes were *only* the end-result of causal environmental forces:

> We are forced to assume . . . that the given brain-structure [which contains the archetypes] does not owe its particular nature merely to the effect of surrounding conditions [i.e. evolutionary forces], but also and just as much to the peculiar and autonomous quality of living matter, i.e. to a fundamental law of life. The given constitution of the organism, therefore, is on the one hand a product of outer conditions, while on the other it is inherently determined by the nature of living matter. Accordingly, the primordial image is just as undoubtedly related to certain manifest, ever-renewing and therefore constantly effective nature processes as it is to certain inner determinants of the mental life and to life in general.[88]

As we have already seen, Jung intensively revised and rewrote his early works. *Psychological types*, however, is one of the few works that was published as part of the *Collected works* with hardly any revisions by Jung. In the *Collected works* version of *Psychological types*, the passage above is left more or less intact. Apart from a few words here and there which are different (which could also be the result of the text having been newly translated) the passage reads almost exactly the same. Jung, however, did add two phrases that I believe support my conclusion that he thought the archetypes could be related to both causal *and* a-causal processes. He introduces the passage in which he starts putting forward his belief that archetypes are shaped by evolution (from which the quote above was taken) as follows:

> From the scientific, causal standpoint the primordial image can be conceived as a mnemic deposit, an imprint or engramm (Semon), which has arisen through the condensation of countless processes of a similar kind.[89]

I have already quoted this passage above, where I used the unrevised, original version of *Psychological types*. When one compares the two quotes, one can see that Jung added the phrase 'from the scientific, causal standpoint', which confirms that Jung thought that theories of evolution are ultimately causal in nature. When we skip forward in the text to the passage also quoted above in which Jung claims that archetypes are also shaped by a 'fundamental law of life', we find that Jung has added a whole extra sentence to introduce this passage. It reads as follows:

> *In view of such questions Semon's naturalistic and causalistic engramm theory no longer suffices* [sentence added by Jung]. We are forced to assume that the given structure of the brain does not owe its peculiar nature merely to the influence of surrounding conditions, but also and just as much to the peculiar and autonomous quality of living matter, i.e., to a law inherent in life itself.[90]

I believe that what Jung is above calling a 'law inherent in life itself' is an early formulation of what would later become his 'a-causal orderedness'. The fact that Jung contrasts it with what he calls a 'causalistic' theory of evolution (Semon's engramm theory) confirms this. Further evidence for this conclusion is given by the fact that Jung stresses that his 'law' (which is a confusing term, as it still gives the impression of a *causal* paradigm) is ultimately *creative* in nature:

> And just as the eye bears witness to the peculiar and spontaneous creative activity of living matter, the primordial image expresses the unique and unconditioned creative power of the psyche.[91]

Synchronicity, too, was seen by Jung as an indication that nature is fundamentally creative. He called it an example of 'acts of creation in time';[92] he also referred to it as 'continuous creation'.[93] Jung's 'law inherent in life itself' and his concept of synchronicity, therefore, should in my opinion be seen as two different formulations of the same idea.

The fact that Jung left *Psychological types* almost completely in tact when adopting it for the *Collected works* seems to me to confirm that he still felt the ideas described above adequately reflected his position at the end of his life. The logical conclusion, therefore, is that Jung felt that the archetypes are not only a reflection of causal forces but also of the *unus mundus*, as it is this metaphysical dimension which he used to explain the synchronicity phenomena. As we will see in the next chapter, this has led Anthony Stevens to write that 'the archetypes which order our perceptions and ideas are themselves the product of an objective order which transcends both the human mind and the external world. At this supreme point physical science, psychology, and theology all coalesce.'[94] It is to a closer examination of his interpretation of Jung that we will now turn.

Notes

1 Mark Whitney, *Matter of heart* (USA: Kino Video), [DVD].

2 Some chapters were written by Jung himself, but most of the chapters were written by his secretary Aniela Jaffé, based on interviews she held with Jung.

3 Jung, *MDF*, p. 158.

4 Ibid.

5 Ibid., p. 159.

6 Ibid., pp. 159, 160.

7 Ibid., p. 160.

8 Anthony Stevens, 'The archetypes', in *The handbook of Jungian psychology*, ed. Renos K. Papadopoulos (New York/London: Routledge, 2006), p. 75.

9 Carl G. Jung, *The psychology of the unconscious*, trans. Beatrice M. Hinkle (London: Kegan Paul, Trench, Trubner & Co. Ltd., 1922 [1912]).

10 Jung, *MDF*, p. 169.

11 Peter Homans, *Jung in context: modernity and the making of a psychology* (Chicago: University of Chicago Press, 1995 [1979]).

[12] Ibid., p. 16.
[13] Stevens, 'The archetypes', p. 75.
[14] Ivan Reitman, *Ghostbusters* (United States: Columbia Tri-Star, 1984).
[15] Christopher Hauke, 'The unconscious: personal and collective', in *The handbook of Jungian psychology*, ed. Renos K. Papadopoulos (New York/London: Routledge, 2006), p. 59.
[16] Jung, *MDF*, p. 107.
[17] *Zur psychologie und pathologie sogenannter occulter phänomene: eine psychiatrische Studie* (1902); English translation 'On the psychology and pathology of so-called occult phenomena', published as part of *Psychiatric studies* (*CW 1*).
[18] *The Freud-Jung letters*, ed. William McGuire, trans. R. F. C. Hull and Ralph Manheim (London: Penguin Books, 1979), p. 244, note 2.
[19] For example: Jolande Jacobi, *The psychology of C.G. Jung* (London: Routledge, 1999 [1942]). Michael Palmer, *Freud and Jung on religion* (London: Routledge, 1997).
[20] Jung, *CW 5*.
[21] Friedrich Nietzsche, *Human, all too Human*, vol. II, p. 27. Quoted in Jung, *The psychology of the unconscious*, p. 14.
[22] Ibid., p. 18.
[23] Ibid., p. 21.
[24] Freud referred to this phylogenetic layer as 'archaic vestiges', sounding very much like the early Jung indeed.
[25] Jung, *The psychology of the unconscious*, p. 13.
[26] Ibid., p. 81.
[27] Ibid., p. 73.
[28] Ibid., p. 72.
[29] Ibid., p. 70.
[30] Jung, *MDF*, p. 208.
[31] Jung, *The psychology of the unconscious*, p. 182.
[32] Whitney, *Matter of heart*.
[33] Jung, *MDF*, p. 161.
[34] Ibid.
[35] Carl G. Jung, *Collected papers on analytical psychology*, ed. Constance E. Long, second edn (London: Baillière, Tindall and Cox, 1922 [1917]), p. 448. Also published in a different translation (in which the term 'primordial idea' is used instead) in Jung, *CW 7*, par. 449.
[36] Jung, *Collected papers on analytical psychology*, pp. 355–444.
[37] Ibid., p. 410.
[38] Quoted in Christopher Badcock, *Evolutionary psychology: a critical introduction* (Cambridge, UK: Polity Press, 2000), pp. 38–40.
[39] Henry Plotkin, *Evolution in mind: an introduction to evolutionary psychology* (Cambridge, MA: Harvard University Press, 1998), p. 27.
[40] Jung, *CW 7*, par. 434. In the second version of the essay, the passage about 'race memories' is edited out. Another phrase, which first read 'the genius of Freud', was changed to simply 'Freud' by Jung after the split.
[41] Jung, *The psychology of the unconscious*, p. 19.
[42] Ibid., p. 20.

[43] Jung, *Collected papers on analytical psychology*, p. 410.
[44] Jung, *CW 8*, par. 263–282.
[45] Ibid., par. 270.
[46] Charles R. Card, 'The Emergence of Archetypes in Present-Day Science and Its Significance for a Contemporary Philosophy of Nature', in *Mind in time*, ed. B. Goertzel, A. Coombs and M. Germine (Creskill: Hampton Press, 2000).
[47] Jolande Jacobi, *Complex, archetype, symbol* (London: Routledge & Kegan Paul, 1959). Quoted in Anthony Stevens, *Archetype revisited – an updated natural history of the self*, second edn (London: Brunner-Routledge, 2002), p. 52.
[48] Jung, *CW 9 part 1*, par. 154.
[49] Ibid., par. 5.
[50] Quoted in Stevens, *Archetype revisited*, p. 50.
[51] Carl G. Jung, *Psychological types* (London: Routledge & Kegan Paul, 1923 [1921]), p. 556.
[52] Ibid., p. 509.
[53] Richard Semon, *The mneme* (London: George Allen & Unwin, 1921), p. 24.
[54] Jung, *CW 9 part 1*, par. 152.
[55] Jung, *CW 7*, par. 109.
[56] Ibid.
[57] Published as part of Jung, *CW 8*, par. 343–442.
[58] Stevens, 'The archetypes', p. 77.
[59] For example, Jacobi, *The psychology of C.G. Jung*. See also: Steven Walker, *Jung and the Jungians on myth and mythology: an introduction* (New York/London: Routledge, 2002), p. 12.
[60] Jung, *MDF*, p. 161.
[61] Jung, *CW 8*, par. 398.
[62] Jung, *CW 18*, par. 1228.
[63] Jung, *CW 8*, par. 398.
[64] Ibid., par. 404.
[65] Ibid., par. 398.
[66] 'Instinct', in Daryl Sharp, *Jung lexicon – a primer of terms and concepts* (Toronto: Inner City Books, 1991).
[67] '*The relations between the ego and the unconscious*', published as part of Jung, *CW 7*, par. 300.
[68] Jung, *CW 8*, par. 416.
[69] Ibid., par. 414.
[70] Ibid., par. 416.
[71] Ibid., par. 398.
[72] Ibid., par. 417.
[73] Ibid.
[74] Stevens, 'The archetypes', p. 77.
[75] Also published as part of *CW 8*, which is the version that I will refer to in this section.
[76] Quoted in Roderick Main, ed., *Jung on synchronicity and the paranormal* (London: Routledge, 1997), p. 35.
[77] Jung, *CW 8*, par. 417.
[78] Ibid., par. 418.

[79] Jung, *MDF*, p. 183.
[80] Jung, *CW 8*, par. 418.
[81] Marie-Louise von Franz, *C.G. Jung – his myth in our time* (New York: Putnam, 1975), p. 237.
[82] Jung, *CW 8*, par. 418.
[83] Jung, *CW 14*, par. 767–769.
[84] Jung, *CW 8*, par. 380.
[85] Jung, *CW 10*, par. 53.
[86] Main, ed., *Jung on synchronicity and the paranormal*, p. 168.
[87] von Franz, *C.G. Jung – his myth in our time*, p. 239.
[88] Jung, *Psychological types*, p. 557.
[89] Jung, *CW 6*, par. 748.
[90] Ibid.
[91] Ibid.
[92] Jung, *CW 8*, par. 965.
[93] Ibid., par. 967.
[94] Quoted in Main, ed., *Jung on synchronicity and the paranormal*, p. 57.

Chapter 3

The ideas of Anthony Stevens

Whereas in the previous chapter I focused on giving an overview of the *development* of Jung's ideas, in this chapter I will be focusing on how to *interpret* these ideas. As the previous chapter has illustrated, interpreting Jung is not always an easy task. Because Jung changed his mind so often and revised his writings so incessantly there are many inconsistencies in his work: what he says in the early phase of his career is not always exactly the same as what he says in the later phases of his career. As I pointed out in Chapter 1, just mapping these changes and pointing out which statement belongs to which phase is not enough to make interpreting his work a completely straightforward task. What makes interpreting Jung's work problematic even *after* one has mapped these changes is that there is also a high degree of ambiguity within some of the key texts themselves. In texts where Jung stresses that the archetype-as-such is equivalent to the biological concept of the 'pattern of behaviour', for example, he sometimes seems to imply that the archetype is a fixed, 'closed system' which isn't 'imprintable' by external stimuli at all. The examples Jung gives when he discusses this topic seem to confirm this. He almost always gives examples of 'patterns of behaviour' from the animal world which are completely innate, and which are not shaped by the organism's experiences during its lifetime in any way. Take, for example, the following passage, which I already quoted in the previous chapter:

> [The archetype] is an inherited mode of functioning, corresponding to the inborn way in which the chick emerges from the egg, the bird builds its nest, a certain kind of wasp stings the motor ganglion of the caterpillar, and eels find their way to the Bermudas.[1]

This passage does seem to confirm that Jung thought that the archetype is an inborn image that is fixed from birth. Yet there is much debate about the level of 'innateness' of Jung's archetypes. Anthony Stevens, whose work I will focus on in this chapter, claims that the archetypes found in the human nervous system aren't 'closed systems' at all: they are open to imprinting, and are therefore determined in content by the experiences of the individual who is born with them. Robert Segal, however, does seem to think that the archetype is a closed system, and that an organism's experiences therefore play no part in determining the way a particular archetype manifests itself:

> Like Tylor, Frazer, and Freud, Jung attributes the similarities in myths to independent invention. But unlike them he attributes independent invention to heredity rather than experience. He claims that everyone is born not just with a need of some kind that the invention of myth fulfils but with the myths, or the contents of myths, themselves. More precisely, everyone is born with the contents of myths already elevated to the level of myth.
>
> . . .
>
> For Tylor, Frazer, and Freud, experience, even if it is of innate needs, provides the impetus for the creation of myth. For Freud, for example, one's experience of one's parents' reaction to one's incestuous drives spurs the creation of myth. For Jung, by contrast, experience provides only an occasion for the expression of pre-existent archetypes. Archetypes shape experience rather than, as for Freud and the others, derive from it.[2]

As both of these men are renowned scholars who know Jung's work well, I am inclined to lay the cause for the discrepancy between their views squarely at Jung's feet. The Jung scholar Anthony Storr once wrote that 'Jung was not a good exponent of his own ideas',[3] and I think that he was right. If Jung had managed to explain himself better then there certainly wouldn't have been so many opposing interpretations of his work. Jung himself was aware of this problem: 'Nobody reads my books', he once said, 'and I have such a hell of a trouble to make people see what I mean.'[4] As I already mentioned in Chapter 1, when one writes about Jung a question that will therefore inevitably come up is this: '*Whose* Jung are you talking about?' Two scholars who have both invested an equal amount of time in researching his ideas might still arrive at two different, incompatible conclusions about what the true meaning of his words.

In this book, then, I have decided to focus on a single interpreter of Jung's work to enable a comparison between the ideas of Jung and Campbell: Anthony Stevens. It is his interpretation of Jung that I will present in this chapter. Stevens is a Jungian analyst who is also an experienced psychiatrist; he holds a doctorate in medicine, and besides having written numerous books about Jung he has also written extensively about psychiatry (e.g. *Evolutionary psychiatry*,[5] together with John Price). He offers an interpretation of Jung that, as I will argue in the chapters to come, matches very closely the interpretation of Jung that Joseph Campbell came to adopt in phase three of his career. As I will also argue, it is this interpretation that lies at the very root of Campbell's theory of myth and religion in this phase of his career.

The first aspect of Stevens' work that I will focus on in this chapter is his claim that Jung's concept of the archetype should be related to the ethological concept of the 'innate releasing mechanism' (IRM):

> Once one conceives of archetypes as the neuropsychic centres responsible for co-ordinating the behavioural and psychic repertoires of our species in response to whatever environmental circumstances we may encounter, they become directly comparable to the 'innate releasing mechanisms' responsible for Lorenz's 'species-specific patterns of behaviour' and Bowlby's 'goal-corrected behavioural systems'.[6]

Stevens wrote about these ideas for the first time in his book *Archetype – a natural history of the self*,[7] published in 1982. In this chapter, however, I will make use of the rewritten version titled *Archetype revisited*, which I will abbreviate from hereon as *Archetype*. In section 3.1, I will give an overview of the core ideas Stevens puts forward in this book.

The second aspect of Stevens' work that I will focus on in this chapter is his interpretation of Jung's concept of the *unus mundus*, to which he attaches primary importance. In section 3.2, I will deal with Stevens' discussion of this concept, focusing specifically on his paper 'Thoughts on the psychobiology of religion and the neurobiology of archetypal experience',[8] published by the academic journal *Zygon* in 1986.

3.1 *Archetype*

I have divided this section into two subsections. In section 3.1.1, I will give a general introduction to Stevens' book *Archetype*; in section 3.1.2, I will focus on the claim Stevens makes in this book that Jung's concept of the archetype should be thought of as equivalent to the concept of the open IRM.

3.1.1 Overview of *Archetype*

Many of the scientific paradigms that held sway while Jung was still alive ran completely counter to the ideas that he was endorsing. Although Freud recognized that there are basic drives which all of us inherit, he still placed much more emphasis on personal experience to account for human behaviour than Jung did. As Anthony Stevens puts it, he saw psychological development as 'a process of accretion or absorption occurring in an unstructured personality'.[9] When behaviourism became the dominant psychological movement in the 1950s and 1960s , the paradigm shifted even more towards what the psychologist Steven Pinker calls the 'blank slate' outlook:[10] the notion that the human psyche is infinitely malleable, and that innate dispositions play no part in determining human behaviour. According to the behaviourists, the only thing that should be taken into account are observable phenomena: such vague and fuzzy entities as 'mental states' were therefore written off as unscientific. The human personality was seen, consequently, as the result of nothing but 'learning'. One of the founders of behaviourism (John B. Watson, 1878–1958), for example, is famous for having said the following:

> Give me a dozen healthy infants, well-formed, and my own specified world to bring them up in and I'll guarantee to take any one at random and train him to become any type of specialist I might select – doctor, lawyer, artist, merchant-chief, and yes, even beggar-man and thief, regardless of his talents, penchants, tendencies, abilities, vocations, and race of his ancestors.[11]

In other disciplines besides psychology, the 'blank slate' paradigm was dominant as well. The founding fathers of anthropology and sociology, Franz Boas and Emile Durkheim, both stressed the dominance of culture over the individual. Durkheim, for example, wrote the following: 'The determining cause of a social fact should be sought among the social facts preceding it and not among the states of individual consciousness.'[12] Although Boas himself did not explicitly deny that there was an inherited structure to the human mind, many of Boas' followers as well as their subsequent pupils did. Margaret Mead, for example, who studied with Ruth Benedict (who, in turn, was trained by Boas) wrote the following:

> We are forced to conclude that human nature is almost unbelievably malleable, responding accurately and contrastingly to contrasting cultural conditions.[13]

It isn't hard to see how different this model of the human mind is from Jung's. Where Jung was proclaiming that the mind had an inborn structure that, like the human body, was a product of evolution, many of his contemporaries didn't even acknowledge that there was such a thing as an inborn structure of the mind to begin with. As Anthony Stevens claims in *Archetype*, this fundamental difference in outlook between Jung and his contemporaries was the main reason why he was never really accepted by the scientific community during his lifetime:

> With hindsight one can see that Jung suffered ostracism by the academic establishment not because he was a mystic but because his ideas ran counter to the intellectual currents of his time. The academic psychologists insisted that the behavioural repertoire of human beings was infinitely plastic, almost completely subject to the vicissitudes of the environment, and relatively uninfluenced by innate or predetermined structures, whereas Jung persisted all his life in advancing the opposite view.[14]

The point Stevens wants to make in *Archetype* is that a new paradigm arose during the final two decades of the twentieth century which is radically different from the 'blank slate' paradigm, vindicating Jung in the process. Stevens calls this paradigm shift the 'ethological revolution'. He claims that the field of ethology – the study of the behaviour of animals in their natural environment, made famous by writers like Konrad Lorenz and Niko Tinbergen – had a strong impact on the study of human behaviour from the beginning of the 1980s, primarily on psychology and sociology. In the 1990s it also had a strong influence on the development of fields like evolutionary psychology and evolutionary psychiatry. Stevens claims that the view of human nature that lies at the root of this new 'ethological' paradigm is radically opposed to that of the 'blank slate' paradigm. Human nature, as seen through the eyes of the ethologists and those they inspired, is not 'infinitely malleable' at all. Like Jung, these thinkers claim that human beings are born with a host of inborn mechanisms which prepare them for the common problems they are likely to encounter during their lifetime: learning a language, finding a mate, or adapting to the norms and values of a specific culture, for example. For Stevens, the findings of these contemporary scientists 'amplify and corroborate'[15] Jung's archetypal hypothesis, and it is this resonance between the new ethological perspective and Jung's theories which Stevens seeks to highlight in *Archetype*. He does not do this just because he wants to educate his readers about this new 'ethological' perspective: more than anything else, he wants to highlight that these ideas prove that, in hindsight, Jung was right. As Stevens himself puts it:

> For most of the twentieth century it was fashionable to focus on environmental influences and to ignore the hereditary ones. This is one reason why Jung's theory of archetypes, which postulated innate structures, was ignored or rejected. Now that hereditary forces are receiving as much attention as environmental factors, evidence is accumulating that Jung was right.[16]

So how similar to Jung's ideas are the findings of the 'ethological' thinkers Stevens discusses in *Archetype*? To start with, let us look at the following quote from the work of one of the heroes of Stevens' book, the psychologist John Bowlby. Stevens offers this quote at the beginning of chapter four.

> Man's behaviour is very variable, it is true, but not infinitely so; and, though cultural differences are great, certain commonalities can be discerned. For example, despite obvious variability, the *patterns of behaviour* [my italics], often very intensely motivated, that result in mating, in the care of babies and young children, and in the attachment of young to parents are found in almost all members of the human race and seem best considered as expressions of *some common plan* [Stevens' italics] and, since they are of obvious survival value, as instances of instinctive behaviour.[17]

'If for "some common plan" we substitute archetype', Stevens writes after he has quoted this passage, 'this passage is completely in accord with the Jungian position.'[18] It is indeed striking to notice how similar the passage in question is to Jung's ideas about the concept of the archetype, especially in the later stages of his career. Bowlby, in the quote above, even calls the instinctive behaviour which he claims lies at the root of the myriad different forms of human culture 'patterns of behaviour', which, as we have seen in the previous chapter, was one of Jung's preferred terms for the concept of the archetype in his later years. As Stevens points out, however, Bowlby is not alone in making such claims. He distinguishes a host of other writers who have discovered, in his words, 'propensities in human subjects which are virtually indistinguishable from Jung's archetypes'.[19] He continues:

> Different workers have called them by different names but all are referring to similar structures with parallel functions. While Paul

> Gilbert (1997) refers to them as 'mentalities', Russell Gardner (1988) of Galveston, Texas, calls them 'master programmes' or 'propensity states' and Brant Wenegrat (1984) of Stanford University calls them 'genetically transmitted response strategies'. David Buss (1999) of Austin, Texas, who has done most to elucidate the archetypes underlying characteristic features of masculine and feminine psychology, refers to them as 'evolved psychological mechanisms', Randolph Nesse (1987) of the University of Michigan School of Medicine to 'prepared tendencies'. Sally Walters (1994) of Simon Fraser University, British Columbia, to 'algorithms' and Leda Cosmides and John Tooby (1992) of the University of California at Santa Barbara to 'multiple mental modules'.[20]

I think Stevens definitely has a point when he stresses how similar the ideas of the thinkers he deals with in *Archetype* are to Jung's ideas. Take, for example, the following quote Stevens offers from the work of the anthropologist Robin Fox:

> The apparently endless kinds of kinship and marriage arrangements known to men are in fact variations on a few themes. The same can be said of political arrangements, which despite their cultural variety are reducible to a few structural forms. Once one gets behind the surface manifestations, the uniformity of human behaviour and of human social arrangements is remarkable.[21]

Or take the following quote from the work of the ethologist Konrad Lorenz which Stevens also offers:

> The system of sense organs and nerves that enables living things to survive and orientate themselves in the outer world has evolved phylogenetically through confrontation with an adaptation to that form of reality which we experience as phenomenological space. The system exists a priori to the extent that it is present before the individual perceives anything, and, must be present if experience is to be possible.[22]

Where the 'ethological' thinkers Stevens deals with in *Archetype* differ from Jung, however, is that almost all of them connect their theories to Darwin. Unlike Jung they explicitly state that their 'innate releasing mechanisms' (Lorenz and Tinbergen), 'evolved psychological mechanisms' (Buss) or 'multiple mental modules' (Cosmides and Tooby) are the end-result of natural selection. The theories of the ethological thinkers, therefore, are explicitly (neo-)Darwinian in nature. In order to connect Jung to these theories, however, Stevens has to deal with one crucial problem: Jung never openly connected his findings to Darwin's theories at all. The four references in the *Collected works* to Darwin give no indication at all as to whether Jung thought Darwin's ideas were valid, and although he did relate archetypes explicitly to evolution, Jung never claimed that archetypes are the result of *natural selection*. At first glance, then, Jung and the 'ethologists' (which is how Stevens sometimes refers to the thinkers he is describing, despite the fact that not all of them work in this field) seem to make rather odd bedfellows. To make matters worse, by putting so much emphasis on the fact that he thought of the archetype as an 'image', Jung often seemed to lean towards Lamarckianism. Stevens acknowledges this problem, writing that this was one of the reasons why at first he didn't take Jung very seriously himself:

> How could 'primordial images', as Jung often referred to archetypes, be inscribed in the brain and later be 'developed' by experience? It was this which made one suspect that he believed that experiences acquired by one generation could be transmitted genetically to the next – the discredited view originally advanced by the French biologist, Jean-Baptiste Lamarck (1744–1829). These notions struck me as contrary to the accepted teachings of biology.[23]

However, as we have seen in the previous chapter as well, Jung ultimately made the distinction between the irrepresentable archetype-as-such and the archetypal images and ideas which the *a priori* archetype-as-such gives rise to. According to Stevens, this distinction is crucial if one wants to establish a connection between Jung and the findings of the ethologists. It is the abstract archetype-as-such which is inherited, not the archetypal images and ideas. This, according to Stevens, makes an interpretation possible of Jung that is wholly in line with Darwinism. The archetype-as-such, which as Jung states is 'not an inherited idea, but an inherited mode of functioning',[24] should be seen, according to Stevens, as a biological entity which is the result of natural selection, despite the fact that Jung never explicitly made this claim himself. Once we view the archetype in this way, Jung's concept of the archetype becomes completely compatible with current neo-Darwinian ideas according to Stevens: it is, as he puts it, 'biologically unimpeachable':

> Jung's most effective counter to charges of Lamarckism was the distinction which he made between what he called the archetype-as-such and the

> images, ideas, feelings and behaviours that the archetype gives rise to. The archetype-as-such is the inherent neuropsychic system – the 'innate releasing mechanism' – which is responsible for patterns of behaviour such as the zigzag dance, or patterns of experience such as falling in love, when an appropriate member of the same species is encountered in the environment. . . . Jung's assertion that the archetype does not 'denote an inherited idea, but rather an inherited mode of functioning' was biologically unimpeachable. It was no more Lamarckian than saying that the male stickleback is innately predisposed to dance when he spies a gravid female, or that a child is innately equipped to speak or to run on two legs.[25]

The quote above represents, in a nutshell, the position Stevens defends in *Archetype*. Of all the claims Stevens makes in the book, his statement that 'the archetype-as-such is the inherent neuropsychic system – the "innate releasing mechanism"' is the most important one in light of the topic of this book. This, then, is what I will focus on in the next section.

3.1.2 The 'innate releasing mechanism'

The term 'innate releasing mechanism' is a central concept of classical ethology. It became a well-known term primarily as a result of the work of two men who are generally seen as the founders of the discipline: the Dutchman Nikolaas (or Niko) Tinbergen and the German Konrad Lorenz. Both men were given the Nobel prize for their work in 1972, and as they were lifelong collaborators it should come as no surprise that the respective models which they put forth to explain animal behaviour are very similar. Lorenz's model is usually described as the 'hydraulic reservoir' theory; Tinbergen's model as the 'hierarchical system of centres' theory. R. A. Hinde, himself an ethologist, gives a good summary of the two models in his paper 'Ethological models and the concept of "drive"':

> Lorenz postulates for each instinctive act a particular 'reaction specific energy' which he pictures as accumulating in a reservoir with a spring-valve at its base. In an appropriate stimulus situation, the spring-valve is released partly by the hydrostatic pressure of the reservoir's contents and partly by the action of the external stimulus, which is pictured as a weight on a scale pan pulling against the spring. Tinbergen, considering the total behaviour of the animal, uses a basically similar analogy when he speaks of 'motivational impulses' accumulating in 'nervous centres' where they are held in check by a 'block' which can be removed

> by an 'innate releasing mechanism' responsive to particular external stimuli.[26]

Although the term IRM is only used by Hinde in his description of Tinbergen's model, it should be noted that Lorenz's model expresses basically the same idea. In that model, the external stimulus triggers a spring-valve, which results in the emptying of the reservoir (a metaphor for the specific drive which is set into motion by the stimulus). The releasing mechanism in Lorenz's model, then, is the spring-valve: it 'releases' the emptying of the reservoir in response to a stimulus. Although it seems that Tinbergen was the first one to use the term IRM, it quickly became a standard term used by many writers in the field, Lorenz included. Stevens discusses Tinbergen and Lorenz as if their views were relatively homogeneous, and uses the term IRM in the context of the work of both men. Whether this approach is correct or not is not the issue at stake here. What is important at this point is to present Stevens' point of view, and for this reason I will follow his approach and treat the work of Lorenz and Tinbergen as if the differences between the two men are negligible.

As we can see from the way Hinde describes the models of Lorenz and Tinbergen in the quote above, a key concept in their respective theories is the term 'stimulus'. This is the event, or collection of events, in the environment of the animal that triggers the IRM. According to Lorenz and Tinbergen, the fact that animals have evolved in a specific environment means that the IRMs they are born with are only triggered by a highly specific set of stimuli. The term IRM is therefore, as Hinde puts it, 'a hypothetical construct first introduced to account for the observation that an animal responds to only a limited part of the total stimulus situation when making an inborn response.'[27] Anthony Stevens puts it as follows in *Archetype*:

> Thus, ethology teaches that all organisms are programmed to perceive the world in specific ways, to select and respond to key stimuli which possess special significance within the context of the organism's Umwelt. . . . It was to explain this process that Niko Tinbergen proposed his hypothesis of an innate releasing mechanism (IRM for short). It is through the operation of such innate mechanisms that ethologists believe many patterns of social behaviour to be activated.[28]

Stevens gives many examples of IRMs found in animals in *Archetype*. One classic example he mentions is the way newborn chicks react to the image of a hawk. If you pull a wooden hawk over a hatch of chicks, they will cower and emit screams of terror. This response is innate, as it is obvious that newborn chicks have never seen a hawk before, and even react in this way if the hawk is not a real one but a wooden model. As Stevens claims, one can raise generation after generation of chicks without the IRM disappearing, even if intermittent generations are not exposed to the image of a hawk at all. This strengthens the hypothesis that the behaviour displayed is what the term IRM implies: innate.

Another classic example of an IRM is the 'zig-zag dance' of the stickleback, a fish found abundantly in temperate regions of the Northern Hemisphere.[29] Stevens describes the courting behaviour of the stickleback as follows:

> [The] courting behaviour of the male stickleback on encountering a pregnant female . . . is released by two sign (or 'key') stimuli – the swollen abdomen of the female, and the special posturing movement she makes on sighting the male. For her part, the female's courting behaviour is also released by two sign stimuli the male's red belly and his special movements, the 'zigzag dance'.[30]

These examples of IRMs are exactly the kind of examples Jung gave when he wrote about the archetype as a 'pattern of behaviour'. I already quoted the following passage in the introduction to this chapter:

> [The concept of the archetype] is not meant to denote an inherited idea, but rather an inherited mode of functioning, corresponding to the inborn way in which the chick emerges from the egg, the bird builds its nest, a certain kind of wasp stings the motor ganglion of the caterpillar, and eels find their way to the Bermudas. In other words, it is a 'pattern of behaviour'. This aspect of the archetype, the purely biological one, is the proper concern of scientific psychology.[31]

Jung, of course, was quick to point out that humans are born with such inborn 'patterns of behaviour' as well. As I wrote in the introduction, this has led some of his interpreters to think that Jung claimed that the archetypes found in the human nervous system are all wholly innate and fixed from birth. Stevens, by claiming that what Jung meant by his concept of the archetype is the same as the ethological notion of the IRM, seems to be saying exactly the same at first glance. The problem with making such a claim, however, is that all of the IRMs mentioned above (both by Stevens and by Jung) are IRMs of a specific kind: they are both simple and immutable.

There is absolutely no learning involved in their operation: the animal is born with the pattern, and it can be triggered by events that the animal has never been in contact with before. These particular kinds of IRMs are sometimes referred to as 'key-tumbler' responses, because the sign stimulus that triggers them is always exactly the same and therefore corresponds to the IRM like a key to a lock. They are also sometimes referred to as 'closed' IRMs, because they are not open to 'imprinting' by the environment.

The problem with claiming that human beings contain such 'closed' IRMs is, of course, that human beings are not really like sticklebacks or baby chicks at all. As Steven Pinker puts it rather wittily:

> People can be forgiven for scoffing at the suggestion that human behavior is 'in the genes' or 'a product of evolution' in the senses familiar from the animal world. Human acts are not selected from a repertoire of knee-jerk reactions like a fish attacking a red spot or a hen sitting on eggs. Instead, people may worship goddesses, auction kitsch on the Internet, play air guitar, fast to atone for past sins, build forts out of lawn chairs, and so on, seemingly without limit. A glance at National Geographic shows that even the strangest acts in our own culture do not exhaust what our species is capable of. If anything goes, one might think, then perhaps we are . . . unconstrained agents after all.[32]

Stevens, however, shows himself to be acutely aware of this problem. Like Pinker, he acknowledges that human behaviour is much more open to learning than the behaviour of animals, and therefore much more flexible:

> [It] is undeniable that the cultural and environmental circumstances into which a human child is born will influence his behaviour as an adult to a greater extent than is true of members of other mammalian species.[33]

Stevens points out that even in the animal kingdom there are many examples of IRMs that are not as closed as the IRMs in the examples we have so far discussed. A classic example of such an 'open' IRM which Stevens mentions is the way in which the young gosling attaches itself to the first moving object it sees after it emerges from its egg. Unlike the closed IRMs that we have dealt with above, this is an IRM which is open to imprinting. According to Stevens, probably all of the IRMs found in human beings are of this kind, and it is these kind of open IRMs that he claims are akin to Jung's concept of the archetype. He compares this conception of the archetype – of a *partially* innate structure, which is determined as to its content by the environment of the organism – to the findings of John Bowlby, who, as we have seen, is one of the main influences on Stevens' thought. He quotes the following passage from Bowlby's work:

> Instinctive behaviour is not inherited. What is inherited is the potential to develop . . . behavioural systems, both the nature and form of which differ in some measure according to the particular environment in which development takes place.[34]

We can now see why Stevens attaches such tremendous importance to the distinction Jung made between the archetype-as-such and the archetypal images and ideas the archetype gives rise to. This distinction corresponds very neatly to the distinction Bowlby makes above: between an inherited *potential* to develop behavioural systems on the one hand, and the actual behaviour which that potential gives rise to on the other hand. The difference between Bowlby and Jung is a matter of focus: Jung, being a naturally introverted psychologist, was interested in the 'inner': the contents of consciousness that accompany instinctive processes in the unconscious. Bowlby, as a man of 'hard' science, is interested in the 'outer': the empirically observable behaviour that is the end-result of the instinctive process. Both, however, acknowledge that there is an inborn potential which gives rise to the different images (Jung) and forms of behaviour (Bowlby). Bowlby, as we can see in the quote above, stresses that instinctive behaviour is not wholly innate: it is influenced by the environment as well. As Stevens claims, Jung too acknowledged this fact, and it is here that he departs from interpreters of Jung's work who claim that Jungian archetypes are fixed from birth. To back up his claims, Stevens offers the following quote from Jung's work:

> Again and again I encounter the mistaken notion that an archetype is determined in regard to its content, in other words that it is a kind of unconscious idea (if such an expression be permissible). It is necessary to point out once more that archetypes are not determined as to their content, but only as regards their form, and then only to a very limited degree. *A primordial image is determined as to its content only when it has become conscious and is therefore filled out with the material of conscious experience* [my italics].[35]

The last sentence of this quote is especially revealing. It seems to confirm that Jung, contrary to what is sometimes claimed, does indeed grant that human experience plays a large role in the way the archetype takes shape. Archetypes are not 'wholly innate': although there is an innate component to them (the archetype-as-such), the archetype itself is 'determined as to its content only when it has become conscious and is therefore filled out with the material of conscious experience'.[36]

This, in broad strokes, is Stevens' interpretation of Jung's concept of the archetype. As we will see in the chapters to come, it is an interpretation which matches very closely the interpretation of the concept of the archetype which Joseph Campbell arrived at in the final phase of his career. Because of the emphasis Stevens puts on the distinction Jung made in 1946 between the archetype-as-such and the archetypal images and ideas, this is an interpretation that focuses primarily on the ideas of the late Jung. It can be summed up by the following statements:

- *The archetype is essentially a biological concept: it is a 'neuro-psychic centre'.*
- *The archetype is the result of evolution. More specifically, it is the product of natural selection.*
- *The concept of the archetype is equivalent to the concept of IRM.*
- *The archetype is not wholly innate: it is open to imprinting. It is therefore to be thought of as the equivalent of an 'open' IRM.*
- *The archetype is therefore what makes an organism respond in a highly, but not wholly, preprogrammed way to certain key stimuli in the organism's environment.*

I will now move on to the next section, in which I will deal with Stevens' interpretation of Jung's concept of the *unus mundus*.

3.2 Why religion?

J. J. Clarke, in his book *In search of Jung*, describes Jung's concept of the archetype as follows:

> [The archetype is] the uniquely human means whereby instinctual, biological energy is transformed into the meaningful symbolic life of the human psyche.[37]

For some scholars this is where their interpretation of Jung ends: they only focus on this biological dimension of his ideas. The fact that the terms we have dealt with so far in this chapter are all rooted squarely in the world of instinct and biology seems to lend strong support to this view of

Jung's theories. When Jung writes that the true meaning of the term archetype is the biological 'pattern of behaviour', we could conclude with some justification that Jung saw the psyche as 'nothing but' biology. Seen this way, Jung's position wouldn't be so different from Freud's position after all. This becomes especially clear when we apply this 'biological interpretation' of the archetype to religion. If religion is 'nothing but' archetypal images, and if archetypal images are 'nothing but' a symbolic reflection of biological processes, then one would have to conclude that for Jung, too, religion is ultimately an illusion. He would differ only from Freud in that for him this would be a *beneficial* illusion: being exposed to religious motifs is healthy for the psyche, even though the motifs themselves are 'nothing but' psychology or biology. Some scholars who endorse this view of Jung's theories – the theologian Michael Palmer, for example – therefore claim that Jung isn't really a 'friend' of religion at all: by stating that religious experience is shaped by archetypes, they claim, Jung is reducing religion to 'nothing but' psychology.[38]

For Stevens, however, this interpretation of Jung does not do justice to the facts. According to him, Jung's concept of the archetype is not just 'the human means whereby instinctual energy is transformed into the symbolic life of the psyche', as Clarke puts it; it is also an expression of what Jung (as we have seen in the previous chapter) called the *unus mundus*: a transcendent dimension which lies not only at the root of the psyche but at the root of the material world as well. Read this way, Jung's concept of the archetype becomes not just a psychology but also a cosmology. Although Stevens deals with these ideas briefly in *Archetype* as well, it is only in his paper 'Thoughts on the psychobiology of religion and the neurobiology of archetypal experience'[39] (from hereon abbreviated as 'Thoughts') that he deals with them in depth. In this paper, written in 1986 for the academic journal *Zygon*, Stevens focuses primarily on this metaphysical dimension of Jung's ideas. Whereas in *Archetype* he often seems to give the impression that he himself falls in the 'biology only' camp as well, in the *Zygon* paper he makes it obvious that for him there is much more to be said about Jung's ideas than that. In this section I will give an overview of the ideas put forward by Stevens in this paper.

3.2.1 Thoughts on the psychobiology of religion and the neurobiology of archetypal experience

Stevens first delivered 'Thoughts' at a conference organized by *Zygon* in memory of the renowned cultural anthropologist Victor Turner, who died in 1983. Turner, before his death, had been an important contributor to *Zygon* himself. In an article titled 'Body, brain and culture',[40] published in the September issues of 1983, Turner took up a position remarkably similar to the one Stevens defends in *Archetype*. David Glover, editorial assistant for *Zygon*, calls this paper by Turner 'a radical breakthrough':

> Turner's 1983 *Zygon* article was a radical breakthrough for the cognitive sciences. Here was a renowned cultural anthropologist calling for more attention to the biogenetic approaches to his field – prior to this, the two camps were at odds with each other.[41]

Stevens begins 'Thoughts' by reflecting on the fact that Turner not only defended a similar position to his own one in 'Body, brain and culture', but even explicitly mentioned his book *Archetype*. Stevens writes that the fact that Turner endorsed the ideas he put forward in this book came as something of a surprise to him:

> Victor Turner was kind enough to mention my book *Archetype* (1982) in his paper 'Body, Brain, and Culture in the Ritual Process' (1983). Surprisingly, he did not seem adverse to the suggestion which I develop in my book that essential features of the human life cycle are predetermined from the moment of conception – not only anatomically and physiologically, but psychologically as well. That so eminent an anthropologist should not be outraged by such an idea was a source of delight and encouragement to me.[42]

After this introduction, Stevens then once more presents what is one of the central hypotheses of *Archetype*: that throughout most of the twentieth century the 'blank slate' paradigm was the dominant one. Writing in 1986, four years after the first edition of *Archetype* was published, Stevens is also once again claiming that this paradigm is increasingly under fire. He stresses that Turner agreed with him that this was a highly important development for the humanities:

> We [Stevens and Turner] both saw that psychology and psychiatry, as well as sociology and anthropology, were in danger of becoming self-serving and sterile because of a form of selective myopia which resulted in a refusal to examine their data in a biological or phylogenetic perspective. By denying the phylogenetic dimension they rendered themselves incapable of seeing the wood for the trees. They could not perceive the phenomena of human life *sub specie aeternitatis*.[43]

It is within the context of this 'paradigm shift' that Stevens wants to discuss what was the topic of the conference where he presented his paper: the relevance of neurobiology for the study of religious phenomena. In order to deal with this topic, he turns to the work of the thinker with which he is most familiar: Jung.

> That religion does possess an archetypal basis in human nature Jung was in no doubt. His extensive studies in comparative mythology and religion, as well as his clinical insights into the function of religious symbolism in his patients and in himself, convinced him that all religions are true expressions of the biological reality of the Self. (The Self is Jung's term for the central coordinating nucleus of the entire archetypal endowment of the human individual.)[44]

Even though, as we will see, Stevens does not claim that a Jungian interpretation of religion reduces religion to 'nothing but' biology, he does stress that Jung thought that religious phenomena are to a large extent determined by biological processes. Stevens writes that he agrees with Jung in this regard. For him, the fact that religious ideas are both as widespread and persistent as they are gives strong support to the hypothesis that there is an innate component to the way in which individuals 'learn' religion. In 'Thoughts', Stevens calls this innate component 'the rule-learning device':[45] as he puts it, this is 'an imperative already present in the genome – a phylogenetic instruction *to learn the rules* [Stevens' italics].'[46] Stevens states that he thinks this 'rule-learning device' functions as an 'open program', much like Noam Chomsky's language acquiring device. It is an innate complex 'primed to be programmed with the religious/mythological/moral "vocabulary" of the culture'.[47]

One can clearly see the echoes of the ideas Stevens put forward in *Archetype* in these statements: what Stevens is here calling the 'rule-learning device' is quite obviously the equivalent of what in *Archetype* he called the open IRM. This, in turn, is the equivalent of Jung's the archetype-as-such. As Stevens claimed in *Archetype*, the IRMs (or archetypes-as-such) found in the human nervous system are open to imprinting: they are not fixed, 'key-tumbler' IRMs like those found predominantly in animals, but 'open IRMs' which are programmed by the experiences of the individual who is born with them. Religious and mythological images, therefore, should be seen as having a cultural *and* an innate component. Although the blueprint that enables the learning is there from birth, the specific shape the religious image takes on is nonetheless determined by the culture (as well as the environment) in which the individual in question is born.

At the root of the ideas Stevens puts forward in 'Thoughts' about the 'rule-learning device', then, lies once again Jung's distinction between the archetype-as-such and the archetypal image. What we find on the psychobiological level are archetypes-as-such; what we find on the cultural level are archetypal images. As such, Stevens' claims about the relationship between Jung's concept of the archetype and myth and religion are almost exactly the same as the Jungian interpretation of 'mythmaking' Steven Walker puts forward in his book 'Jung and the Jungians on myth and mythology':

> Mythmaking thus has to be viewed as an archaic form of artistic activity. As the active and conscious elaboration of an archetypal image, mythmaking brings what is relatively timeless (the archetypal image as a representation of the instinctual world of the archetypes) into the world of human history; mythmaking brings what is pre-cultural into the world of human culture. Since the archetypal image as archetypal motif becomes represented in a myth in the terms of a particular culture and of a particular moment in history, it is improper to consider a myth as ageless or as universal as an archetype, since it bears the particular stamp of the specific age and culture that produces it.[48]

After this discussion of the 'rule-learning device' Stevens then asks the question I already dealt with briefly in the introduction to this section: is this all to be said about Jung's ideas about religion? Can religion be reduced to 'nothing but' neurobiology, or does religious experience have an ontological 'referent' (my term) as well? As Stevens himself rephrases this question: 'does the fact that I experience God mean that there must be a God out there for me to experience?'[49]

Stevens stops short of claiming that the experience of God proves that God exists, however. He agrees with Jung on this topic, who wrote that 'the idea of God is an absolutely necessary psychological function of an irrational nature, which has nothing whatever to do with the question of God's existence. The human intellect can never answer this question, still less give any proof of God.'[50] On the other hand, Stevens isn't claiming that a Jungian interpretation of religion forces one to conclude that religion can be defined solely in neurobiological terms either. On the contrary, the key point that Stevens wants to make in 'Thoughts' is that this isn't the case. For Stevens, Jung's concept of the archetype ultimately represents much more than just a psychology:

> Followed to its logical conclusion, Jung's seminal concept [of the archetype] carries us out of the realms of psychology and anthropology, and beyond the confines of biology itself. Jung's view of the material, non-psychic aspect of the archetype was embraced by the physicist and Nobel Laureate Wolfgang Pauli, who saw it as a major contribution to our understanding of the laws of nature. For Pauli the archetype represented a sort of 'missing link' between the material world, which is the legitimate study of physical science, and the mind of the scientist who studies it. Jung's postulate was not just 'the bridge to matter in general' but to a 'cosmic order independent of our choice and distinct from the world of phenomena'.[51]

This cosmic order that so impressed Wolfgang Pauli, of course, is none other than the *unus mundus*. For Stevens, this concept is of vital importance if one wants to truly understand Jung's ideas about religion. For him, this concept shows that a Jungian interpretation of religious experience does not reduce religion to 'nothing but' psychological or neurological structures. As Stevens puts it, this concept shows that Jung thought that 'the archetypes which order our perceptions and ideas are *themselves* the product of an objective order which *transcends* both the human mind *and* the external world.'[52] According to Stevens, then, J. J. Clarke's statement that '[the archetype is] the uniquely human means whereby instinctual, biological energy is transformed into the meaningful symbolic life of the human psyche'[53] does not represent the ultimate truth about Jung's concept of the archetype. Although he acknowledges that there is most definitely a link between religion and the innate structures of the mind (which have been shaped by our evolutionary history), religion cannot be reduced to these structures. This, in a nutshell, is the ultimate point that Stevens is trying to make in 'Thoughts'. The summary that he gives at the beginning of the paper conveys this very neatly:

> There is good reason to suppose that religious belief and ritual are manifestations of the archetypal blueprint for human existence encoded in the genetic structure of our species. As a consequence, religion has become a focus of study for psychobiologists and neuroscientists. However, scientific explanations of religious experience do not 'explain away' such experience nor are they substitutes for the

experience itself. On the contrary, scientific discoveries may be seen as corroboration of religious insights into the *unus mundus*, the essential oneness of all experience, which links human nature with the nature of the cosmos.[54]

3.3 Conclusion

Summing up, I believe Stevens' interpretation of Jung is distinctive from other interpretations in two regards:

The archetype-as-such and the archetypal image

First of all, Stevens' interpretation differs from other interpretations in the emphasis it places on Jung's distinction between the archetype-as-such and the archetypal image. It is this distinction that lies at the root of all the ideas he puts forward in *Archetype*, and most of the ideas he puts forward in 'Thoughts'. Stevens believes that this distinction makes Jung's concept of the archetype 'biologically unimpeachable', and makes an interpretation of Jung possible that is fully in line with the findings of contemporary psychologists and ethologists. The archetype-as-such should be seen as the equivalent of the concept of the 'innate releasing mechanism', and even though Jung frequently gave examples of 'closed' IRMs when discussing his concept of the archetype, Stevens believes that Jung's archetypes should instead be seen as equivalent to so-called open IRMs. Stevens therefore calls the archetype-as-such an innate complex, 'primed to be programmed with the religious/mythological/moral "vocabulary" of the culture'.[55]

The **unus mundus**

The second aspect of Stevens' interpretation of Jung that distinguishes him from other interpreters is the emphasis he places on the concept of the *unus mundus*. The *unus mundus* is an aspect of Jung's theoretical framework that not many Jung scholars write about.[56] According to Stevens, however, this concept is crucial if one wants to truly understand Jung's ideas, especially his ideas about religion. For him, the *unus mundus* makes it clear that Jung's theory of religion is not just psychological in nature but metaphysical as well. A Jungian theory of religion, therefore, does not 'explain away' religion.

In part two of this book (to which we will now turn) I will relate these two aspects of Stevens' thought to the work of Joseph Campbell. As I will show, Campbell's interpretation of Jung is similar to that of Stevens in both regards. I will also argue that there is ample evidence to suggest that Campbell was aware of the fact that this interpretation leads to the conclusion that his own most important ideas can be seen as highly similar to Jung's ideas, even though he himself sometimes protested that he wasn't a Jungian.

Notes

1 Jung, *CW 18*, par. 1228.
2 Robert Segal, *Introduction*, pp. 249–250.
3 Quoted in Anthony Stevens, *Archetype revisited – an updated natural history of the self*, second edn (London: Brunner-Routledge, 2002).
4 Quoted in Anthony Stevens, *Jung – a very short introduction* (Oxford: Oxford University Press, 2001).
5 Anthony Stevens and John Price, *Evolutionary psychology: a new beginning*, second edn (London: Routledge, 2000).
6 Stevens, *Archetype revisited*, p. 17.
7 Anthony Stevens, *Archetype – a natural history of the self* (London: Routledge & Kegan Paul, 1982).
8 Anthony Stevens, 'Thoughts on the psychobiology of religion and the neurobiology of archetypal experience', *Zygon* 21 (March 1986).
9 Stevens, *Archetype revisited*, p. 16.
10 Steven Pinker, *The blank slate: the modern denial of human nature* (London: Allen Lane, 2002).
11 J. B. Watson, *Behaviorism*, second edn (New York: Norton, 1930). Quoted in Pinker, *The blank slate: the modern denial of human nature*, p. 11.
12 Emile Durkheim, *The rules of sociological method*, trans. S. S. Solvay and J. H. Mueller (New York: Free Press, 1950 [1895]). Quoted in Pinker, *The blank slate: the modern denial of human nature*, p. 24.
13 Margaret Mead, *Sex and temperament in three primitive societies* (New York: Harper Perennial, 2001 [1935]). Quoted in Pinker, *The blank slate: the modern denial of human nature*, p. 25.
14 Stevens, *Archetype revisited*, p. 23.
15 Ibid., p. xii.
16 Ibid.
17 Ibid., p. 56.
18 Ibid., p. 57.
19 Ibid., p. 53.
20 Ibid.
21 Ibid., p. 59.
22 Ibid., p. 66.

[23] Ibid., p. 16.
[24] Jung, *CW 18*, par. 1228.
[25] Stevens, *Archetype revisited*, p. 18.
[26] R. A. Hinde, 'Ethological models and the concept of "drive"', *The British journal for the philosophy of science* 6, no. 24 (February 1956), pp. 321–322.
[27] Ibid., p. 328.
[28] Stevens, *Archetype revisited*, p. 63.
[29] 'Stickleback.' Encyclopædia Britannica Deluxe Edition CD (2005). Copyright © 1994–2004 Encyclopædia Britannica, Inc. 30 May 2004.
[30] Stevens, *Archetype revisited*, p. 64.
[31] Jung, *CW 18*, par. 1228.
[32] Pinker, *The blank slate: the modern denial of human nature*, p. 36.
[33] Stevens, *Archetype revisited*, p. 25.
[34] Quoted in ibid., p. 58.
[35] Jung, *CW 9 part 1*, par. 155.
[36] Ibid.
[37] J. J. Clarke, *In search of Jung* (New York: Routledge, 1992), p. 136.
[38] Michael Palmer, *Freud and Jung on religion* (London: Routledge, 1997).
[39] Stevens, 'Thoughts on the psychobiology of religion and the neurobiology of archetypal experience.'
[40] Victor Turner. 1983. 'Body, brain, and culture', *Zygon* 18 (September): 221–245.
[41] http://www.zygonjournal.org/archive/cognitive_sciences.html [accessed 1 September 2008].
[42] Stevens, 'Thoughts on the psychobiology of religion and the neurobiology of archetypal experience', p. 9.
[43] Ibid., p. 11.
[44] Ibid., p. 14.
[45] Ibid., p. 15.
[46] Ibid.
[47] Ibid., pp. 15–16.
[48] Steven Walker, *Jung and the Jungians on myth and mythology: an introduction* (New York/London: Routledge, 2002), p. 19.
[49] Stevens, 'Thoughts on the psychobiology of religion and the neurobiology of archetypal experience', p. 19.
[50] Jung, *CW 7*, par. 110.
[51] Stevens, 'Thoughts on the psychobiology of religion and the neurobiology of archetypal experience', pp. 18–19.
[52] Ibid., p. 19.
[53] Clarke, *In search of Jung*, p. 136.
[54] Stevens, 'Thoughts on the psychobiology of religion and the neurobiology of archetypal experience', p. 9.
[55] Ibid., pp. 15–16.
[56] Marie-Louise von Franz is a notable exception. She devotes an entire chapter to the *unus mundus* in her book *C.G. Jung: his myth in our time.* [Marie-Louise von Franz, *C.G. Jung – his myth in our time* (New York: Putnam, 1975).]

Part Two

Campbell

Chapter 4

Campbell's life

In this chapter I will give a brief overview of the most important events in Joseph Campbell's life. As such, it contains no information that is essential for the arguments that I will be making further on in this book. It has been included merely to provide the reader who does not know much about Campbell's life with some of the most important details. That said, I would like to point out that I have also included some information which I obtained while doing research at the Campbell Archive in California, some of which may be new even to the reader who already has an extensive background knowledge of the key events in Campbell's life.

4.1 Boyhood and student years

Joseph Campbell was born in New York City on 26 March 1904. His father, of Irish descent, was a salesman for a warehouse specializing in hosiery, and his mother, of Scottish-Irish descent, was a full-time housewife. There were no major traumas to speak of in Campbell's early childhood: the family was comfortably upper middle-class, with a vacation home, private education and frequent holidays to Europe to enjoy for all. Campbell went to a day-school convent run by nuns until he was 15, and later attended a prestigious Catholic preparatory school in New Milford, Connecticut, for 2 years. Although Campbell broke with the Catholic church while in college and remained critical of the more dogmatic aspects of the tradition throughout the rest of his life, he nevertheless spoke fondly later on about its emphasis on symbolism and ritual. He also related these aspects of the Catholic church to his lifelong interest in mythology:

> And when you're born in an Irish Catholic family and environment and spend your boyhood with nuns, and you're serving mass (I was a little altar boy), you're studying the Catholic doctrine all the time with deep belief. And I think anyone who has not been a Catholic in that sort of

substantial way has no realization of the ambience of religion within which you live. It's powerful; it's potent – it's life-supporting. And it's beautiful. The Catholic religion is a poetic religion. Every month has its poetic and spiritual value. Boy, that got into me. I'm sure that my interest in mythology comes out of that.[1]

Another formative influence which helped to spark an interest in mythology in the young Campbell was his interest in Native American traditions. After allegedly reading every single book on the subject in his local library, Campbell by age 13 had begun to think of himself as an expert in the field:

By the time I was thirteen I knew about as much about the American Indian as a good many anthropologists that I have met since. They know the sociological interpretations of why the Indians are the way they are or were, but they don't know much about Indians. And I did know.[2]

From an early age on, then, Campbell was in a position to compare the mythological motifs of two wholly different traditions. What would become one of his trademark ideas – that there are similar motifs in traditions from all over the world – was something that seems to have occurred to him even when he was a young boy. As he put it in an interview later on in his life:

[I]t didn't take me long to realize there were virgin births, deaths and resurrections, in both mythological systems. So very early on I became interested in this comparative realization, and by the age of eleven or twelve, I was pretty well into the material.[3]

A third determining factor in Campbell's early life besides his obsession with Native Americans and his Catholic upbringing was his fascination with the world of nature. The Campbell family had a holiday house in the Pocono mountains in Pennsylvania, where Campbell spent a lot of time as a boy. One of the occupants of a nearby cottage was Elmer Gregor, an author of books about Native Americans who also knew a lot about the local wildlife. Gregor would become Campbell's first mentor: they went fishing together, studied the local animals and plant life and talked for hours on end about Native Americans.

And so this beautiful place [the Campbell's holiday house] became my real discovery of nature. My emphasis on biology and nature and the body in my writing about myth comes out of those years. It is really a combination that comes from this man, who was a naturalist as well as an Indian scholar. He put me right on the road. Elmer Gregor. I remember him as a great. We used to communicate across the dining room with Indian sign language, and all that kind of thing.[4]

So inspired was Campbell by his boyhood exposure to the animal and plant kingdom that he decided to make biology one of his main subjects when he enrolled as a freshman at Dartmouth, an Ivy League college in Hanover, New Hampshire. After having been given a copy of *The romance of Leonardo da Vinci* by Dimitri Merejkowski, however, Campbell decided to stop studying biology and transfer to a course in the humanities instead:

When I was in prep school I was interested in biology and mathematics, and that was also true in my freshman year in Dartmouth. But in the interval between my freshman and sophomore years somebody gave me Dimitri Merejkowski's *The Romance of Leonardo da Vinci.* That is what turned me on. My God, I discovered that I didn't know anything about the world of art and culture and civilization. I knew about American Indians but not about art and civilization. My whole world shifted with that book.[5]

After having studied at Dartmouth for only one year Campbell went to Columbia, where he signed up for a Bachelor in English literature. During his years at Columbia Campbell also took a more practical interest in the arts, particularly in music. His diaries show that he took up playing the piano, often playing it for hours on end; he also started to play saxophone in a Jazz combo. Besides these instruments Campbell also learned how to play the violin, banjo, guitar, mandolin and ukulele.[6]

After having successfully obtained his B.A. in 1925 Campbell stayed on at Columbia to do his M.A., this time specializing in medieval literature (with a special focus on Arthurian romances). Once again, a comparative outlook seems to have come naturally to him:

Well, when I started reading the medieval material I became so excited. There were the old myth motifs again which I remembered from my Indian days, particularly in the Arthurian stuff.[7]

His thesis on '*Le morte d'Arthur*' won him a Proudfit travelling scholarship, which he used to study in Paris for a year in 1927. It was here that Campbell received his initiation into a world about which he knew almost nothing at that point in time: the world of modern art.

> The discovery of modern art happened when I was in Paris. . . . Well, I had come over from good ole rural America, you might say, and this whole world of far-out, avant-garde, well . . . bohemians was totally new. And my opening up to the world of art and its relationship to my life took place there.[8]

Campbell came to Paris to study Old French and Provencal, but left the city with a number of completely unrelated discoveries under his belt that would stay with him for the rest of his life. Stephen and Robin Larsen argue in their biographical 'guest' chapter written for John Lobell's *Joseph Campbell – the man and his ideas* that it was here that Campbell's lifelong fascination with 'the creative journey of the artist' [Stephen and Robin Larsen's words] began:

> While in Paris from 1927–1928, Campbell socialized with artists and scholars and renewed his friendship with Krishnamurti.[9] Their creative group socialized together, discussing philosophy and art. It was very likely here that Campbell s lifelong fascination with the creative journey of the artist began. Here also he broke with the Catholicism of his upbringing.[10]

Although it could be argued that this pivotal moment had taken place earlier (e.g. with Campbell's discovery of Leonardo da Vinci) his time in Paris certainly had a defining influence when it came to his later ideas. It was in Paris that Campbell first discovered the novels of James Joyce, about whom he would eventually write a book and to whom he would devote countless essays and lectures; it was in Paris, also, that Campbell came into contact with Antoinne Bourdelle, a famous sculptor and painter who shared with Campbell his ideas about the nature of art and the role of the artist. This event in particular would have a defining influence on the way Campbell later came to see myth: not as a divine revelation, but as a natural product of the human imagination – as art.

> One phrase of [Bourdelle's] got into my mind and it's been there as a kind of a guiding phrase ever since: '*L'art fait ressortir les grandes lignes de la nature.*' 'Art brings out the grand lines of nature.' And this is what myths are also about.[11]

After having discovered that a great many books about the subjects he was interested in (which included, increasingly, everything to do with mythology) were published only in German, Campbell wrote to Columbia to ask if they would extend his scholarship so that he might study in Germany for a while. His request was granted, and in 1928 Campbell left Paris for Munich, where he would stay for another year.

> Then I went the next year [fall of 1928] to Munich. There I discovered what we didn't know in the United States at that time: I discovered Freud, I discovered Jung, I discovered Thomas Mann, and I started my study of Sanskrit. One of the wonderful things about coming all at once out of the realm of Columbia University into the world of what one of my professors called 'the castle of German scholarship' – and Sanskrit at the same time – was an awakening that you can't imagine. And there it was that I found what the depths were in the richness of the world that I had been dealing with in dealing with Arthurian romance, and the Celtic material that I had loved ever since early boyhood, and the American Indian myths where the same motifs existed.[12]

After his year in Germany was over Campbell returned to the United States. Having already decided that he was going to take his Ph.D. at Columbia before he went to Europe, Campbell now wanted to incorporate all the different influences he had soaked up during his stay on the continent in his upcoming thesis. He went back to Columbia to discuss these plans, but discovered that Europe had made him somewhat incompatible with the academic *milieu* at Columbia:

> I went back up to Columbia to go on with my work on the PhD and told them, 'This whole thing has opened out.'
>
> 'Oh, no', they said. 'You don't follow that. You stay where you were before you went to Europe.'
>
> Well, I just said, 'To hell with it.'[13]

This clash with the academic establishment would prove to be a fateful event in Campbell's life. Although he would later teach at a small New England college for girls (Sarah Lawrence), Campbell would never really fit in again with the academic crowd after he came back from Europe. He would find his main audience elsewhere, although after he had just come back from Europe he still had no idea about where to find it.

> The world had blown open. I'm no longer in the Ph.D. bottle. I don't want to go on with my little Arthurian pieces. I had much more exciting things to do – and I didn't know what they were.[14]

4.2 Development of core ideas

As far as career prospects were concerned Campbell couldn't have chosen a worse time to come back to the United States. He arrived in New York on 23 August 1929; three weeks later, the stock market crashed and the great depression began.[15] Because Campbell was lucky enough to have a rather large sum of money to his name (which he had earned while playing in his Jazz band while at Columbia) he was able to support himself for several years, which meant he could continue his intensive reading program on his own.

> I left Europe three weeks before the Wall Street crash. The only money I had was what I'd made playing in a jazz band in college. I'd earned several thousand dollars – which was a lot in those days – and that was what I had until it disappeared. I didn't make another cent for five years.[16]

He retreated to a cabin in Woodstock, a small village in upstate New York mostly populated by artists. Here Campbell continued his love affair with the world of modern art and bohemia that he had started on the continent. Almost everyone in the community was working in some creative field or other, with people engaging in everything from music to dance to creative writing and sculpting. In Woodstock Campbell became acquainted with the novelist Henry Morton Robinson, like Campbell a Joyce aficionado. It was with Robertson that Campbell would later write his first book, a companion to Joyce's *Finnegan's wake.* Robinson's wife, Gertrude Robinson, wrote the following about the atmosphere in the community at the time that Campbell was there:

> Everybody was poor. Nobody had money. Everybody was an artist. Nobody had a bathroom, running water. Electricity came through sometime in the thirties.
>
> . . .
>
> And we had all kinds of musicians coming up from New York. [The Woodstock concert hall] is where we used to give our festivals, and the Maverick Festivals[17] were marvellous. All the artists would do drawings and decorate the whole hall with these great big murals, and everybody would work on everybody else's mural. And we would have these terrific parties to raise money for some indigent artist, and these parties were fantastic. The musicians would play, we'd dance, we'd have all kinds of games going on, and there was a very free spirit, everybody in costume always.[18]

So infected had Campbell become with the artistic spirit, that he had at this point decided that he was going to become one himself. During his time in Woodstock Campbell worked night and day on what had at this point become his dream: to become a writer of fiction. He wrote numerous short stories, one of which he was later able to sell for about $300 – a considerable amount of money at the time. This story was called 'Strictly Platonic', and it was published in 1933 by *Liberty magazine.* Because it is very hard to find, I have decided to quote the opening passage here to give an idea of Campbell's fiction writing style.

> Across the campus from the Gothic gym was the Georgian red-brick Philosophy Building, where Old Dittman spent his office hours filling an oblong book-lined room with a stinking brand of tobacco smoke. By a window he sat with his long thin legs crossed; a saxophone pipe curled down against his silky fraying beard.
>
> Jim Weston sat in a hamstrung chair, watching him; a big-shouldered young fellow, threadbare in his dark suit, his shoes down at the heels.
>
> Old Dittman said: 'So I can't advise you, Weston, to be too stubborn about this thing.'
>
> Old Dittman frowned. 'I like your ideals – and – well – your spunk; but, just the same, Weston, your attitude seems to me to be altogether injudicious.'
>
> Jim opened his broad hands. 'But why is it injudicious?'
>
> The old smoky man smacked and rumbled. 'Because, Weston, these fellows have the power and will to break you.' He pointed with the moist stem of his pipe, rounding his eyes. 'This football crowd's been closing around our throats here like a garrotte. You ought to know, Weston – you played for them yourself once. They're fanatics. They've a stadium now worth more than any three buildings on the campus. They've a coach – my Lord, they pay him more than any ten professors! They've the alumni, the students, the trustees on their side; so they're the masters, that's all.' Dittman settled back. 'And we? You and I? The mere professors?' He answered himself rhetorically: 'We're the hired bits of camouflage stuck around to give an athletic club the complexion of a college.'
>
> Jim said: 'But Sir!' He rubbed his neck. 'We can't just let these fellows wipe their feet on – on scholarship – on everything Wilton College used to stand for! Now can we? Why *have* these eligibility rules if we're not to flunk a football man when he flunks?'
>
> Dittman was impatient. 'Those rules are part of the camouflage. Those rules don't mean a thing when a man like Cobb comes into question. Do you realize who he is?'

'Yes', Jim answered, ' I realize. All-American halfback two seasons in a row.'

Dittman nodded, looking grim. 'Tickets for this game are going at fifty dollars apiece because it's Larry Cobb's last game. And now your flunk makes him ineligible. Weston, they'll kill you! Kid these playboys, can't you? No use just being stubborn.'[19]

After two years in Woodstock Campbell moved to Monterey, California, where he once again lived in a small community of like-minded free-spirited individuals. One of them was the novelist John Steinbeck,[20] with whom Campbell became close friends for a while. Campbell stayed in Monterey for one year. After a brief and unsatisfying spell of teaching at his old prep-school (Canterbury) Campbell went back to Woodstock, where he once again returned to what was by this time his usual daily routine: read books, often for up to nine hours each day. Campbell had by now decided that writing fiction was not for him. Instead, his interest had returned to scholarly works, specifically those dealing with history, religion and mythology. The great thinkers he had discovered on the continent – Joyce, Mann, Jung and Freud – were still with him, but by this time Campbell had discovered other writers who would turn out to be just as influential. The two most important of these were Oswald Spengler and Leo Frobenius.

I remember that I just didn't have anybody to tell me what to read and so I began pulling these things together. The realization I discovered during those years – Oswald Spengler's *The Decline of the West*, and the marvellous work of Leo Frobenius, seeing these men talking about historical forms, and seeing how it all went with Jung and Freud and Mann and Joyce. . . . Those were great illuminations. And I didn't have to write a thesis. I didn't have to write anything. All I did was underline sentences and take notes.[21]

It was especially after the reading of Leo Frobenius' works – the scholar of African history and mythology whose concept of 'the night sea journey' also had a profound influence on Jung – that things started to fall into place. Having just read through most of Frobenius's 15 volumes, Campbell wrote the following in his diary:

I learned that the essential form of the myth is a cycle, and that this cycle is a symbolic representation of the form of the soul, and that in the dreams and fancies of modern individuals (who have been brought up

> along the lines of a rational, practical education) these myth-symbols actually reappear – giving testimony of a persistence, even into modem times, of the myth power.[22]

More and more, Campbell was able to combine his different influences and turn them into a coherent system. He was beginning to find his voice, and he was exhilarated to have done so. 'I begin to realize that if possible [this] has been an even bigger year than the one I spent in the West', he wrote to a friend. 'I feel it rolling me forward like a snowball gathering weight. I cannot possibly tell you what deep tones I feel resounding inside me.'[23]

To make things even better, Campbell was also offered a job at a small, progressive college for girls in 1934: Sarah Lawrence, in Bronxville, New York, which had opened its doors only eight years earlier. Campbell accepted, and started to prepare for his first course with great enthusiasm. After five years of living in relative poverty with nothing to do other than read and write his career was finally taking off, and this added to the enthusiasm he had felt about his recent insights. The above-quoted letter continues as follows:

> I like the job very much. Having an income and a set of limited working hours takes a good deal of the adventure out of the picture, but it is a pleasant rest for a change. So I am now a recognized member of the community with at least 9 months of future ahead of me. [24]

Despite his initial disappointment about the lack of adventure, Campbell would stay at Sarah Lawrence for the next 34 years. He often stressed later on that his particular approach to mythology – focusing specifically on the practical relevance for day-to-day life – was an outcome of the fact that he had taught the subject to women for such a long time. In an interview from 1977 he said that his students 'wanted to know how the myths I was teaching related to their lives. I could never get off into a little academic hole in the ceiling because they were always asking what it all meant.'[25]

Campbell, by all accounts, seems to have been a hugely popular teacher at Sarah Lawrence. Nancy Sureck, a former student of Campbell's, wrote a short article for the 1987 edition of *Sarah Lawrence College magazine* about Campbell as a teacher. She opens her article by writing the following:

> The influence of Professor Joseph Campbell on his students throughout his teaching career was extraordinary. I have my own memories of attending his classes thirty-eight years ago, but as memory is a fallible instrument,

> I tapped the recall of classmates. It did not surprise me that we have so many recollections in common: the electricity of Joseph Campbell's lectures, his profound mark on our spiritual lives and thinking process, the battles we waged to get into his class. Our respect was akin to worship and we all appreciate that we studied with a unique mind.[26]

Another student of Campbell's, Sarah Hunter, had this to say about Campbell's lectures in a *New York times* article published just after Campbell's death:

> I walked away from his conferences and I felt like doing cartwheels. I felt my work with him was the apex of my intellectual experience, not only at Sarah Lawrence, but of my whole life. He really taught you to think and gave you confidence to go into the depths of your mind.[27]

4.3 Professional career

Campbell's job at Sarah Lawrence was only the first of several professional and personal successes that would come his way during the mid-1930s and 1940s. In 1938 Campbell married Jean Erdman – a former student of his at Sarah Lawrence – who had gone on to become a professional dancer with the Martha Graham dance company in New York. In 1943, together with his friend Henry Morton Robinson, Campbell wrote *A skeleton's key to Finnegan's wake*,[28] a companion to what is arguably Joyce's most difficult book to read. It was published to critical acclaim in 1944. He was also asked to write an introduction to *The complete Grimm's fairytales*,[29] published in 1944 by Pantheon.

His own career now firmly established, it is perhaps somewhat ironic that Campbell would spend most of the 1940s and early 1950s editing the work of another scholar. In the early 1940s Campbell came into contact with a man who is described by John Lobell in his *Joseph Campbell – the man and his ideas* as 'probably the single most important influence on his scholarship':[30] the prolific German scholar of Indian mythology and culture Heinrich Zimmer. Zimmer had fled Germany during the Second World War and had ended up at Columbia, where Campbell attended one of his lectures. Having similar interests, the two men quickly became good friends, and when Zimmer died unexpectedly of pneumonia in 1943 Campbell took on the job of editing and rewriting the manuscripts for the books that Zimmer had planned to publish in the coming years. It was a huge task, which would keep Campbell occupied for the next 13 years. Campbell later often claimed that it was Zimmer who gave him the impetus to really start interpreting myths in his own unique way. As he put it in an interview once:

> If I do have a guru . . . it would be Zimmer – the one who really gave me the courage to interpret myths out of what I knew of their common symbol.[31]

Through Zimmer, a connection was also established that would prove to be crucially important for Campbell's professional career: his long-lasting association with the Bollingen foundation, an institution founded by the wealthy American couple Paul and Mary Mellon in the late 1930s which had as its goal 'to develop scholarship and research in the liberal arts and sciences and other fields of cultural endeavour generally'.[32] The Mellons had been patients of Jung, and it is often claimed that they started the foundation upon recommendation of Jung himself. Even though they did not restrict their list of publications to Jungian scholars only, many of the authors who have been published by the Foundation did have a profoundly Jungian outlook. Zimmer, who was on the early board of directors of the foundation during the last years of his life,[33] recommended that Campbell be asked to write the introduction to what would become the very first publication of the foundation: *Where the two came to their father: a Navaho war memorial*,[34] published in 1943. Campbell would also come to edit six books containing translations of lectures given at the yearly Eranos conferences in Ascona, Switzerland, which were published by Bollingen. The seven volumes of Zimmer's work that Campbell edited were published by Bollingen as well, and when Campbell visited India and Japan in 1954 it was the Bollingen foundation which funded the trip. Most importantly, however, it was the Bollingen foundation which published what would be Campbell's first book written on his own, after two other publishers had refused to do so: *The hero with a thousand faces*, which came out in 1949.

After *Hero* had been published another memorable event took place: Campbell had his first and only meeting with Jung himself. Zimmer had been a close friend of Jung's, and because Campbell had edited Zimmer's work he had come to Jung's attention. Consequently, Campbell and his wife were invited to afternoon tea at Jung's famous Bollingen tower, an event about which Campbell later told the following in an interview:

> I had the real pleasure, many years ago of having an invitation to tea, my wife and I, with Dr. and Mrs. Jung. And this was at his place outside

> Zurich called Bollingen, after which the Bollingen Foundation was named. It's at the far end of Lake Zurich. . . . We drove up to the place where Jung's little castle was that he had built with his own hands, this stone castle that was part of his opus to find what his mythology was. We drew up there and got out of the car and began walking up the path, but so many people had walked there that the path was worn too deep to reach the door – I didn't know how to get in. Well, Jean knows how to do things, so finally she found the bell and rang it, and we came in and were greeted by Dr. and Mrs. Jung. We had tea there, and now this is the man's character: No 'Herr Doktor Professor.' He was just a genial host. I had no trouble with him because by that time I had published four volumes of Heinrich Zimmer's work. Zimmer was a friend of his. And Jung had published one of Zimmer's German works. So we were coeditors, you might say, of Heinrich Zimmer. . . . Jung was a beautiful man to be with. That's all I can say.[35]

After their meeting Campbell sent Jung a copy of *Hero* to thank him. The Campbell Archive owns the letter that Jung sent in response (dated 4 November 1953), in which he writes the following:

> Thank you ever so much for kindly sending me your very beautiful book. I had already seen it before and have duly admired it. You are certainly shaping after my late friend Heinrich Zimmer. It is the same style and outlook. I am glad to have made your personal acquaintance this summer.[36]

After he had finished writing *Hero*, Campbell began work on what would eventually become the four-volume series *The masks of God*. With the help of financial aid from the Bollingen Foundation he was able to start working part-time at Sarah Lawrence, which meant that he could now devote the remainder of his time to the writing of what turned out to be a very demanding project indeed. Even though he had originally envisioned *Masks* as a single book, the project quickly grew out of control, with Campbell working on it for about twelve years. About this time in his life he would later say: 'It was horrible, really, carrying one idea around in your head for twelve years, and never being able to allow yourself to think of anything else during that time.'[37]

The years during which Campbell worked on the *Masks of God* were also the years during which Campbell began to achieve a higher level of professional and popular success than he had previously experienced. He served as President of the American Academy for the Study of Religions for several years, and also became a highly sought-after public speaker, lecturing twice at the Eranos conference for which he had previously edited the yearbooks. *The hero with a thousand faces* became an unexpected best-seller when it struck a chord with a younger generation during the 1960s, and he was made a Bollingen trustee in 1960.

In 1972, after having worked at Sarah Lawrence for more than 30 years, Campbell retired from teaching. Rather than resting on his laurels, he went on the lecture circuit, giving a great many lectures around the United States despite his increasingly old age. He also spent a large portion of his time writing and studying. In an article about Campbell for Harper's Bookletter, Sally Helgesen writes the following about Campbell's schedule at this point in his career:

> Campbell begins work every morning at about 7:30 A.M. and stops around 4:00 P.M. to go for a swim and sauna at the New York Athletic Club. He's kept to this schedule since he quit teaching at Sarah Lawrence. . . . During his thirty-eight years on the faculty there he spent his weekends, his vacations, and his summers writing from early morning until late at night. He says he's never had difficulty writing because 'there so much material it just writes itself'. This has been true ever since he began writing on mythology. 'There was a time though, before I knew what I was doing, when I just sat in front of a blank sheet of paper and stared for two years – I mean that literally, I just stared. It was a pitiful performance. But then I decided to read and study and organize my notes, and doing that gave me something to say.[38]

Campbell stuck to this intense schedule until he was well into his eighties, even beginning work on a large project that would be the last one he ever worked on: *The historical atlas of world mythology*, a series of broadsheet books in full-colour which combined text, images and charts to shed more light on the different world-mythologies than would be possible by using text alone. Campbell hoped desperately that he would be able to finish the project during his lifetime, and worked maniacally on its completion throughout the middle and late 1980s. Despite his best efforts, however, the project remains uncompleted: only the first two volumes of the planned four were published. The Joseph Campbell Foundation,[39] a voluntary organization set up after Campbell's death, has plans to edit the remaining documents and publish them on a date that has yet to be set.

As I already mentioned in the preface, in 1988 what is perhaps the single most important event related to Campbell's career took place: the airing of *The power of myth*, a series of interviews with Campbell conducted by TV-journalist Bill Moyers. The interviews were watched by an audience of millions, and the book containing a transcription of the interviews went on to sell well over a million copies worldwide.[40] Stories abound about people whose lives have been touched by the interviews, with many reporting the uplifting effect they have had on their lives. Bill Moyers even told a *New York times* journalist about a woman who had told him that she had decided not to commit suicide after seeing one of the episodes:

> Mr. Moyers told of encountering a woman on Eighth Avenue who related how years before she had reached such despair with her acting career that she went home and turned on the gas, hoping to die. As the gas spread, she noticed Mr. Moyers on television 'talking to a wonderful man'. . . . At the end of the show, Mr. Moyers said he would be back next week with the rest of the conversation. 'I thought, "I've got to hear that" ', the woman told Mr. Moyers. 'I turned off the gas and opened the windows.'[41]

Campbell didn't live to see the show's success. He died after a brief struggle with cancer in the autumn of 1987.

Notes

1 Joseph Campbell, *The hero's journey: Joseph Campbell on his life and work*, ed. Phil Cousineau (San Francisco/London: Harper & Row, 1990), p. 6.
2 Ibid., pp. 3, 4.
3 Joseph Campbell, *An open life – Joseph Campbell in conversation with Michael Toms*, ed. John M. Maher and Dennie Briggs (New York: Harper & Row, 1990), p. 119.
4 Campbell, *The hero's journey*, p. 5.
5 Ibid., p. 27.
6 Stephen Larsen and Robin Larsen, *A fire in the mind – the life of Joseph Campbell* (New York: Doubleday, 1991), p. 16.
7 Donald Newlove, 'Interview with Joseph Campbell', *Esquire* 88 (September 1977), p. 102. Quoted in Robert Segal, *Introduction*, p. 15.
8 Campbell, *The hero's journey*, p. 30.
9 Campbell had befriended Krishnamurti three years earlier on an ocean liner and met up with him again in Paris.
10 John Lobell, *Joseph Campbell – the man and his ideas* (San Anselmo: Joseph Campbell Foundation, 1993), p. 4.
11 Campbell, *The hero's journey*, p. 32.
12 Ibid., p. 33.
13 Ibid. p. 52
14 Newlove, 'Interview with Joseph Campbell', p. 103. Quoted in Segal, *Introduction*, p. 16.

[15] Lobell, *Joseph Campbell – the man and his ideas*, p. 6.
[16] Joseph Campbell, *A Joseph Campbell companion – reflections on the art of living*, ed. Diane K. Osbon (New York: HarperCollins, 1991), p. 58.
[17] Maverick is the name of the community at Woodstock in which Campbell was living.
[18] Quoted in Larsen and Larsen, *A fire in the mind*, pp. 220, 222.
[19] Joseph Campbell, 'Strictly platonic', *Liberty magazine* 1933 (Campbell Archive: box 107, folder F12).
[20] The community in Monterey was the inspiration for one of Steinbeck's most famous books, *Cannery row*.
[21] Campbell, *The hero's journey*, pp. 54, 55.
[22] Larsen and Larsen, *A fire in the mind*, p. 224.
[23] Ibid., p. 230.
[24] Ibid.
[25] Sally Helgesen, 'Every day column', *Harper's bookletter*, 14 February 1977 (Campbell Archive: box 113, folder A33).
[26] Nancy Sureck, 'In class with Joseph Campbell', *Sarah Lawrence College magazine* 1986 (Campbell Archive: box 106, folder AA33).
[27] Joseph Berger, 'A teacher of legends becomes one himself', *New York times*, 10 December 1988 (Campbell Archive: box 106, folder AA18).
[28] Joseph Campbell and Henry Morton Robinson, *A skeleton key to Finnegan's wake* (New York: Harcourt, Brace & Co., 1944).
[29] Padraic Colum, ed., *The complete Grimm's fairy tales* (New York/Toronto: Pantheon, 1944).
[30] From the introduction, written by Robin and Stephen Larsen, in Lobell, *Joseph Campbell – the man and his ideas*, p. 6.
[31] Campbell, *An open life*, p. 123.
[32] Larsen and Larsen, *A fire in the mind*, p. 321.
[33] Ibid.
[34] Joseph Campbell et al., *Where the two came to their father: a Navaho war memorial*, Bollingen Series I (Richmond: Old Dominion Foundation, 1943).
[35] Campbell, *The hero's journey*, pp. 47–48.
[36] Carl G. Jung, 'Letter to Joseph Campbell', 4 November 1953 (Campbell Archive: box 116, folder L694a).
[37] Helgesen, 'Every day column.'
[38] Ibid.
[39] www.jcf.org
[40] Larsen and Larsen, *A fire in the mind*, p. 556.
[41] Berger, 'A teacher of legends becomes one himself.'

Chapter 5

Phases one and two of Campbell's career

As I already pointed out in Chapter 1, one of the most important points that I will be making in this part of the book is that Campbell's reception of Jung changed significantly over time. A close analysis of the most important changes has led me to divide his career into three phases. As these three phases form the backbone of the structure of this part of the book, I will repeat the summary I gave of them in Chapter 1 here:

Phase one: 1943–1959

In this phase of his career Freud and Jung were both of equal importance to Campbell, and his theoretical position is an amalgamation of both Jungian and Freudian ideas. This phase contains all of Campbell's early works, and ends with the publication of the first volume of the *Masks of God*, which marked a change of direction for Campbell. The most important work written in this phase is *Hero*.

Phase two: 1959–1968

In this phase Campbell dismissed Jung's concept of the archetype as irreconcilable with his own ideas. The most important works written during this phase are the first three volumes in the *Masks of Gods* series. This phase ends with the publication of *Masks: creative* (volume 4 in the series, published in 1968), in which Campbell suddenly claims that his ideas and Jung's concept of the archetype are compatible after all. It is with the publication of this book that what I am calling the 'Jungian turn' (see Chapter 1) begins.

Phase three: 1968–1988

From 1968 onwards Campbell became highly positive about Jung. He also arrived at an interpretation of Jung which is different from the one he had in phase two, and which is almost completely identical to Anthony Stevens' interpretation of Jung. In this phase (which, as I will argue, lasts until his death in 1988) Campbell consistently associated Jung with all of his key ideas.

In this chapter I will deal with the ideas of phases one and two. I will deal with the ideas of phase three in the next chapter (Chapter 6).

The interpretation of Campbell's reception of Jung that I am putting forward in these two chapters has not been argued before by other scholars. As I also mentioned in the introduction, the scholar who in my opinion has so far most adequately dealt with Campbell's reception of Jung is the Religious Studies scholar Robert Segal (currently at the University of Aberdeen). Because my interpretation of Campbell's reception of Jung differs from Segal's interpretation regarding a number of key issues, I will return to his work throughout this chapter and the next one. Where relevant, I will briefly describe his interpretation of these issues, and compare them to my own conclusions. In this way I will attempt to show that my conclusions offer an original contribution to the field.

I have divided this chapter into the following three sections. In section 5.1, I will give an overview of all the books by Jung that Campbell owned at the end of his life. I will draw on this section throughout this chapter and the next one to establish which books by Jung Campbell might have had access to during the various phases of his career. After this section I will deal with Campbell's reception of Jung in phase one (section 5.2) and phase two (section 5.3).

5.1 Which books by Jung did Campbell own?

Campbell was often asked whether he did any spiritual exercises like yoga or meditation. Surely someone as interested in Eastern mysticism and spirituality as himself would have only attained the charisma and energy levels for which he was renowned by doing some form of spiritual training? When Campbell was asked this question, he would often recount that he had once answered it by saying: 'Yes – I underline sentences.' In an interview with the psychologist Jeffrey Mishlove he put it as follows:

> I remember when Alan Watts one time asked me, 'Joe, what yoga do you practice?' I said, 'I underline sentences.' And that's all I'm doing. I'm no guru or anything of the kind. I've just had the great good fortune to find this golden world of myth, and I was also well trained in how to write a

book. And so all I've done is gather what has excited me into my books, and by God, it works for other people just as well as it worked for me.[1]

And underline sentences Campbell did: the Joseph Campbell Library, based on the campus of the Pacifica Graduate Institute, bears witness to that. The library owns the entire collection of books put together by Campbell during his lifetime. As such, it provides a unique opportunity to ascertain just what books Campbell owned; by using the publication dates in the volumes he possessed, one has also some indication as to when Campbell *could* have read a certain book. The fact that Campbell owned a certain book doesn't automatically imply that he read it, of course. Because of the fact that Campbell underlined key passages in the books he read so vigorously, however, one is able to draw much more accurate conclusions as to which books Campbell owned were actually read by him. Needless to say, this information is only of limited use: it does not establish, for example, at which date Campbell read the book in question, nor does it reveal very much about the way he interpreted a certain text. On a similar note, the fact that a certain text has *not* been underlined by Campbell does not prove that he did not read the text. That said, having a rough idea of which books by Jung Campbell actually owned and which parts of those books were definitely read by him is still incredibly helpful when one is trying to assess why Campbell's attitude towards Jung changed so significantly. When Campbell wrote *Hero*, for example, he drew heavily on a book by Jung called *The integration of the personality*, which contains an early version of the essay 'The archetypes of the collective unconscious.' The version of this text which is part of the *Collected works*, however, was heavily revised by Jung. Both texts were underlined heavily by Campbell, which shows he read them both. Comparing the differences in the two texts, as I will do in the next chapter, is very helpful when one is trying to assess why Campbell became more favourable to Jung later on in his career.

In the first version of the text, which Campbell would have read in the first phase of his career, Jung does not yet make any distinction between the archetype-as-such and the archetypal image; in the second version (which Campbell would have had access to from 1959 onwards), however, he has added a passage which makes it obvious to the reader that he feels that this distinction is highly important. As this distinction is a crucial part of Anthony Stevens' interpretation of Jung, having an indication as to when Campbell became aware of it is important, and only by drawing on the material found in the Campbell Library can topics such as this one be dealt with. For this reason I will now give an overview of the books by Jung

Campbell owned, sorted by their publication date. As I was able to verify in person which parts of these books were underlined and which parts were not when I visited the Campbell Library in May 2007, I will also give a brief indication about the extent to which the books in question have been underlined. Although I have sorted the list of books by publication date, I have decided to group the volumes of the *Collected works* together for reasons of clarity.

Wandlungen und symbole der libido. *1925*[2]

This is, in all likelihood, the first book by Jung that Campbell read. It is the original German edition, which was – as I discussed in Chapter 2 – published in English as *Psychology of the unconscious*.[3] The book is in a very fragile state, and is heavily underlined throughout.

Dream symbols of the individuation process. *1936*[4]

This book was never officially published. It is a transcription of a seminar Jung gave in 1936 on Bailey Island, Maine. This seminar, in turn, was based on an essay Jung delivered at the Eranos conference in 1935. This essay was published in *The integration of the personality*, which Campbell also owned (see below). It was also published, in a revised form, as part of *CW 12*. Even though the text in this book is roughly the same as the text in *Integration of the personality*, it is still heavily underlined.

The integration of the personality. *1939*[5]

This book is a collection of essays Jung delivered at the Eranos conference. Almost all of these were – mostly in rewritten form – published in one of the volumes of the *Collected works*. The book is heavily underlined throughout. It contains the following essays:

'On the meaning of individuation.' Not published in *Collected works*.
'A study in the process of individuation.' Published in *CW 9 part 1* in revised version.
'The archetypes of the collective unconscious.' Published in *CW 9 part 1* in revised version.
'Dream symbols of the process of individuation.' Published in *CW 12* in revised version.

'The idea of redemption in alchemy.' Published in *CW 12* in revised version.
'The development of the personality.' Published in *CW 17.*

Essays on a science of mythology ***(together with C. Kerényi). 1949***[6]

Heavily underlined throughout.

Introduction to Zen Buddhism ***by Daisetz Teitaro Suzuki. 1949***[7]

Jung wrote a lengthy introduction to this classic work on Zen Buddhism. This introduction is not underlined.

The interpretation of nature and the psyche ***(with W. Pauli). 1955***[8]

This book contains two essays, one by Jung and one by Pauli. Jung's essay ('Synchronicity: an acausal connecting principle') was published as part of *CW 8.* Campbell only underlined Pauli's essay ('The influence of archetypal ideas on the scientific theories of Kepler'), which probably means that he read this book after *CW 8* had been published.

Gegenwart und Zukunft. ***1955***[9]

This book was translated by R. F. C. Hull and published as *The undiscovered self* (Boston and London, 1958). Campbell has the original German edition. The book is not underlined.

The trickster: a study in American Indian mythology,
by Paul Radin. 1956[10]

This book contains an essay by Jung: 'On the psychology of the trickster figure.' This was later published as part of *CW 9 part 1.* Jung's essay is heavily underlined, but not the other sections of the book.

Memories, dreams, reflections. ***1963***[11]

Jung's famous semi-autobiography. Underlined throughout.

Analytical psychology – its theory and
practice – the Tavistock lectures. ***1968***[12]

No underlining.

The visions seminars – ***book 2, parts eight – thirteen. 1976***[13]

This is book two in a series of two volumes. The books contain a transcription of a seminar given by Jung in 1930. The book is not underlined.

Flying saucers: a modern myth of things seen in the sky. ***1978***[14]

No underlining.

Psychology and the East. ***1978***[15]

This is a collection of texts taken from the *Collected works* (volumes 10, 11, 13 and 18). Since Campbell already had these texts, it is likely that the book was sent to him as a gift, probably from the publisher. There is no underlining in the book.

Collected works ***[abbreviated as CW followed by volume number]***

Campbell owned most of the volumes of the *Collected works* (only volumes 19 and 20 are absent). Almost all of them are first editions; only his copies of *CW 12* and *CW 16* are second editions.

CW 1 (1957) Underlined throughout.
CW 2 (1973) No underlining.
CW 3 (1960) Underlined throughout.
CW 4 (1961) Underlined throughout.
CW 5 (1956) Underlined until page 66.
CW 6 (1971) No underlining.
CW 7 (1953) Not much underlining.
CW 8 (1960) Most texts underlined.
CW 9 (1959) Most texts underlined.
CW 10 (1964) Not much underlining.
CW 11 (1958) Underlined throughout.
CW 12 (1968 – second edition) Not much underlining.
CW 13 (1968) No underlining.
CW 14 (1963) Most texts underlined.
CW 15 (1966) No underlining.
CW 16 (1966 – second edition) Not much underlining.
CW 17 (1954) Not much underlining.
CW 18 (1976) No underlining.
Supplement volume A: The Zofingia lectures (1983) No underlining.

5.2 Phase one (1943–1959)

As I will argue in the next section (5.3), the second phase of Campbell's career began in 1959. This is the year in which the first volume of the *Masks of God* series was published (*Primitive mythology*,[16] from hereon abbreviated as *Masks: primitive*), which as I will show in that section marked a radical departure from the theoretical approach he had taken during the years before. As Campbell's first published text is from 1943 (his introduction to *Where the two came to their father*,[17] from hereon abbreviated as *Where the two*), this means that the first phase of Campbell's career lasts approximately 16 years. As this was also the period in which Campbell was editing the posthumously published works of Heinrich Zimmer, it is perhaps unsurprising that Campbell published very little under his own name during this time. The main text from this period is obviously *The hero with a thousand faces* (*Hero* for short), published in 1949. Apart from the introduction to *Where the two*, Campbell published only two texts before 1949: *A Skeleton's key to Finnegan's wake*,[18] co-written with Henry Morton Robinson, and the introduction to the Pantheon edition of *Grimm's fairytales* (1944, from hereon abbreviated as *Grimm*).[19] After *Hero*, Campbell published only one text: the article 'Bios and mythos',[20] written for a *festschrift* dedicated to the Freudian scholar Geza Roheim. Because Campbell does not present any ideas that radically differ from the ideas in *Hero* in this text, I have decided not to dedicate a section to it. *Hero* is by far the best work available to us to analyse Campbell's ideas in the first phase of his career, and for this reason I have predominantly focused on this work to offer an overview of the relationship between Campbell's work and Jung's ideas in phase one. I have also decided to devote a short section to the works published before *Hero*, as I believe having an understanding how Campbell arrived at the ideas outlined in *Hero* makes grasping the essence of these ideas easier. I will deal with the texts written before *Hero* in section 5.2.1, and with the ideas propagated in *Hero* in section 5.2.2. In section 5.2.3, I will give a brief general summary of Campbell's ideas in phase one.

5.2.1 Early works: *Where the two* and *Grimm*

Apart from his short story 'Strictly platonic' (see Chapter 4), *Where the two* was Campbell's first published work. It was also the very first publication of the Bollingen Foundation, with which Campbell's career would remain inextricably connected throughout his life (his *The mythic image*, for example, was chosen as the capstone volume of the 100-volume series, volume C, published in 1974). *Where the two* is, strictly speaking, a work of ethnography. It was put together by the American artist Maud Oakes, who had won the trust of the Navaho shaman Jeff Oakes and had been given permission by the latter to study and record the sand paintings he made as part of a Navaho war memorial. The ritual was based on the hero myth of two young demi-Gods who go in search of their father the Sun God. Campbell was chosen to write an academic introduction to the story of the two young heroes, which in turn was written down by Oakes. He was given the job primarily because of his friendship with Heinrich Zimmer, who recommended him to the editorial board of the Bollingen Foundation. Even though it is Campbell's first published text on mythological themes, it contains many ideas that would later become classic Campbell hallmarks. As such, it is an ideal text to begin our discussion of Campbell's ideas in the first phase of his career.

In the introduction to his book *Myths to live by*, a collection of speeches published in 1972, Campbell wrote the following about the way his ideas had developed during the years before 1972:

> My notion about myself was that I had grown up during that time, that my ideas had changed, and, too, that I had progressed. But when I brought these papers together, they were all saying essentially the same thing – over a span of decades. I found out something about the thing that was moving me. I didn't even have a very clear idea of what it was until I recognized those continuities running through that whole book. Twenty-four years is a pretty good stretch of time. A lot had happened during that period. And there I was babbling on about the same thing.[21]

Looking at *Where the two* now, in full knowledge of the works that were to come after it, one gets the impression that Campbell was right: from the beginning there were certain key themes which ran through Campbell's work. One of these themes, as shall become apparent in this chapter and the next one, is Campbell's assertion that myth isn't merely a collection of irrational, unscientific statements that can be refuted by modern science: on the contrary, mythological symbols represent metaphysical intuitions that have as their connotation a 'plane of reference' that 'transcends all categories of knowledge and thought', as Campbell put it in an interview he gave towards the end of his life:

> [Interviewer]: *What does myth do for us? Why is it so important?*
>
> [Campbell]: It puts you in touch with a plane of reference that goes past your mind and into your very being, into your very gut. The ultimate

> mystery of being and nonbeing transcends all categories of knowledge and thought. Yet that which transcends all talk is the very essence of your own being, so you're resting on it and you *know* it. The function of mythological symbols is to give you a sense of 'Aha! Yes. I know what it is, it's myself.' This is what it's all about, and then you feel a kind of centering, centering, centering all the time. And whatever you do can be discussed in relationship to this ground of truth. Though to talk about it as truth is a little bit deceptive because when we think of truth we think of something that can be conceptualized. It goes past that.[22]

From hereon I shall refer to this idea as the 'metaphysical theme' in Campbell's work. In *Where the two* it is clear that Campbell had already developed this idea as early as 1944, even though he doesn't yet call his metaphysical 'plane of reference' by the name which he would later use for it: the 'transcendent'. Instead, he chooses to use a term which he probably borrowed from Schopenhauer: the 'Will'.

> Since early ages, and throughout the world, it has been a function of myth and rite to bring the human mind and heart into concord with the mighty Will. An individual or a community knowing such concord becomes – according to the ancient wisdom – a conduit of world-renewing power. There are many ways to state this truth. The different cultures have so inflected the basic symbolical imagery that the various mythologies and rites of the peoples of the world apparently offer contrasting, even conflicting, forms. Nevertheless, the tenor of the richly orchestrated statements is ever the same; it is the message of a life-abundance through a fundamental concord with the Will Supreme.[23]

The similarity with Jung's first book, *Wandlungen und symbole der libido,* is striking: in this work Jung focused on Schopenhauer's notion of the Will as well, linking it to his own ideas about the psychoanalytical concept of libido. The result is a world-view which is highly reminiscent of Campbell's in *Where the two.* As Jung wrote in *Wandlungen*:

> This view brings us to a conception of libido, which extends over the boundaries of the physical sciences into a philosophical aspect – to a conception of the will in general. I must give this bit of psychological 'Voluntarismus' into the hands of the philosophers for them to manage. For the rest I refer to the words of Schopenhauer relating to this.[24]

Jung also refers to the libido as the 'universal creative power existent everywhere',[25] and also as 'the creative strength existent in man'[26] and the 'driving strength of our own soul'.[27] Campbell's choice of words in *Where the two* is remarkably similar:

> The landscape of the myth is the landscape of the human spirit. The way of the god is the way to the seat of energy within the soul. The priest, chanting and praying, is the guide to conduct the imagination across every threshold of inner resistance to the secret of the life that built the body – not man's body only, but the body of the world.[28]

This similarity, however, is probably not a coincidence. Of all the books by Jung Campbell owned, only three would have been available to him while he was working on *Where the two*: *Wandlungen* (1925), *Dream symbols of the individuation process* (1936) and *The integration of the personality* (1940). In interviews, Campbell only ever referred to *Wandlungen* as having had any influence on him. Campbell knew the book well (as the amount of underlining in the book shows), and it is likely that he had read it intensively by the time he started to work on *Where the two*. It should be stressed, however, that apart from the similarities mentioned above, Campbell doesn't take an overly Jungian approach in *Where the two*. It is certainly true that he makes it obvious that, like Jung, he believes that it is highly significant that there are similarities to be found in myths from all over the world: he is constantly 'amplifying'[29] the motifs from the Navaho hero myth by offering similar motifs from other myths, and stresses that for him these similarities cannot just be explained by a theory of diffusion. What Campbell doesn't yet do, however, is attach these archetypal motifs (a term which Campbell does use in *Where the two*) to the findings of psychoanalysis in general or to Jung's findings in particular. In his later works Campbell never fails to make this connection. Consider this statement, for example, from *Hero*:

> It is not difficult for the modern intellectual to concede that the symbolism of mythology has a psychological significance. Particularly after the work of the psychoanalysts, there can be little doubt, either that myths are of the nature of dream, or that dreams are symptomatic of the dynamics of the psyche.[30]

Statements such as this one abound in almost all of Campbell's works. For this reason I have chosen it – along with the metaphysical theme mentioned above – as the second theme to structure my overview of the three phases of Campbell's career in this chapter and the next one. I will refer to it from hereon as the 'psychological theme'. Given the fact that it is such an important part of Campbell's theoretical framework, it is surprising that it is almost completely absent in *Where the two*. The closest Campbell comes to making any connection between myth and psychoanalysis is in the following passage:

> But in the depths [of the psyche] the energies of nature persist in their elemental, wildest mode, totally ignorant of, and indifferent to, the weal and woe of bounded forms. . . . These energies are the source energies of existence. Without them there is nothing; but they cannot be carelessly challenged, evoked, or neglected.[31]

It is only in another text, published one year after *Where the two*, that Campbell explicitly makes the connection between myth and psychology for the first time: his foreword to *Grimm*, published in 1944. In contrast to *Where the two*, which isn't that easy to get hold of, this text is widely available, as Campbell decided to contain it in his collection of essays *Flight of the wild gander* (from hereon abbreviated as *Gander*). In *Grimm* Campbell does, for the first time in a published work, make the assertion for which he would become famous: that myths and fairytales are of the order of dream, and can therefore by illuminated by the findings of the psychoanalysts:

> [*The psychoanalysts have demonstrated that*] dreams are precipitations of unconscious desires, ideals and fears, and furthermore, that the images of dream resemble – broadly, but nevertheless frequently to the detail – the motifs of folk tale and myth. Having selected for their study the symbol-inventing, myth-motif-producing level of the psyche – source of all those universal themes ('Elementary Ideas') which men have read into the phenomena of nature, into the shadows of the tomb, the lives of the heroes, and the emblems of society – the psychoanalysts have undoubtedly touched the central moment of the multifarious problem.[32]

Campbell takes an approach in *Grimm* which is highly characteristic of his position in the rest of phase one: he talks about the psychoanalytical movement as if the ideas held by the various 'schools' are relatively homogeneous. He does not yet establish a preference for Freud, Jung or anyone else; instead he chooses to speak about 'the psychoanalysts' as if there is somehow a central point of view to be distilled from their various theories. What he also does, however, is claim that the psychoanalytical school does not represent the last word about the nature of myth: instead, he claims that a further step has yet to be taken in order to accurately understand it. Myth is not just 'psychology, misread as cosmology, history and biography',[33] as Campbell claims the psychoanalysts hold; instead, myths also 'present in pictorial form cosmogonic and ontological intuitions'.[34] Campbell states that although myths contain motifs that are similar to those found in dreams, their ultimate meaning is nonetheless different. This is because the creators of myth *consciously* used the picture language of the unconscious to convey a message of metaphysical import.

> Myth, as the psychoanalysts declare, is not a mess of errors; myth is a picture language. But the language has to be studied to be read. In the first place, this language is the native speech of dream. But in the second place, it has been studied, clarified, and enriched by the poets, prophets, and visionaries of untold millenniums. Dante, Aquinas, and Augustine, al-Ghazali and Mohammed, Zarathustra, Shankaracharya, Nagarpna, and Tai Tsung, were not bad scientists making misstatements about the weather, or neurotics reading dreams into the stars, but masters of the human spirit teaching a wisdom of death and life. And the thesaurus of the myth-motifs was their vocabulary.[35]

Just what exactly Campbell thinks this 'wisdom of life and death' represents, however, remains unclear in *Grimm*. It is fairly obvious that there is a connection to the metaphysical assertions he made in *Where the two*; but just what exactly the connection is between myth and what I have called the 'metaphysical theme' above remains unclear. To shed more light on this topic we will now turn to the most important work Campbell wrote during the first phase of his career: *The hero with a thousand faces.*

5.2.2 *The hero with a thousand faces*

Campbell started to work on what would eventually become *Hero* after his friend Henry Morton Robinson (with whom he had written *A skeleton's key to Finnegan's wake*) had brought him into contact with the publisher Simon and Schuster, who were interested in publishing a book about myth.

> So we get a phone call from my friend Robinson, and he says, 'Joe, Simon & Schuster's interested in a book on mythology and if you get up on your high horse and knock 'em down I'll never talk to you again.' We

> arranged for a publisher's luncheon and they said, 'Yes, we'd like a book on mythology.'
>
> 'What kind of book do you want?'
>
> 'We want a sort of modern Bullfinch.'
>
> I said, 'I wouldn't touch it with a ten-foot pole.'
>
> They said, 'What would you like to do?'
>
> I said, 'I'd like to write a book on how to read a myth.'
>
> 'A sort of self-help book?'
>
> 'Yeah, okay.'[36]

Campbell was offered a generous contract for the book and started to work on it straight away, basically using what was his introductory class in comparative mythology at Sarah Lawrence as his raw material. Ever the perfectionist, he worked on the book for five years, only to discover that by that time Simon and Schuster had changed management and were no longer interested in publishing the book. After one other publisher rejected the book, the Bollingen Foundation finally accepted it in 1949. It has been a steady seller ever since, even appearing on the *New York times* best-seller list in 1989 as a result of Campbell's unexpected posthumous fame. According to the April 2007 newsletter of the Joseph Campbell foundation, the book has sold nearly one million copies to date.[37]

In *Hero*, Campbell is once again concerned with the observation that there are common motifs in stories from all over the world. In the introduction, Campbell makes it clear that for him these patterns are ubiquitous: they occur not only in religious texts and myths, but also in fairytales and even in philosophical texts.

> Whether we listen with aloof amusement to the dreamlike mumbo jumbo of some red-eyed witch doctor of the Congo, or read with cultivated rapture thin translations from the sonnets of the mystic Lao-tse; now and again crack the hard nutshell of an argument of Aquinas, or catch suddenly the shining meaning of a bizarre Eskimo fairy tale: it will be always the one, shape-shifting yet marvellously constant story that we find, together with a challengingly persistent suggestion of more remaining to be experienced than will ever be known or told.
>
> . . .
>
> All the religions of all time, the social forms of prehistoric and historic man, the arts, the philosophies, the prime discoveries in science and technology, the very dreams that blister sleep boil up from the simple basic, magic ring of myth.[38]

The mythological motif which Campbell focuses on in *Hero* is that of the 'hero's journey'. In its essence, the 'hero's journey' is a story that describes the adventure of a hero who, after having received what Campbell calls 'the call to adventure', sets off for the unknown, faces a series of trials and tribulations, and returns – transformed – to his everyday surroundings. Campbell labels these three stages 'Separation', 'Initiation' and 'Return'.

> The standard path of the mythological adventure of the hero is a magnification of the formula represented in the rites of passage: separation-initiation-return: . . . A hero ventures forth from the world of common day into a region of supernatural wonder: fabulous forces are there encountered and a decisive victory is won: the hero comes back from this mysterious adventure with the power to bestow boons on his fellow man.[39]

Perhaps because of this strong emphasis on the common motifs of myth, Hero has been predominantly perceived as Jungian in nature throughout the years. The critic Max Radin, for example, said the following about it in his review of the book for the *New York times*:

> There is so much in this book and the analogies and comparisons are so interesting and stimulating, that it is too bad that it is all presented in the mystical and pseudo-philosophic fog of Jung.[40]

As I already mentioned in Chapter 1, another example is the *Macmillan encyclopaedia of religion*, which contains the following description of *Hero*:

> Many excellent and widely acclaimed studies of religious myths have been created that utilize Jung's psychology. Of these, the best known are the works of Joseph Campbell, in particular *The hero with a thousand faces*.[41]

It is certainly not the case, however, that Campbell relies solely on Jung to interpret the mythological patterns he is dissecting in *Hero*: Freud plays an equally important role, as do many other well-known psychoanalytical thinkers (Rank, Roheim and Stekel being the most frequently quoted). The book opens, for example, with the following quote from Freud:

> The truths contained in religious doctrines are after all so distorted and systematically disguised, that the mass of humanity cannot recognize them as truth.[42]

Geza Roheim is listed in the index as many times as Jung (13 times), and Freud is quoted even more times than Jung (17 times). From the outset, then, it is rather clear that *Hero* isn't overtly Jungian, with Campbell himself claiming throughout the book that he does not prefer one psychoanalytical school over the other. This attitude is similar to the one he adopted in *Grimm*, in which he chose to refer simply to 'the psychoanalysts' without taking sides. Just like he did in that work, Campbell stresses in *Hero* that the psychoanalytical schools can be seen as one big movement, with a 'body of common principles':

> It is not difficult for the modern intellectual to concede that the symbolism of mythology has a psychological significance. Particularly after the work of the psychoanalysts, there can be little doubt, either that myths are of the nature of dream, or that dreams are symptomatic of the dynamics of the psyche. Sigmund Freud, Carl G. Jung, Wilhelm Stekel, Otto Rank, Karl Abraham, Geza Roheim, and many others have within the past few decades developed a vastly documented modern lore of dream and myth interpretation; and though the doctors differ among themselves, they are united into one great modern movement by a considerable body of common principles.[43]

Even though it is obvious, then, that Campbell relies heavily on psychoanalysis to interpret myth in *Hero*, Campbell somewhat surprisingly states several times that he is not interested in interpreting myth. Instead, he claims that he is merely trying to show that common motifs or archetypes exist, for example, when he writes that 'the present volume is a comparative, not genetic, study. Its purpose is to show that essential parallels exist in the myths themselves.'[44] As Robert Segal quite rightly points out in his *Introduction*, however, Campbell does not make true on this claim.[45] From the first page of the book he goes well beyond merely pointing out similarities. He is therefore not merely an anthologist of myth (as he claims in the beginning of the book), but also an interpreter of myth, and it is in this regard that psychoanalysis plays its part. The role of psychoanalysis in *Hero*, however, is not so much to offer a consistent, uniform theory; it is used more as a hermeneutical tool. Campbell is not yet really concerned with presenting the foundations of a 'Campbellian' theory of myth; he is merely trying to give the reader an inkling as to the meaning of the 'hero's journey', and to this end he uses a variety of different psychoanalytical theories, Freud's and Jung's among them. His approach in *Hero*, therefore, is eclectic, pragmatic: he uses whatever theory might shed some light on his subject matter, and therefore ends up quoting a wide range of different thinkers one wouldn't necessarily think of as being compatible. This perhaps explains why critics have accused the book of being 'vague and shadowy',[46] as one critic put it when the book came out in 1949. This same approach, however, is also what has won him a lot of praise for being 'open-minded' and 'syncretistic' throughout the years.

Summing up, we could say that Campbell deals with two tasks in *Hero*:

1. To establish to what kind of underlying structure the similarities between stories that deal with a 'hero's journey' adhere to
2. To attempt to make an educated guess as to the meaning of this underlying structure, for which end he makes use of the 'tool' of psychoanalysis.

I will now give a short explanation of how Campbell deals with each of these two tasks. It is in my explanation of the second task that I will deal with Campbell's reception of Jung in phase one.

Task 1

As I already explained, Campbell divides what he called 'the hero's journey' into three stages: separation, initiation and return. He based this tripartite structure on Arnold van Gennep's theory about rites of passage, who labelled these three stages separation, transition and incorporation. In most rites of passage, according to van Gennep, the neophyte is separated from his community (separation stage); undergoes a series of tests or ordeals with an aim to transform him (transition stage); and is brought back to his or her everyday surroundings, reborn (incorporation stage). Campbell sees this same structure in stories which are characterized by the 'hero's journey' motif: the hero leaves home (separation), undergoes a series of tests and/or ordeals in some strange, unknown domain (initiation), and returns home as a transformed individual.

> Prometheus ascended to the heavens, stole fire from the gods, and descended. Jason sailed through the Clashing Rocks into a sea of marvels, circumvented the dragon that guarded the Golden Fleece, and returned with the fleece and the power to wrest his rightful throne from a usurper. Aeneas went down into the underworld, crossed the dreadful river of the dead, threw a sop to the three-headed watchdog Cerberus, and conversed, at last, with the shade of his dead father. All things were unfolded to him: the destiny of souls, the destiny of Rome, which he was

> about to found. . . . He returned through the ivory gate to his work in the world.[47]

Campbell not only finds this pattern in the more obvious hero myths he mentions in the quote above, but also, more conspicuously, in the story of Jesus (who undergoes a series of tests by the devil, dies and is 'reborn') and in the story of the Buddha (who separated himself from the world, attained enlightenment under the Bo tree, and went back into the world to share his teaching). In contrast to Frazer, who focused on the God who dies and is reborn in *The golden bough*, Campbell focuses instead on the hero (who can be a god, but is mostly human) as the subject of a symbolical 'rebirth'. In the initiation stage, the hero has to face dark forces of terrible power, which more often than not leave him on the brink of death; the hero (usually with the help of magical helpers) then finds light within the darkness and manages to return from – sometimes literally – the land of the dead, reborn. This pattern then – of a hero who, like the shaman who during his initiation is dissected and put back together by his spirit helpers, dies to the world and is reborn – is for Campbell the archetypal 'hero's journey'. Campbell gives the following summary of the pattern, which although it is a bit lengthy, I have decided to include here so as to offer the reader a more detailed outline of the patterns described in *Hero*.

> The mythological hero, setting forth from his commonday hut or castle, is lured, carried away, or else voluntarily proceeds, to the threshold of adventure. There he encounters a shadow presence that guards the passage. The hero may defeat or conciliate this power and go alive into the kingdom of the dark (brother-battle, dragon-battle; offering, charm) or be slain by the opponent and descend in death (dismemberment, crucifixion). Beyond the threshold, then, the hero journeys through a world of unfamiliar yet strangely intimate forces, some of which severely threaten him (tests), some of which give magical aid (helpers). When he arrives at the nadir of the mythological round, he undergoes a supreme ordeal and gains his reward. The triumph may be represented as the hero's sexual union with the goddess-mother of the world (sacred marriage), his recognition by a father-creator (father atonement), his own divinization (apotheosis), or again – if the powers have remained unfriendly to him – his theft of the boon he came to gain (bride-theft, fire-theft); intrinsically it is an expansion of consciousness and therewith of being (illumination, transfiguration, freedom). The final work is that of the return. If the powers have blessed the hero, he now sets forth under their protection

(emissary); if not, he flees and is pursued (transformation flight, obstacle flight). At the return threshold the transcendental powers must remain behind; the hero re-emerges from the kingdom of dread (return, resurrection). The boon that he brings restores the world (elixir).[48]

Task 2

We have seen above that Campbell primarily uses psychoanalysis to interpret the 'hero's journey' motif in *Hero*, and that he does not really take preference for any particular psychoanalytical school. In an interview given during the final phase of his career, Campbell confirmed that he felt that Freud and Jung were both of equal value to him while he was writing *Hero*:

> When I wrote *The Hero With A Thousand Faces* in the early '40s, these two men were sort of equal in my thinking. But then in the years following, Jung became more and more eloquent to me. My feeling is that Freud tells us what myths mean to neurotics, and Jung gives us a clue how to let the myth talk to us in its own terms without putting a formula on it. Jung is not the final word at all – I don't think there is a final word. But he opened me up to new prospects and vistas.[49]

Despite this claim on Campbell's part, there are nevertheless a lot of hints that Campbell was already leaning more towards Jung at the time of *Hero*. To begin with, there is a strong parallel between Campbell's 'hero's journey' and Jung's concept of individuation. Jung stressed that an important part of individuation is the letting go of, or going beyond, culturally defined norms and restraints, claiming that '[individuation] is the process by which individual beings are formed and differentiated; in particular, it is the development of the psychological individual as a being distinct from the general, collective psychology.'[50] Campbell makes similar claims about the 'hero's journey' throughout *Hero*, for example, when he states that 'everywhere . . . the really creative acts are represented as those deriving from some sort of dying to the world.'[51] In a speech given about the 'hero's journey' when he was already in his eighties, Campbell expressed this idea with even greater clarity than he does in *Hero*:

> It's always a dangerous adventure because you're moving out of the familiar sphere of your community. In myths, this is represented as moving out of the known sphere altogether into the great beyond. I call this

> crossing the threshold. This is the crossing from the conscious into the unconscious world, but the unconscious world is represented in many, many, many different images, depending on the cultural surroundings of the mythos.[52]

Jung also wrote about individuation as a process of 'turning inward'. For Campbell, the true reference of the 'hero's journey' motif is exactly such a process:

> Hence the incidents are fantastic and 'unreal'; they represent psychological not physical triumphs. Even when the legend is of an actual historical personage, the deeds of victory are rendered, not in lifelike, but in dreamlike figurations; for the point is not that such-and-such was done on earth; the point is that, before such-and-such could be done on earth, this other, more important, primary thing had to be brought to pass within the labyrinth that we all know and visit in our dreams. The passage of the mythological hero may be over ground, incidentally; fundamentally it is inward – into depths where obscure resistances are overcome, and long lost, forgotten powers are revivified, to be made available for the transfiguration of the world.[53]

Robert Segal mentions another aspect of Campbell's position in *Hero* which he claims is similar to Jung's ideas. According to him, a Freudian hero figure would be in the first stage of life, dealing with the concerns of how to integrate successfully into society; a Jungian hero, however, would be in the second stage of life, dealing with concerns of how to go beyond the norms of society and of how to integrate the ego with the unconscious. He then quite rightfully points out that the heroes Campbell deals with in *Hero* are almost all dealing with the concerns of the second stage of life.[54] For this reason he claims that Campbell's hero is a Jungian hero.[55]

There are several other 'clues' that show that during this early phase of his career Campbell was already leaning more towards Jung. What I consider to be the most important one is the fact that Campbell's view of the unconscious is ultimately a highly positive one. I already dealt with the difference between Freud and Jung regarding their attitude to the unconscious when writing about Jung's ideas in *Wandlungen*. Even though Jung still espoused many Freudian ideas in that book, he did put forward a radically different view of the nature of the unconscious in it, especially in the second part of the book. Where Freud saw the unconscious as something which needed to be overcome through use of the rational ego – 'where Id was, there ego will be', as he put it famously – Jung stressed that the unconscious should be seen more as a source of creativity and transformation, capable of refreshing and reviving the conscious life. What Campbell writes in *Hero* reveals that he shares this positive view of the unconscious with Jung. He claims repeatedly that the function of mythological symbols has always been to 'carry the human spirit forward' (something which Freud never would have claimed); like Jung, he also stresses that an inability to 'connect' with the source of these symbols – the unconscious – might lead to a neurosis, thus indicating that the unconscious is for him more healing balm than threat:

> It has always been the prime function of mythology and rite to supply the symbols that carry the human spirit forward, in counteraction to those other constant human fantasies that tend to tie it back. In fact, it may well be that the very high incidence of neuroticism among ourselves follows from the decline among us of such effective spiritual aid.[56]

It is obvious, then, that Campbell shares Jung's positive evaluation of the nature of the unconscious. Even though Campbell never writes whether he thinks that the contents of the unconscious are predominantly inherited (which would establish without any shadow of a doubt that he is taking a Jungian approach), he even gives hints that the unconscious the hero travels into has a layer which consists of archetypes, for example, when he writes the following:

> In a word: the first work of the hero is to retreat from the world scene of secondary effects to those causal zones of the psyche where the difficulties really reside, and there to clarify the difficulties, eradicate them in his own case . . . and break through to the undistorted, direct experience and assimilation of what C. G. Jung has called 'the archetypal images'.[57]

It is quite clear, therefore, that Campbell has much more in common with Jung than he does with Freud in *Hero*. That said, it must be noted that Campbell was not ready to openly embrace Jung at the time of *Hero*. In fact, towards the end of the book Campbell even distances himself from Jung. Although he distances himself from the other psychoanalytical thinkers he has been quoting throughout the book as well, this is still an important 'move' on Campbell's part. The psychoanalysts, Campbell writes, have discovered that the 'patterns and logic of fairytale and myth correspond to those of dream'.[58] However, if we are to understand myth properly, we must first acknowledge that myth is not *completely* of the same order as dreams. Just as in *Grimm*, Campbell stresses that where dreams are spontaneously generated by the unconscious, myths have been *consciously* created by mythmakers:

> [The figures found in dreams and myths] originate from the same sources – the unconscious wells of fantasy – and their grammar is the same, but they are not the spontaneous products of sleep. On the contrary, their patterns are consciously controlled. And their understood function is to serve as a powerful picture language for the communication of traditional wisdom.
>
> . . .
>
> [They are] not only symptoms of the unconscious . . . but also controlled and intended statements of certain spiritual principles which have remained as constant throughout the course of human history as the form and nervous structure of the human physique itself. *Briefly formulated, the universal doctrine teaches that all the visible structures of the world – all things and beings – are the effects of a ubiquitous power out of which they rise, which supports and fills them during the period of their manifestation, and back into which they must ultimately dissolve.* [my italics]
>
> . . .
>
> Myth is but the penultimate; the ultimate is openness – that void, or being, beyond the categories – into which the mind must plunge alone and be dissolved.[59]

Here Campbell finally returns to the metaphysical theme that I identified in section 5.2.1. The symbols found in myths stem from the unconscious; the *meaning* of myth, however, is not psychological at all but metaphysical. Furthermore, myths have this metaphysical meaning because the mythmakers created the myths *consciously* with this metaphysical meaning in mind. This idea is most definitely different from Jung's ideas about myths. Even though, as we have seen in Chapters 2 and 3, metaphysical speculation isn't 'un-Jungian' at all, Jung did stress time and time again that he saw myths as a 'spontaneous' product of the unconscious, and not as a conscious creation (as Campbell claims in *Hero*). For example,

> We can see almost daily in our patients how mythical fantasies arise: they are not thought up, but present themselves as images or chains of ideas that force their way out of the unconscious, and when they are recounted they often have the character of connected episodes resembling mythical dramas. That is how myths arise, and that is the reason why the

> fantasies from the unconscious have so much in common with primitive myths. . . . Myth is nothing but a projection from the unconscious and not a conscious invention at all.[60]

Jung had a lot of experience of working with schizophrenics, and it seems that he interpreted mythmaking as a process that is highly similar to the way a schizophrenic receives his often dreamlike visions. As he once wrote: 'The primitive mentality does not invent myths, it experiences them.'[61] Campbell, perhaps because he had more experience with scholarship than with schizophrenic visions, saw mythmaking as a much more rational process in this phase of his career. As we will see in the next section, Campbell would soon abandon this idea, along with a whole host of other ideas that are characteristic of the first phase of his career. Before we turn to these new ideas in the next section, however, I would first like to give a brief overview of the ideas of phase one.

5.2.3 Overview of phase one

The key concepts Campbell uses in this phase are mostly related to psychoanalysis: he frequently relates that myth is of the order of dream, and he explains the fact that common motifs occur in myths from all over the world by referring to several different theories of the unconscious, without openly choosing sides. Most importantly, however, he distinguishes himself from the psychoanalysts by claiming that myth is not a spontaneous product of the unconscious but that it is reflected upon, and should be seen as a collection of conscious and controlled statements that have been created with the intent to teach a metaphysical truth. 'The old teachers knew what they were saying',[62] Campbell writes in his foreword to *Hero*, and this seems indeed to be the logical implication: myth now becomes something of which the creators *knew* that it was only a 'picture-language'. The masses might have believed that it was all true and that the reference of the symbols was to real gods and goddesses, but the enlightened few who created the myths were conscious of its true point of reference: a metaphysical 'ubiquitous force', which he would later refer to as 'the transcendent'.

5.3 Phase two (1959–1968)

As I already explained in the introduction to section 5.2, phase two of Campbell's career (as I have defined it) began with the publication of the first volume of the *Masks of God* series (*Masks: primitive*), published in 1959. As I will show in section 5.3.1, the ideas which Campbell put forward in this volume of the *Masks* series couldn't be more different from the ideas of *Hero*, and for this reason I feel that it truly marks the beginning of a new phase in Campbell's career. As I will argue in the next chapter (Chapter 6), the third phase of Campbell's career began with the publication of the fourth volume of the *Masks* series, *Creative mythology* (from hereon abbreviated as *Masks: creative*)[63]. In this book Campbell openly re-embraced Jung, whereas he distanced himself from Jung in *Masks: primitive* (as we will see below). The second phase of Campbell's career, therefore, lasts from 1959 to 1968 – nine years in total. Even though this phase is shorter than phase one, Campbell published a great deal more in this phase than he did in that phase. Apart from the first three volumes of the *Masks* series there are also many essays (published in both *Gander* and *The mythic dimension*[64]); Campbell also delivered a lot of lectures, some of which were published in *Myths to live by*.[65] Giving an overview of every single new idea Campbell put forward during phase two, however, is not the goal of this section. My aim here is again to compare Campbell's ideas to Jung's, and for this reason I will focus primarily on *Masks: primitive*, as it is in this book that Campbell deals explicitly with Jung (with a special focus on the concept of the archetype). I will do this in section 5.3.1. I will not devote a section to the other texts published in this period, as these are much less important in light of the overall argument of this book. I will once again finish with a summary of the ideas of this phase in section 5.3.2.

5.3.1 The masks of God

Campbell conceived of the idea for the *Masks of God* series early on in the 1950s, after he had finished editing the *Portable Arabian nights* for Viking press. According to Campbell's biographers Stephen and Robin Larsen, it was Viking editor Pascal Covici who initially came up with the idea, suggesting that Campbell turn his Sarah Lawrence mythology lectures into a book.[66] Although Campbell had drawn on his notes for his course on comparative mythology for *Hero* as well, he had by now much more material to work with. In a letter to Covici from 1957 Campbell wrote:

> This organisation of the material is one that I have developed, during the past twenty-two years, in the course on Comparative Mythology that I have been giving at Sarah Lawrence College; and I am using the notes and wire-recordings of the lectures of this course as the basis for my present plan.
> . . .

> Last year, while working on the volume that I presented for your consideration and for which we have a contract, I found that I had greatly underestimated the density of my materials and plan. I found that a lecture off some twenty-five typed pages, delivered to a group of students who had done collateral reading, required, on the average, well over a hundred pages for proper development in written, rather than oral, prose. . . . The written material that I produced last year comes to some four hundred typewritten pages, and the typescript from the recordings of my lectures to a little over a thousand. These I am using as the raw material for the draft now under weigh.[67]

Perhaps because of the wealth of material at his disposal, Campbell soon thought that the series was going to consist of six volumes. The first two volumes would deal with giving a theoretical introduction to the study of mythology; volume 3 would deal with Oriental thought; volume 4 with Occidental thought; volume 5 with indigenous traditions; volume 6, finally, would deal with the relationship between mythology and the modern world. In the end, however, Campbell's plan for a six-volume series was changed somewhat. The *Masks* series, as it was published from 1959 onwards, consists of only four volumes: volume 1 – *Primitive mythology*; volume 2 – *Oriental mythology*; volume 3 – *Occidental mythology*; and volume 4 – *Creative mythology*. The sound theoretical foundation which Campbell had planned on providing for his series was never given a separate volume; instead, it was given only two chapters: chapters one and two of *Masks: primitive*. As we have seen, Campbell never attempted to present a unified theory about the origins of myth in the first phase of his intellectual development. In these two chapters of *Masks: primitive*, however, Campbell sets out to put forward exactly such a theory. He states that it is his aim to present a 'natural history of the gods and heroes',[68] and then goes on to present a theory that is in almost every single way a break with the position adopted in *Hero*. Gone are the numerous quotes of leading writers from the psychoanalytic field; gone, too, are the numerous assertions that myth is of the order of dream, and that psychoanalysis presents a framework to reinterpret its true meaning. From the very first page, however, Campbell does make it clear that he is once again concerned with what has by now become somewhat of a Campbellian *leitmotiv*: the notion of recurring mythological themes.

> The comparative study of the mythologies of the world compels us to view the cultural history of mankind as a unit; for we find that such themes

> as the fire-theft, deluge, land of the dead, virgin birth, and resurrected hero have a worldwide distribution – appearing everywhere in new combinations while remaining, like the elements of a kaleidoscope, only a few and always the same.[69]

Because these two chapters are also the part of *Masks: primitive* in which he deals with Jung's concept of the archetype, I will now give a detailed analysis of them.

Masks of God: Primitive mythology

As we have seen in Chapter 4, Campbell was fascinated as a boy by the world of biology and nature, even going on to study the subject for a brief spell when at College. Now, for the first time in his career, Campbell tried to make this fascination part of the backbone of his theoretical framework. Instead of focusing on the work of Jung, Freud and their myriad 'followers', Campbell's writing is riddled with quotes from the field of ethology in *Masks: primitive*, many of which we have already encountered in the chapter about Anthony Stevens. Like Stevens in his book *Archetype*, Campbell focuses primarily on the ethological concept of the IRM:

> Students of animal behaviour have coined the term 'innate releasing mechanism' (IRM) to designate the inherited structure of the nervous system that enables an animal to respond thus to a circumstance never experienced before, and the factor triggering the response they term a 'sign stimulus' or 'releaser'. It is obvious that the living entity responding to such a sign cannot be said to be the individual, since the individual has had no previous knowledge of the object to which it is reacting. The recognizing and responding subject is, rather, some sort of trans- or superindividual, inhabiting and moving the living creature.[70]

If it wasn't for the fact that *Masks: primitive* was written more than 20 years before *Archetype*, one would suspect that Campbell had drawn on Stevens' book to find inspiration for his writing. Like Stevens, Campbell stresses that the human psyche carries the traces of its evolutionary history: the human nervous system contains IRMs, and the existence of these IRMs can be explained by the fact that humans have evolved in a specific way, in a specific environment.[71] Furthermore, Campbell stresses that the IRMs which are to be found in human beings are of a different nature than those found in animals. Like Stevens, he claims that the IRMs found in animals are mostly 'closed' or 'stereotyped'; the IRMs to be found in human beings, on the other hand, are open to imprinting – they are so-called open IRMs.

> [Two] orders of innate releasing mechanisms have been identified, namely, the stereotyped, and the open, subject to imprint. In the case of the first, a precise lock-key relationship exists between the inner readiness of the nervous system and the external sign stimulus triggering response; so that, if there exist in the human inheritance many – or even any – IRMs of this order, we may justly speak of 'inherited images' in the psyche.
>
> . . .
>
> [However], the human psyche has not yet been, to any great extent, satisfactorily tested for such stereotypes, and so, I am afraid, pending further study, we must simply admit that we do not know how far the principle of the *inherited image* can be carried when interpreting mythological universals. It is no less premature to deny its possibility than to announce it as anything more than a considered opinion.[72]

Even though this passage makes it sound as if Campbell prefers to leave the question regarding the existence of 'closed' IRMs in the human nervous system open, elsewhere in *Masks: primitive* he makes it obvious that he is adamant that such IRMs are not be found in human beings:

> Furthermore, since we now know that no images have been established unquestionably as innate and that our IRMs are not stereotyped but open, whatever 'universals' we may find in our comparative study must be assigned rather to common experience than to endowment.[73]

As we have seen in Chapter 3, Stevens thinks that Jung's theoretical framework is perfectly compatible with this viewpoint. He stresses that Jung's concept of the archetype should be interpreted as the equivalent of an 'open' IRM. Archetypes, therefore, are not to be thought of as wholly innate; rather, they are 'filled out' (Jung's term, see quote below) by the contents of personal experience. Stevens quotes the following passage from Jung's work to back up this interpretation:

> Again and again I encounter the mistaken notion that an archetype is determined in regard to its content, in other words that it is a kind of unconscious idea (if such an expression be permissible). It is necessary to point out once more that archetypes are not determined as to their content, but

> only as regards their form, and then only to a very limited degree. *A primordial image is determined as to its content only when it has become conscious and is therefore filled out with the material of conscious experience* [my italics].[74]

Campbell's discussion about the relationship between myth and the IRMs of the human nervous system is so similar to the ideas of Anthony Stevens that one might expect him to fully endorse Jung's concept of the archetype as well. What is surprising, however, is that Campbell does nothing of the sort. Where in Hero he only separated himself from Jung's ideas in a rather roundabout way – not by attacking Jung's theories themselves, but by stressing that he thinks myths are consciously, as opposed to unconsciously, created – he now dismisses what is arguably the very essence of Jung's theoretical framework: the concept of the archetype. Where for Stevens the ideas of the ethologists are perfectly compatible with Jung's concept of the archetype, Campbell draws the exact opposite conclusion.

As we have seen in Chapter 3, one of the examples Stevens gives of a 'closed' IRM is the fact that chicks cower and duck for cover when a hawk flies over their coop. Campbell uses this example as well in *Masks: primitive.* In the following passage, he states that for him this is an example of what Jung means by his concept of the archetype:

> C.G. Jung . . . identifies two fundamentally different systems of unconsciously motivated response in the human being. One he terms the personal unconscious. It is based on a context of forgotten, neglected, or suppressed memory images derived from personal experience (infantile impressions, shocks, frustrations, satisfactions, etc.), such as Sigmund Freud recognized and analyzed in his therapy. The other he names the collective unconscious. Its contents – which he calls archetypes – are just such images as that of the hawk in the nervous system of the chick. No one has yet been able to tell us how it got there; but there it is![75]

Because Campbell feels that there is no justification for claiming that such 'closed' IRMs (which he also refers to as 'inherited images') are to be found in the human nervous system, he is forced to conclude that his own ideas are at odds with Jung.

As I pointed out in the introduction to Chapter 3, there are two different approaches to interpreting Jung's concept of the archetype: the 'inheritance only' approach, which is the one taken by Robert Segal; and the 'inheritance plus experience' approach, which is the one taken by Anthony Stevens. Campbell, because of the fact that he equates the concept of the archetype with a 'closed' IRM, takes the 'inheritance only' approach in *Masks: primitive.* This does not mean that Campbell now no longer appreciates Jung's work at all: he even calls it 'one of the leading theories in our field'[76] at one point. However, because he feels that Jung does not leave enough room open for personal experience in explaining the common motifs of mythology, he still – politely – shows him the door:

> Tentatively, it might reasonably be supposed that food-seeking, sleep, self-protection, courtship and mating, and some of the activities of parenthood should be instinctive. But the question – as we have seen – remains open as to what precisely are the sign stimuli that generally trigger these activities in man, or whether any of the stimuli can be said to be as immediately known to the human interior as the hawk to the chick. We do not, therefore, speak of inherited images [Campbell's term for 'closed' IRMs] in the following pages.
>
> . . .
>
> Therefore, though respecting the possibility – perhaps the probability – of such a psychologically inspired parallel development of mythological imagery as that suggested by . . . C. G. Jung's of the collective unconscious, we cannot attempt to interpret in such terms any of the remarkable correspondences that will everywhere confront us.[77]

Campbell would have written this section of *Masks* somewhere towards the end of the 1950s; in all likelihood he finished it somewhere in 1958. By that time, he would have had access to a great deal more texts by Jung than at the time he wrote *Hero.* Of all the volumes in the *Collected works*, for example, seven volumes had already been published at that time (volumes 1, 5, 7, 11, 12, 16 and 17, to be precise). Of the books by Jung in Campbell's library, 12 books have a publication date before 1958. Of course, this does not prove that Campbell actually had them in his possession at that time: he may have bought them at a later date. Still, the fact that these books had been published in the English language at that time shows that a great deal more texts by Jung were readily available. Campbell, however, bases his interpretation of Jung's concept of the archetype in *Masks: primitive* on a single text from an early stage of Jung's career: *Psychological types*, published in 1921. He gives the following quote from it to illustrate what he thinks Jung means by his term 'archetype':

> The primary image, which I have termed archetype, is always collective, i.e. common to at least whole peoples or periods of history. The chief

> mythological motifs of all times and races are very probably of this order; for example, in the dreams and fantasies of neurotics of pure Negro stock I have been able to identify a series of motifs of Greek mythology.
>
> The primary image is a memory deposit, an engramm, derived from a condensation of innumerable similar experiences . . . the psychic expression of an anatomically, physiologically determined natural tendency.[78]

The reference Campbell gives for this passage is to the German edition from 1921.[79] It seems as if Campbell has translated the passage himself (something which he did more often), as the translation differs from both the translation found in the *Collected works* edition[80] and the translation of the 1923 English edition by H. Godwin Baynes.[81] In the 1923 Baynes translation, for example, a key passage in the above quote reads as follows:

> The primordial image is a mnemic deposit, an imprint ('engramm' – Semon), which has arisen through a condensation of innumerable, similar *processes* [my italics].[82]

The difference between the two translations might give us some clue as to the reasons behind Campbell's negative evaluation of Jung's ideas. In the *Collected works* translation the archetype is the result of a condensation of 'innumerable, similar *processes*'; in Campbell's translation it is the result of the condensation of 'innumerable similar *experiences*'. The difference between these two passages is crucial. The archetype, when seen as a wholly innate 'inherited image' which is the end-result of the imprinting of the *experiences* of our forebears, comes awfully close to the idea of a Lamarckian 'race memory' of which Jung was accused so much in the beginning of his career. Campbell, who seems to have been acutely aware of the scientific developments of his time, would have rejected such a notion straight away.

This negative judgement of Jung's work, however, is perhaps a bit premature on Campbell's part. As we have seen in Chapter 2, it is highly problematic to base one's interpretation of Jung's ideas solely on a text written as early as 1921. Anthony Stevens, for example, bases his positive evaluation of Jung's ideas on the latter's distinction between the archetype-as-such and the archetypal image which the archetype-as-such gives rise to. As Jung only developed this distinction in 1946 (in 'On the nature of the psyche'; see Chapter 2 for a detailed analysis), it isn't hard to see that Campbell, by basing his judgement on a text written 25 years earlier, is perhaps being a touch unfair on Jung.

In Campbell's defence, it should perhaps be pointed out that the volume of the *Collected works* which contains 'On the nature of the psyche' was only published in 1960; volume 9 of the *Collected works* ('The archetypes and the collective unconscious'), which also contains many key texts which shed light on the exact nature of Jung's ideas about the concept of the archetype, was only published in 1959 – the year of the publication of *Masks: primitive.* At first glance, then, it seems that Campbell simply may not have had access to the right information. When one digs a little deeper, however, it becomes obvious that Campbell did indeed have access to one of the key texts by Jung which deals with this important subject matter, namely 'On the nature of the psyche'. This text was originally delivered by Jung at the Eranos conference of 1946. Campbell, as we have seen in Chapter 4, was given the job of editing the six volume series *Papers from the Eranos yearbooks.* For these books, a selection was made of what the publishers deemed the best lectures; these were then grouped according to a similar theme. Campbell's job as editor was to read through all of the original German yearbooks and then to write a short report on each lecture contained in them. The Joseph Campbell Archive at the Pacifica graduate institute has the original copies of these reports by Campbell, and there is indeed a report on 'On the nature of the psyche' among these rather lengthy, typewritten reports as well.[83] As Campbell had already completed the task of editing the yearbooks in 1958, this means that he was certainly aware of the contents of the text at the time he was writing *Masks: primitive.* The fact that he seems to have interpreted it differently than Stevens proves perhaps what I have already argued in the introduction to Chapter 3: that the fact that different interpretations of Jung's work are possible is predominantly Jung's own fault. His texts were sometimes highly ambiguous, and for this reason they can often be read in more than one way. This is particularly true in the case of 'On the nature of the psyche'. The examples Jung gives in that text of the concept of the 'pattern of behaviour' (Jung's term for the archetype-as-such; see section 2.2), for example, are all what in the language of the ethologists would be called a 'closed' IRM. Take, for example, the following passage:

> Instinct and the archaic mode meet in the biological conception of the 'pattern of behaviour'. There are, in fact, no amorphous instincts, as every instinct bears in itself the pattern of its situation. Always it fulfils an image, and the image has fixed qualities. The instinct of the leaf-cutting ant fulfils the image of ant, tree, leaf, cutting, transport, and the little antgarden of fungi. If any one of these conditions is lacking, the instinct

> does not function, because it cannot exist without its total pattern, without its image.[84]

Even though Jung does make the important distinction in 'On the nature of the psyche' between the archetype-as-such and the archetypal image, he never really makes it clear that he thinks that the archetype-as-such is 'imprinted' by experience, like Stevens claims. The examples from the animal kingdom such as the one in the quote above seem, at first glance, to confirm that he *doesn't* think that the archetype-as-such is open to imprinting. A leap of interpretation is necessary to arrive at the conclusion that this is indeed the case, and this is a leap that does not always follow logically from Jung's writings. We should not blame Campbell, then, for thinking that Jung's concept of the archetype is the equivalent of a 'closed' IRM. Even though he certainly could have been more careful in his treatment of Jung in *Masks: primitive* – he could, for example, have quoted from a later text than *Psychological types* – the fact that he arrives at the conclusions outlined above should not be dismissed as nonsensical.

Robert Segal's interpretation of **Masks** *as 'un-Jungian'*

Robert Segal's interpretation of Jung, as we have already seen, is very similar to Campbell's in *Masks: primitive.* He, too, claims that Jung's concept of the archetype should be thought of as a wholly innate psychological structure:

> Like Tylor, Frazer, and Freud, Jung attributes the similarities in myths to independent invention. But unlike them he attributes independent invention to heredity rather than experience. He claims that everyone is born not just with a need of some kind that the invention of myth fulfils but with the myths, or the contents of myths, themselves. More precisely, everyone is born with the contents of myths already elevated to the level of myth.
>
> . . .
>
> For Tylor, Frazer, and Freud, experience, even if it is of innate needs, provides the impetus for the creation of myth. For Freud, for example, one's experience of one's parents' reaction to one's incestuous drives spurs the creation of myth. For Jung, by contrast, experience provides only an occasion for the expression of pre-existent archetypes. Archetypes shape experience rather than, as for Freud and the others, derive from it.[85]

Because of this interpretation of Jung's ideas, Segal draws the conclusion in his *Introduction* that Campbell's ideas in *Masks* are not in line with Jung's ideas at all. Where Jung claims that the similarities found in myths are due to common psychological inheritance, Segal states, Campbell draws the exact opposite conclusion, claiming that these similarities should primarily be explained by focusing on common *experience*. According to Segal, this conclusion on Campbell's part is a distinctly 'un-Jungian' one. The fact that Campbell stresses that every generation creates their archetypes anew from conscious experience is something that Jung would never have concluded:

> Campbell might here seem no different from early Jung, but for even early Jung the archetypes formed out of the experiences of prehistoric humans get inherited in turn. For Campbell, by contrast, each generation creates archetypes anew out of its own experiences. Imagination takes significant experiences and makes them mythical, or archetypal. Only the mechanisms for activating emotions and actions, the IRMs, are inherited. Archetypes themselves, which activate the IRMs, are not.[86]

Segal attaches considerable importance to the question whether Campbell is a Jungian or not, as he devotes an entire chapter to the subject matter in *Introduction*. He acknowledges, too, that Campbell's ideas have changed over time, for he deals with the question whether Campbell is taking a Jungian approach or not for all of Campbell's most important works separately. About the *Masks of God* series Segal writes that 'Campbell is less Jungian in *Masks* than in any other work except "Bios and Mythos" '.[87] He gives two reasons for this. The first reason is one I have just dealt with above: that Campbell states that experience, not inheritance, is central if one wants to explain the common motifs of world mythology. The second reason he offers, however, is one that I haven't dealt with thus far: the fact that Campbell also focuses heavily on diffusion when explaining the archetypal images he deals with in *Masks*. Diffusion as an explanation for the recurring motifs found in mythology plays an important role in all of Campbell's works. Although it remained in the background in *Hero*, even in that work he makes it obvious that he feels that some similarities between myths simply cannot be explained by referring to common inheritance or experience, for example, when he states that 'few (if any) of the so-called "primitive cultures" studied by our anthropologists represent autochthonous growths. They are, rather, local adaptations, provincial degenerations, and immensely old fossilizations, of folkways that were developed in very different lands, often under much less simple circumstances, and by other races.'[88] In *Masks* this theme is much more prominent. This leads Segal to claim that '[Campbell] is so intent on tracing cultural influences that he might well seem to be attributing the similarities to diffusion rather than independent invention.'[89] In my opinion, however, acknowledging that some similarities between myths are not due to independent invention but due to diffusion is not distinctly un-Jungian at all. In fact, Jung himself acknowledged that his own theoretical framework did not oppose theories of diffusion. Rather, he felt that the two could, and should, go hand in hand:

> The first investigator in the field of ethnology to draw attention to the widespread occurrence of certain 'elementary ideas' was Adolf Bastian. Two later investigators, Hubert and Mauss, followers of Durkheim, speak of 'categories' of the imagination. And it was no less an authority than Hermann Usener who first recognized unconscious preformation under the guise of 'unconscious thinking'. If I have any share in these discoveries, it consists in my having shown that archetypes are not disseminated only by tradition, language, and migration, but that they can rearise spontaneously, at any time, at any place, and without any outside influence.[90]

Anthony Stevens, too, stresses that Jung was not 'against' diffusion:

> Jung was not so naïve as to deny that this universal parallelism of motifs, ideas and images could be brought about by the combined operation of tradition and migration, but he argued that some form of transmission through heredity must also occur since he was able to discover numerous instances where such motifs arose spontaneously, without any previous encounter with them on the part of the subject. Jung, therefore, concluded that they must correspond to 'typical dispositions', 'dominants' or 'nodal points' within the structure of the psyche itself.[91]

In my opinion, therefore, the fact that Campbell focuses heavily on theories of diffusion in *Masks* does not mean his approach is 'un-Jungian' at all. The question whether Campbell is indeed taking an approach which can be thought of as compatible with Jung in *Masks*, therefore, depends solely on one's evaluation of the ideas he puts forward regarding the psychobiological roots of the archetypal images. Robert Segal, given his interpretation of the concept of the archetype, draws the conclusion that

Campbell's ideas about this topic in *Masks* are not in line with Jung's ideas at all; Anthony Stevens, however, would in all likelihood draw a very different conclusion. Campbell himself, at this point in time, still shares Segal's point of view.

The position of Anthony Stevens, as I argued at the end of section 3.1, can be summed up by the following statements:

- *The archetype is essentially a biological concept.*
- *The archetype is the result of evolution. More specifically, it is the product of natural selection.*
- *The concept of the archetype is equivalent to the concept of the innate releasing mechanism.*
- *The archetype is not wholly innate: it is open to imprinting. It is therefore to be thought of as the equivalent of an 'open' IRM.*
- *The archetype is therefore what makes an organism respond in a highly, but not wholly, preprogrammed way to certain key stimuli in the organism's environment.*

I think that Campbell, at the time of *Masks: primitive*, would have readily conceded that these statements accurately reflect his own ideas about the ground structures of the human nervous system. What he would have objected to, however, is the fact that Stevens claim that they accurately describe the 'essence' of the concept of the archetype. As I will argue in the next chapter, however, this judgement on Campbell's part would change drastically. Campbell changed from Segal's interpretation of Jung to the one that Stevens propagates, and consequently arrived at the conclusion that he could endorse Jung's ideas after all. In the first three volumes of *Masks*, however, Campbell does no such thing. Instead of linking his ideas about the 'open' IRM to Jung, he links them to another thinker which he would refer to again and again throughout his career: the nineteenth-century German explorer Adolf Bastian. Campbell, from *Masks: primitive* onwards, made heavy usage of Bastian's terms 'elementary ideas' and 'ethnic ideas' to explain the exact nature of his ideas about mythic symbols. In *Masks: primitive* he gives the following description of these terms:

> Adolf Bastian (1826–1905) . . . recognized, in the course of his extensive travels, the uniformity of what he termed the 'elementary ideas' (Elementargedanke) of mankind. Remarking also, however, that in the various provinces of human culture these ideas are differently articulated and elaborated, he coined the term 'ethnic ideas' (Völkergedanke)

> for the actual, local manifestations of the universal forms. Nowhere, he noted, are the 'elementary ideas' to be found in a pure state, abstracted from the locally conditioned 'ethnic ideas' through which they are substantialized; but rather, like the image of man himself, they are to be known only by way of the rich variety of their extremely interesting, frequently startling, yet always finally recognizable inflections in the panorama of human life.[92]

He then links these two terms to his own ideas about the 'open' IRM. According to him, the fact that the IRMs in the human nervous system are all 'open' explains why we find different inflections of mythic symbols all over the world, as opposed to symbols which are exactly the same. The concept of the open IRM thus leads to a dichotomy comparable to Bastian's dichotomy of the elementary and the ethnic idea: of the innate factor on the one hand (the IRM 'as-such', which is the same in all cultures), and the various 'imprints' on the other hand (which are different from culture to culture). He therefore arrives at the following schema:

Elementary idea	–	*ethnic idea*
Open IRM	–	*imprint*

As we will see in the next chapter, Campbell would eventually add Jung's concepts of the archetype-as-such and the archetypal image to this schema as well. Before we move on to the next chapter to see how this came about, however, we must look into one more subject matter: the metaphysical theme, which played such a prominent role in the previous section.

The metaphysical theme in phase two

Reading the discussion about Campbell's ideas about IRMs above (which summarizes Campbell's ideas about the *psychological* theme in phase two), one might get the impression that Campbell has undergone a sudden conversion to scientific naturalism. This is not the case, however: the metaphysical theme is still present, although it remains very much in the background in *Masks: primitive.* In the next volume of the series (*Masks: oriental),* however, Campbell makes it much more obvious that this theme still plays an important role in his thinking. In Chapter 2 of that book he compares his own ideas about the metaphysical connotation of mythic symbols to the ideas of Rudolf Otto, the famous theologian who so heavily influenced Mircea Eliade. 'Following Rudolf Otto, I shall assume the root of mythology as well as of religion to be an apprehension of the numinous', Campbell writes. He then gives the following quote from Otto's *The idea of the holy*:

> This mental state [the numinous] is perfectly sui generis and irreducible to any other; and therefore, like every absolutely primary and elementary datum, while it admits of being discussed, it cannot be strictly defined. There is only one way to help another to an understanding of it. He must be guided and led on by consideration and discussion of the matter through the ways of his own mind, until he reach the point at which 'the numinous' in him perforce begins to stir, to start into life and into consciousness. We can cooperate in this process by bringing before his notice all that can be found in other regions of the mind, already known and familiar, to resemble, or again to afford some special contrast to, the particular experience we wish to elucidate. Then we must add: 'This X of ours is not precisely this experience, but akin to this one and opposite to that other, cannot you now realize for yourself what it is?' In other words our X cannot, strictly speaking, be taught, it can only be evoked, awakened in the mind; as everything that comes 'of the spirit' must be awakened.[93]

Campbell then explains how, for him, Otto's position is reflected in his own approach to the study of mythology:

> The symbolism of the temple and atmosphere of myth are, in this sense, catalysts of the numinous – and therein lies the secret of their force. However, the traits of the symbols and elements of the myths tend to acquire a power of their own through association, by which the access of the numinous itself may become blocked. And it does, indeed, become blocked when the images are insisted upon as final terms in themselves: as they are, for example, in a dogmatic credo.[94]

Campbell, towards the end of his life, frequently stated that to read a myth correctly one must make it 'transparent to the transcendent'. Myth, properly understood, refers not only to the dynamics of the psyche but to a transcendent dimension as well; adherents of religions, however, often fail to see this, thus reducing their tradition to nothing but empty dogma. As this is exactly the same argument which Campbell makes in *Masks: oriental* about the proper way to understand the 'numinous', it is clear that this concept is an earlier equivalent of his concept of the 'transcendent'. As

I argued in the previous section, the 'transcendent' is also the equivalent of what he referred to in *Hero* as a 'ubiquitous force'. The role Campbell assigns to this metaphysical dimension in *Masks*, however, differs slightly from the way he dealt with it in *Hero*. Where in *Hero* the meaning of myth was metaphysical because its creators created it consciously with this meaning in mind, Campbell now claims that the 'symbolism of the temple and the atmosphere of myth' lead to a direct *experience* of the metaphysical. He also claims that an experience of the metaphysical is what brought about the myths in the first place: 'Following Rudolf Otto, I shall assume the root of mythology as well as of religion to be an apprehension of the numinous.'[95] This focus on the experience of the metaphysical, however, was already part of the discussion found in *Hero* as well, albeit in a different context. This experience, namely, is what the hero's journey is all about: after going deep within his own unconscious, the hero is able to break through to a realization that he contains a divine spark – is able, in other words, to experience the numinous. What is different from his approach in *Hero*, however, is that Campbell no longer puts as much emphasis on the notion that myth is *consciously* created in *Masks*. He now takes a much more Jungian approach and focuses more on the spontaneous generation of myth, for example, when he writes:

> Mythology is not invented rationally; mythology cannot be rationally understood. Theological interpreters render it ridiculous. Literary criticism reduces it to metaphor. A new and very promising approach is opened, however, when it is viewed in the light of biological psychology as a function of the human nervous system, precisely homologous to the innate and learned sign stimuli that release and direct the energies of nature – of which our brain itself is but the most amazing flower.[96]

This leaves us with the following question: if the meaning of myth is no longer metaphysical because myths were created consciously, how exactly does Campbell connect the psychological and the metaphysical themes in phase two? Even though at first glance the two themes may appear to be completely at odds with each other in the first three volumes of *Masks*, Campbell does indeed establish a connection between the two. After having completed his discussion of the IRMs of the human nervous system in chapter one of *Masks: primitive*, in which he establishes that the archetypal images of myth should be explained by focusing on common experience rather than common inheritance, Campbell devotes a very long second chapter to establishing what exactly this common experience consists of.

It is in this chapter (called 'The imprints of experience') that Campbell combines his view of the human psyche as containing 'open' IRMs with the metaphysical theme, and he does this in a way that is distinctly different from the approach he took in *Hero.* Campbell now stresses that experience of a metaphysical dimension is one of the most important *imprints* of experience. To give an example of one who thinks has had such an experience, Campbell offers a quote from the writings of Nicholas of Cusa:

> Thy face, [Lord], which a young man, if he strove to imagine it, would conceive as a youth's; a full-grown man, as manly; an aged man as an aged man's! Who could imagine this sole pattern, most true and most adequate, of all faces – of all even as of none other? He would have need to go beyond all forms or races that may be formed, and all figures. And how could he imagine a face when he must go beyond all faces and all likenesses and figures of all faces and all concepts which can be formed of a face, and all color, adornment and beauty of all faces? Wherefore he that goeth forward to behold Thy face, so long as he formeth any concept thereof, is far from Thy face. For all concept of a face falleth short, Lord, of Thy face, and all beauty which can be conceived is less than the beauty of Thy face; every face hath beauty yet none is beauty's self, but Thy face, Lord, hath beauty and this having is being. Tis therefore Absolute Beauty itself, which is the form that giveth being to every beautiful form. O face exceedingly comely, whose beauty all things to whom it is granted to behold it, suffice not to admire! In all faces is seen the Face of faces, veiled, and in a riddle: howbeit unveiled it is not seen, until above silence where there is no knowledge or concept of a face. This mist, cloud, darkness, or ignorance into which he that seeketh Thy face entereth when he goeth beyond all knowledge or concept is the state below which Thy face cannot be found except veiled; but that very darkness revealeth Thy face to be there, beyond all veils.[97]

Campbell then gives the following commentary on this quote, revealing that he thinks of this kind of experience as a *mystical* experience:

> Here is the secret cause – known not in terror but in rapture. And its sole beholder is the perfectly purified spirit, gone beyond the normal bounds of human experience, thought, and speech. 'There the eye goes not', we read in the Indian Kena Upanishad, 'speech goes not, nor the mind'. And yet the impact has been experienced by a great many on this earth. It has been rendered . . . in many mythologies and many paeans

of the mystics, in many times and many lands. Without question, it is an available experience.[98]

The role which Campbell now assigns this experience is rather different from the role it plays in Jung's theoretical framework. For the late Jung, the archetype is *inherently* metaphysical; it points to a transcendent dimension not because the person who is born with it has had an experience of this dimension, but because the archetype itself is, as Anthony Stevens puts it, 'the product of an objective order which transcends both the human mind and the external world'.[99] For the late Jung, therefore, *all* archetypes point towards the metaphysical, or, in his terminology, the *unus mundus*. If we follow Campbell's argument that mysticism is but one of the many 'imprints of experience', however, an archetype points to the metaphysical only if it has been imprinted by an individual's *experience* of it. As we have seen above, however, Campbell stresses at the same time (in *Masks: oriental*) that *all* religious symbols refer to the numinous: 'The symbolism of the temple and atmosphere of myth are . . . catalysts of the numinous – and therein lies the secret of their force.'[100] How should we deal with this obvious inconsistency in what is arguably one of the most important series of books written by Campbell? My suggestion is this: we can't. Campbell at this time was still searching, circling his subject matter from several different perspectives, and he had yet to arrive at a unified point of view which incorporates in a non-contradictory way the two themes which have played such a central role in this chapter: the psychological and the metaphysical theme. For this unified theory, however, we must jump forward into time to the next phase of Campbell's career. Before we do so in the next chapter, I would again like to offer a brief overview of Campbell's position in this phase of his intellectual development.

5.3.2 Overview of phase two

In this phase we can clearly see that Campbell distances himself from the ideas expressed in *Hero*. He dismisses Jung because he feels that there are no 'closed' IRMs in the human psyche; he also aligns himself with Rudolf Otto, but never deals with the question whether these two perspectives (Otto and his focus on the ethological concept of the IRM) are really all that compatible. There is a tension, then, in Campbell's thought at this point in his career: between the metaphysical theme on the one hand and the psychological theme on the other hand. To see how Campbell finally resolved this tension we will now turn to the last phase of his intellectual development.

Notes

[1] Jeffrey Mishlove, *Thinking allowed: conversations on the leading edge of knowledge and discovery* (Tulsa: Council Oak books, 1995), p. 91.
[2] Jung, *Wandlungen und symbole der libido* (Leipzig: F. Deuticke, 1925 [1912]).
[3] Carl G. Jung, *The psychology of the unconscious,* trans. Beatrice M. Hinkle (London: Kegan Paul, Trench, Trubner & Co. Ltd., 1922 [1912]).
[4] Carl G. Jung, *Dream symbols of the individuation process* (New York: Private copyright, 1937).
[5] Carl G. Jung, *The integration of the personality,* trans. Stanley M. Dell (New York: Farrar & Rinehart, 1939).
[6] Carl G. Jung and C. Kerényi, *Essays on a science of mythology: the myth of the divine child and the mysteries of Eleusis* (New York: Pantheon Books, 1949).
[7] D. T. Suzuki, *Introduction to Zen Buddhism (with a foreword by C.G. Jung).* (New York: Philosophical Library, 1949 [1934]).
[8] Carl G. Jung et al., *The Interpretation of nature and the psyche* (New York: Pantheon Books, 1955).
[9] Carl G. Jung, *Gegenwart und zukunft* (Zürich: Rascher-Verlag, 1957).
[10] Paul Radin, *The trickster: a study in American Indian mythology* (New York: Philosophical Library, 1956).
[11] Carl G. Jung, *Memories, dreams, reflections* (New York: Random House, 1965 [1961]).
[12] Carl G. Jung, *Analytical psychology: its theory and practice; the Tavistock lectures* (New York: Pantheon Books, 1968).
[13] Carl G. Jung, *The visions seminars* (Zürich: Zürich Spring Publications, 1976).
[14] Carl G. Jung, *Flying saucers: a modern myth of things seen in the skies* (Princeton: Princeton University Press, 1978).
[15] Carl G. Jung, *Psychology and the East* (Princeton: Princeton University Press, 1978).
[16] Joseph Campbell, *Masks: primitive.*
[17] Joseph Campbell et al., *Where the two came to their father: a Navaho war memorial,* Bollingen Series I (Richmond: Old Dominion Foundation, 1943).
[18] Joseph Campbell and Henry Morton Robinson, *A skeleton key to Finnegan's wake* (New York: Harcourt, Brace & Co., 1944).
[19] Published as part of Joseph Campbell, *Gander.*
[20] Ibid.
[21] Joseph Campbell, *Pathways to bliss – mythology and personal transformation,* ed. David Kudler, The collected works of Joseph Campbell (Novato: New World Library, 2004), p. xi.
[22] Tom Collins, 'Mythic reflections – an interview with Joseph Campbell', *The new story* 12 (winter 1985).
[23] Campbell et al., *Where the two came to their father,* p. 33.
[24] Jung, *The psychology of the unconscious,* p. 81.
[25] Ibid., p. 73.
[26] Ibid., p. 72.
[27] Ibid., p. 70.
[28] Campbell et al., *Where the two came to their father,* p. 33.

[29] The Jungian term for the technique in which the analyst tries to clarify a dream or story motif by offering archetypal parallels from myths and fairytales from all over the world.
[30] Joseph Campbell, *Hero,* p. 255.
[31] Campbell et al., *Where the two came to their father,* p. 36.
[32] Campbell, *Gander,* p. 32.
[33] Ibid., p. 33.
[34] Ibid., p. 16.
[35] Ibid., p. 33.
[36] Joseph Campbell, *The hero's journey: Joseph Campbell on his life and work,* ed. Phil Cousineau (San Francisco/London: Harper & Row, 1990), p. 119.
[37] *Joseph Campbell Foundation update April 2007* [online] (21 April 2007, accessed 30 April 2007); available from http://tinyurl.com/5rqg37
[38] Campbell, *Hero.*
[39] Ibid., p. 30.
[40] Quoted in Stephen Larsen and Robin Larsen, *A fire in the mind – the life of Joseph Campbell* (New York: Doubleday, 1991), pp. 347, 348.
[41] Peter Homans, 'C.G. Jung', in *The encyclopaedia of religion,* ed. Mircea Eliade (editor-in-chief) (New York: Macmillan, 1987).
[42] Campbell, *Hero,* p. vii.
[43] Ibid., p. 255.
[44] Ibid., p. 39, note 43.
[45] Robert Segal, *Introduction,* p. 30.
[46] Unnamed critic, quoted in Larsen and Larsen, *A fire in the mind,* 347.
[47] Campbell, *Hero,* pp. 30, 31.
[48] Ibid., pp. 245, 246.
[49] Michael Toms, 'Interview with Joseph Campbell', *Sunrise,* August–September 1979 (Campbell Archive: box 113, folder A1), p. 329.
[50] Jung, *CW 6,* par. 757.
[51] Campbell, *Hero,* p. 35.
[52] Campbell, *Pathways to bliss,* p. 114.
[53] Campbell, *Hero,* p. 29.
[54] Segal, *Introduction,* p. 43.
[55] Ibid.
[56] Campbell, *Hero,* p. 11.
[57] Ibid., pp. 17, 18.
[58] Ibid., p. 255.
[59] Ibid., pp. 256–258.
[60] 'On psychic energy', in Jung, *CW 8,* par. 38.
[61] 'The psychology of the child archetype', in Jung, *CW 9 part 1.*
[62] Campbell, *Hero,* p. vii.
[63] Joseph Campbell, *Masks: creative.*
[64] Joseph Campbell, *The mythic dimension – selected essays 1959–1987,* ed. Antony van Couvering, The collected works of Joseph Campbell (New York: Harper Collins, 1997).
[65] Joseph Campbell, *Myths to live by* (New York: Bantam Books, 1972).
[66] Larsen and Larsen, *A fire in the mind,* p. 426.

[67] Joseph Campbell, 'Letter to Pascal Covici', 4 January 1957 (Campbell Archive: box 108, folder P1).
[68] Campbell, *Masks: primitive*, p. 5.
[69] Ibid., p. 3.
[70] Ibid., p. 31.
[71] Ibid., p. 34.
[72] Ibid., pp. 44–45.
[73] Ibid., p. 48.
[74] Jung, *CW 9 part 1*, par. 155.
[75] Campbell, *Masks: primitive*, pp. 32–33.
[76] Ibid., p. 32.
[77] Ibid., p. 48.
[78] Quoted in ibid., p. 32.
[79] It reads as follows: 'C.G. Jung, Psychologischen Typen (Zürich: Rascher-Verlag, 1921), p. 598.'
[80] Jung, *CW 6*.
[81] Carl G. Jung, *Psychological types* (London: Routledge & Kegan Paul, 1923 [1921]).
[82] Ibid., p. 556.
[83] Campbell derives the name for the paper from the original German title and calls it instead 'Spirit in psychology' (Campbell Archive: box 129, folder Eranos 13–16 [1945–1948]).
[84] Jung, *CW 8*, par. 398.
[85] Segal, *Introduction*, pp. 247–248.
[86] Ibid., p. 253.
[87] Ibid.
[88] Hero, p. 142.
[89] Segal, *Introduction*, p. 253.
[90] Jung, *CW 9 part 1*, p. 79.
[91] Anthony Stevens, *Archetype revisited – an updated natural history of the self*, second edn (London: Brunner-Routledge, 2002), p. 46.
[92] Campbell, *Masks: primitive*, p. 32.
[93] Rudolf Otto, *The idea of the holy* (London: Oxford University Press, 1925), p. 7. Quoted in Joseph Campbell, *Masks: oriental*, p. 45.
[94] Campbell, *Masks: oriental*, p. 46.
[95] Ibid., p. 45.
[96] Campbell, *Masks: primitive*, p. 42.
[97] Quoted in ibid., p. 51.
[98] Ibid.
[99] Anthony Stevens, 'The archetypes', in *The handbook of Jungian psychology*, ed. Renos K. Papadopoulos (New York/London: Routledge, 2006), p. 88.
[100] Campbell, *Masks: primitive*, p. 46.

Chapter 6

Phase three of Campbell's career

As I already mentioned in Chapter 4, Campbell retired from Sarah Lawrence College in 1972. Finally free to devote all his time to what, by now, had become his main source of income – his scholarly work – Campbell embarked on a rigorous program of lecturing and writing. He started to give many, many lectures, sometimes giving more than 200 a year;[1] also, as he started to become more and more well known, he started to give a lot more interviews than he did before he went into retirement. These interviews are particularly revealing in regard to Campbell's attitude to Jung. There are hardly any interviews from before 1972; after that date, however, the number of interviews increases significantly, and as Jung often came up as a subject matter, these interviews offer one an excellent opportunity to explore what Campbell's exact ideas were about Jung. In one of the first interviews Campbell gave after his retirement he was asked by the interviewer in what way myth can still be relevant today. Part of Campbell's response was the following:

> [The] myths originally came out of the individual's own dream consciousness. Within each person there is what Jung called a collective unconscious. We are not only individuals with our unconscious intentions related to a specific social environment. We are also representatives of the species homo sapiens. And that universality is in us whether we know it or not. We penetrate to this level by getting in touch with dreams, fantasies and traditional myths; by using active imagination.[2]

Given Campbell's dismissal of Jung's concept of the archetype (which lies at the root of his theory of the collective unconscious) in *Masks: primitive*, this answer is surprising to say the least. Of course, we could explain Campbell's assertion that 'within each person there is what Jung called a collective unconscious' as a mere slip of the tongue, uttered by someone who hasn't realized that what he is saying is the exact opposite of what he has claimed in a book written 12 years earlier. If this were the case, then we might expect Campbell to go back and forth between the two positions at random; we would expect him to deny the existence of the collective unconscious at certain times, while endorsing the idea at other times. As I will be arguing in this chapter, however, this is not the case. From 1968 onwards (a date that I will clarify below) Campbell consistently displayed a highly positive attitude towards Jung's core ideas, specifically the concept of the archetype and the theory of the collective unconscious. Thus, we find him saying the following in an interview from the 1980s:

> Now, my own discovery of Jung happened when I was a student in Germany in the 1920s. I was interested in mythology at that time. But I had never found any relationship of psychology to mythology in the literature that I was introduced to in college or graduate school. But, my god, when I began reading Jung's works – particularly the work that's been translated as *Symbols of Transformation* – that was just one of those things that sends all the lights up in all directions! I knew that a whole new dimension of understanding of what mythology was all about had come to me. So as far as the psychological interpretation of mythology and elucidation and evaluation go, I find Jung the base.[3]

In this chapter I will offer many more passages from interviews, books and lectures in which Campbell makes similar, highly positive comments about Jung. The earliest example that I have been able to find of such a comment is a passage from *Masks: creative*, published in 1968. As I will show in this chapter, the highly positive evaluation of Jung's core ideas displayed for the first time in that book would remain a feature of Campbell's ideas until his death in 1988. *Masks: creative* thus represents the beginning of the third and final phase of Campbell's career.

The reason that this shift in Campbell's attitude to Jung took place, as I will be arguing, is the fact that Campbell's interpretation of Jung also changed in 1968. As I already stated in Chapter 1, an interpretation of Jung is possible which (in contrast to the interpretation of Jung which Campbell subscribed to in phase two) does lead to the conclusion that Campbell's own ideas are highly similar to Jung's. The most well-known scholar who defends such an interpretation is Anthony Stevens, whose work I have already dealt with in Chapter 3. In this chapter I will show that Campbell came to adopt an interpretation of Jung that is strikingly similar to Stevens' interpretation, and argue that this is what led him to conclude that his own ideas were compatible with Jung's core ideas after all. These conclusions – that his former interpretation of Jung was inaccurate, and that some of Jung's concepts can in actual fact be seen as direct equivalents of his own most important concepts – is what I feel is the most likely explanation for Campbell's shift in attitude towards Jung.

These changes on Campbell's part – characterized by both a highly positive attitude to Jung as well as a new interpretation of Jung's core ideas – is what I am referring to in this book as the 'Jungian turn'. In the first section of this chapter (6.1) I will gather as much evidence as I can to establish that it actually took place. I will start by looking at *Masks: creative* (6.1.1), and show that it marks a distinct change of direction from the other three *Masks* books as far as the attitude to and interpretation of Jung displayed in it is concerned. I will then deal with all the relevant sources from the 1970s (6.1.2) and 1980s (6.1.3), showing that these sources all confirm that Campbell's positive evaluation of Jung remained constant during these last two decades of his career.

After having established that the Jungian turn actually took place and remained constant throughout the rest of Campbell's career, I will be offering some suggestions as to what may have caused Campbell to change his interpretation of Jung in the next section (6.2). There are two main factors which I consider to be likely causes for the Jungian turn: first of all, the editing by Campbell of the *Portable Jung* (published in 1971), for which he had to reread a lot of Jung's work; and second of all, the publication of Jung's *Collected works*, in which Jung included many extra footnotes and rewritten sections to clarify the ins and outs of his theoretical framework. These changes, added by Jung in order to further clarify his ideas, may have led Campbell to reinterpret certain key concepts as well.

These two sections, however (6.1 and 6.2), deal primarily with the psychological dimension of Campbell's work. The subject matter here is the concept of the archetype, especially in relationship to Campbell's own ideas about IRMs. As has become obvious in the previous chapter, however, there is also a metaphysical theme in Campbell's work. In section 6.3, I will deal with the relationship between Jung's ideas and this equally important theme in Campbell's work, focusing again on phase three of Campbell's career. In this section I will show that Campbell's ideas about the metaphysical theme become highly similar to Jung's metaphysical ideas (which revolve around the concept of the *unus mundus*) in this phase. I will also show that Campbell himself acknowledged these similarities, and that we can therefore conclude that in this phase of his career Campbell thought of his own ideas as compatible with Jung's not only as far as the psychological theme is concerned, but also as far as the metaphysical theme is concerned. However, as I feel that I cannot say with certainty that this realization played any part in causing him to become so highly positive about Jung in 1968, I have decided to devote a separate section to this topic.

In section 6.4, finally, I will focus once more on the work of Anthony Stevens. Although I will refer to Stevens throughout this chapter, this section will be specifically devoted to comparing his ideas to Campbell's. In it, I will show that the 'essence' of Campbell's theoretical framework in phase three of his career is almost completely identical with Stevens' interpretation of Jung. I will do this by showing that both men give identical accounts of both the origins and functions of myth and religion.

6.1 Establishing proof for the Jungian turn

As I already indicated above, the earliest example of the Jungian turn that I have been able to find occurs in the fourth volume of the *Masks of God* series, *Masks: creative.* In this book Campbell suddenly endorses Jung's concept of the archetype, suddenly claiming the following:

> Dr. Jung used the terms 'archetype' and 'primordial image' interchangeably, to designate those formative powers of the psyche that have been discussed at length in the first chapters of the opening volume of this study: *Primitive Mythology*, Chapter I, 'The Enigma of the Inherited Image', and II, 'The Imprints of Experience'.[4]

As we have seen in the previous chapter that Campbell actually stated in those chapters that he felt that the concept of the archetype was *not* an accurate way to describe the 'formative powers of the psyche', it is obvious that a change has taken place. In section 6.1.1, I will attempt to give an indication of the exact nature of this change by analysing the chapter from which the quote above was taken. I will then deal with the relevant sources from the 1970s in section 6.1.2, followed by a section on the relevant sources from the 1980s (6.1.3). As I will show, both these categories of sources confirm that Campbell's new reception of Jung remained constant throughout these two final decades of his career.

6.1.1 Creative mythology

Masks: creative is a pivotal work in Campbell's career. Several ideas which he would come back to again and again throughout the final phase of his career make their appearance for the first time in this book: the notion that the artist is the one who communicates myth for today; the four functions of mythology; the assertion that Joyce and Mann have provided a blueprint for what a 'modern myth' should look like. It is by no means the case, however, that the exact meaning of these ideas is made crystal clear. *Masks: creative* is a long and somewhat chaotic book, which is bound to leave many readers who encounter it for the first time in a state of bewilderment. This is perhaps due to the fact that Campbell was under tremendous pressure to finish the book when he wrote it. In an interview given in 1983 to the *New York times book review*, he had this to say about this time in his life:

> Remember those little Japanese things they used to have where you drop them in a cup of tea and they open out into a flower? The books grow like that. . . . On the last couple of chapters of 'Creative Mythology' I wrote for 38 hours without a stop, eating coffee pills to keep me awake.[5]

Whatever the reason may be, the chaotic nature of *Masks: creative* means that it is far from obvious when one starts reading the book that it marks an important shift in Campbell's thinking. The section in which Campbell suddenly endorses Jung's concept of the archetype only occurs at the very end of the book, right in the middle of a chapter about something completely different. To make matters worse, Campbell never even mentions that he had previously claimed something completely different about the concept of the archetype. Despite this fact, however, it is certainly obvious from the outset that Campbell's ideas come very close to Jung's in *Masks: creative.* Even though he doesn't exactly spell out his position, there are many statements in the book that are strikingly Jungian in tone, for example, the assertion that all religions start with someone who has had a personal religious experience,[6] that one of the results of our current lack of a shared myth is that 'the mad-houses are full',[7] and that mythological symbols usually arise as a compensation to the conscious attitude of the time.[8] Campbell especially makes much reference to Jung when he is dealing with the Jungian topic *par excellence*, alchemy. Even here, however, Campbell keeps his reader in the dark about the exact relationship between his ideas and Jung's. This is a topic that he only sheds some light on in the final chapter of the book, titled 'The earthly paradise'. This chapter is a somewhat messy amalgam of different perspectives and theories in which Campbell skips from thinker to thinker, from theory to theory, from myth to myth, in typical 'Campbellian' eclectic–syncretistic fashion. Joyce, Mann, Frobenius, Zimmer, Jung, Freud, even

Wittgenstein: all make an appearance. He combines excerpts from the works of these thinkers with an analysis of the mystic syllable AUM, which he bases on the exposition about the same topic found in the Indian Mandayuka Upanishad (this, too, would become a favourite topic which Campbell would return to again and again in his later years). As confusing as all of this sounds (and which it, admittedly, often is), Campbell does mention to bring clarity here to the topic that lies at the very root of this book: the relationship between his own ideas and Jung's concept of the archetype. He does this in section two of the chapter in question, which is titled 'Symbolization' and starts on page 647. It is in this section that Campbell makes the statement that I quoted in the introduction of this section (in which he suddenly endorses the concept of the archetype). I will now give a short analysis of it.

Campbell starts the section in question by pointing out that the difference between Freud and Jung is that the former stresses that dreams and myths can be reduced to personal experience of the dreamer or mythmaker; the latter, as Campbell puts it, 'gives stress in his interpretations of both dreams and myth not so much to history and biography as to biology and those initiations into the nature and sense of existence that all, in the course of a lifetime, must endure'.[9] To put it in Jungian terms: Freud claims that myths stem from the personal unconscious, whereas Jung stresses that they come from the collective unconscious. Campbell then gives a very long quote from Jung's work, in which the latter explains what the difference is between these two concepts. It is a bit too long to quote in its entirety here; I will leave out the passage in which Jung explains his concept of the personal unconscious, and quote only the part in which he explains his concept of the collective unconscious:

> The other part of the unconscious is what I call the impersonal or collective unconscious. As the name indicates, its contents are not personal but collective; that is, they do not belong to one individual alone but to a whole group of individuals, and generally to a whole nation, or even to the whole of mankind. These contents are not acquired during the individual's lifetime but are products of innate forms and instincts. Although the child possesses no inborn ideas, it nevertheless has a highly developed brain which functions in a quite definite way. This brain is inherited from its ancestors; it is a deposit of the psychic functioning of the whole human race. The child therefore brings with it an organ ready to function in the same way that it has functioned throughout human history. In the brain the instincts are preformed, and so are the primordial

> images which have always been the basis of man's thinking – the whole treasure-house of mythological motifs. [10]

Campbell has taken this quote from *CW 8*, titled *Structure and dynamics of the psyche*. The essay from which it was taken is called 'The psychological foundation of belief in spirits', originally written by Jung in 1919 but heavily revised in 1946. It is therefore a much later text than the one Campbell used in *Masks: primitive* to explain Jung's ideas (where he quoted from the 1921 edition of *Psychological types*). In that book Campbell stated that Jung's concept of the archetype was an 'inherited image', the equivalent of a 'closed' IRM which is not open to imprinting by the environment at all. If we look at the quote above, however, it might seem logical that Campbell still interprets Jung in this way. In this quote, namely, Jung seems to say that he does believe in 'inherited images', particularly when he says that 'in the brain the instincts are preformed, and so are the primordial images which have always been the basis of man's thinking – the whole treasure-house of mythological motifs.'[11] A little further down in the same section, however, Campbell reveals for the first time that he is now reading Jung in a different way. Instead of claiming that the archetype is an inherited image, he now stresses that 'the archetypes . . . are not to be thought of as of determined content.'[12] He then offers a quote from Jung's work which is absolutely crucial to this discussion:

> Again and again I encounter the mistaken notion that an archetype is determined in regard to its content, in other words that it is a kind of unconscious idea (if such an expression is admissible). It is necessary to point out once more that archetypes are not determined as regards their content, but only as regards their form and then only to a very limited degree. A primordial image is determined as to its content only when it has become conscious and is therefore filled out with the material of conscious experience. Its form, however, might perhaps be compared to the axial system of a crystal, which, as it were, performs the crystalline structure in the mother liquid, although it has no material existence of its own. This first appears according to the specific way in which the ions and molecules aggregate. The archetype in itself is empty and purely formal, nothing but a facultas praeformandi, a possibility of representation which is given a priori. The representations themselves are not inherited, only the forms, and in that respect they correspond in every way to the instincts, which are also determined in form only. The existence of the instincts can no more be proved than

> the existence of the archetypes, so long as they do not manifest themselves concretely.[13]

As we have seen in Chapter 3, this is the exact same quote which Anthony Stevens uses to back up his claim that one should read Jung's archetypes as the equivalent of an 'open' IRM instead of a 'closed' IRM. As I argued in the previous chapter, Campbell's ideas about the IRMs of the human nervous system are exactly the same in *Masks: primitive* as the ideas which Anthony Stevens puts forward in his book *Archetypes*, with one crucial difference: Stevens claims that these ideas are compatible with Jung's, whereas Campbell claimed the exact opposite. Now, however, it seems that Campbell has come round to Stevens' point of view completely. Without indicating that this claim represents a radical change of position, he writes the following:

> Dr. Jung used the terms 'archetype' and 'primordial image' interchangeably, to designate those formative powers of the psyche that have been discussed at length in the first chapters of the opening volume of this study: *Primitive Mythology*, Chapter I, 'The Enigma of the Inherited Image', and II, 'The Imprints of Experience'.[14]

This statement (which I already quoted in the introduction to this section) is almost a case of intellectual dishonesty, as anyone familiar with *Masks: primitive* will see immediately that Campbell made no such claim in that work. As I already pointed out above, in that work Campbell dismissed Jung's archetype as the equivalent of a 'closed' IRM, while at the same time stressing that the IRMs of the human nervous system are to be thought of as open. For reasons of clarity I will briefly recap Campbell's position in that work, and compare it to Anthony Stevens' ideas. I will then relate both these positions to Campbell's new position as put forward in *Masks: creative*.

In *Masks: primitive* Campbell made an important distinction which he would come back to again and again later on in his career. Drawing on the work of the nineteenth-century German thinker and explorer Adolf Bastian, Campbell pointed out that there are two orders of mythic images: what Bastian called the *elementary ideas* and the *ethnic ideas*. Every culture puts its own stamp on the mythic images: these are the ethnic ideas. According to Bastian, however, there are also certain elementary ideas that lie at the root of these ethnic ideas. What one encounters on the level of the various cultures of the world are not elementary ideas but ethnic ideas;

however, at the root of these ethnic ideas lie the elementary ideas, which are the same for every culture. In *Masks: primitive* Campbell connected this dichotomy to another concept which he attaches primary importance to that of the open IRM. As he states again and again in the first chapter of the book, Campbell is of the opinion that the defining characteristic of the human psyche is that its ground structures are open to imprinting. Unlike the instinctive structures found in animals, which are usually fixed from birth, the instincts found in man are infinitely more flexible: they are open, not closed. As Campbell put it in a speech given in 1962:

> As it turns out, we have found it impossible to determine any stereotyped images in the human psyche. For our discussion, then, we will have to assume that there are no stereotyped innate releasing images in the human psyche of very much significance. The imprint factor is the dominant one.[15]

This openness of the IRMs found in the human nervous system explains, according to Campbell, why we find different inflections of mythic symbols all over the world, as opposed to symbols which are exactly the same. This concept of the open IRM thus leads to another dichotomy, which Campbell then links to that of the elementary and the ethnic idea: of the innate factor on the one hand (the IRM 'as-such', which is the same in all cultures), and the various 'imprints' on the other hand (which are different from culture to culture). He therefore arrives at the following schema:

Elementary idea	–	*ethnic idea*
Open IRM	–	*imprint*

Campbell then draws the following conclusion: if one wants to study the various ethnic ideas of mankind (which is his goal in the *Masks* series) one should focus on the different imprints which have led to the differing symbols of world mythology. For this reason Campbell says in the speech quoted above that 'the imprint factor is the dominant one'; for this reason, too, Campbell named the second chapter of *Masks: primitive* (which follows the chapter in which he deals with the ethological theory of the IRM, and which is by far lengthier) 'The imprints of experience'.

As we have seen in Chapter 3, Anthony Stevens has exactly the same view of the nature of the human psyche. He too stresses that the imprint factor is the dominant one for human beings; he even uses the exact same ethologically inspired terminology as Campbell to express this idea (which revolves around the notion of the 'open' IRM). Where Stevens differs from Campbell's position in *Masks: primitive*, however, is that he feels that these ideas are perfectly compatible with Jung's ideas. Campbell stresses in *Masks: primitive* that Jung's archetypes are *not* open to imprinting: they are a wholly innate psychological structure. Because he draws the conclusion that 'the imprint factor is the dominant one', he is forced to conclude that Jung's ideas are not compatible with his own:

> Therefore, though respecting the possibility – perhaps the probability – of such a psychologically inspired parallel development of mythological imagery as that suggested by . . . C. G. Jung's of the collective unconscious, we cannot attempt to interpret in such terms any of the remarkable correspondences that will everywhere confront us.[16]

Stevens, however, interprets the concept of the archetype differently. According to him, the archetype is not wholly innate. One must distinguish between the archetype-as-such (which *is* wholly innate, but which is nevertheless open to imprinting; it is therefore, according to Stevens, the equivalent not of a closed but of an open IRM) and the archetypal image which the archetype-as-such gives rise to. The archetype-as-such is an abstract structure, a mere form without content. To back up this interpretation of Jung he offers the following quote:

> Again and again I encounter the mistaken notion that an archetype is determined in regard to its content, in other words that it is a kind of unconscious idea (if such an expression be permissible). It is necessary to point out once more that archetypes are not determined as to their content, but only as regards their form, and then only to a very limited degree. *A primordial image is determined as to its content only when it has become conscious and is therefore filled out with the material of conscious experience* [my italics].[17]

Now we have finally come full circle. As we have seen above, this is the exact same passage which Campbell quotes in the final chapter of *Masks: creative* when discussing Jung's concept of the archetype. He even introduces this quote with the following statement: 'the archetypes . . . are not to be thought of as of determined content.'[18] It seems, therefore, that Campbell has now arrived at the exact same interpretation of Jung as the one Anthony Stevens defends. He realizes, therefore, that the ideas he put forward in *Masks: primitive* can be thought of as compatible with Jung's ideas after all. What has changed as far as Campbell's theoretical framework is concerned, then, is not his ideas about IRMs, but his interpretation of Jung. As Campbell writes in *Masks: creative*: '[the concept of the archetype is the equivalent of] those formative powers of the psyche that have been discussed at length in the first chapters of the opening volume of this study: *Primitive Mythology*.'[19] This makes it obvious that he still endorses the views he expressed in that work. Campbell, therefore, still believes that a distinction should be made between ethnic ideas on the one hand (which he relates to the imprints of experience) and the elementary ideas on the other hand (which he relates to the open IRM). However, he now connects Jung's concept of the archetype to this schema as well, which is something he never did in *Masks: primitive*. The following quote establishes this with great clarity:

> Adolf Bastian (1825–1905) coined the term 'ethnic ideas' (Volkergedanke) for the local, historic transformations of the archetypes, and the term 'elementary ideas' (Elementargedanke) for the archetypes themselves.[20]

In conclusion, therefore, we can state that the basic outline of Campbell's new position is the following list of synonymous dichotomies:

Elementary idea	–	*ethnic idea*
Open IRM	–	*imprint*
Archetype-as-such	–	*archetypal image*

As I pointed out in both Chapters 3 and 5, there are two different approaches to interpreting Jung's concept of the archetype: the 'inheritance only' approach, which is the one taken by Robert Segal; and the 'inheritance plus experience' approach, which is the one taken by Anthony Stevens. Because Segal takes the 'inheritance only' approach he is forced to conclude that Campbell's assertion that the IRMs of the human nervous system are open to imprinting is un-Jungian. I do not find fault with Segal for coming to this conclusion. As I have stated several times in the previous chapters, I think that the fact that Jung's work is so ambiguous and sometimes vague makes it inevitable that scholars arrive at different interpretations of his work. I don't think it is 'wrong', therefore, of Segal to arrive at the conclusion that Jung's archetype is a 'closed' psychological structure which is not open to imprinting. What Segal has failed to pick up on, however, is that Campbell himself came to adopt an interpretation of Jung that is different to his own interpretation of Jung. It seems to me that it is extremely important to realize that Campbell, from *Masks: creative* onwards, came to see one of the defining features of this theoretical framework – the open IRM – as a concept which is wholly compatible with Jung's ideas. Although Segal does devote considerable attention to the development of Campbell's ideas in his *Introduction*, he never picks up on the fact that Campbell came to interpret Jung differently, and that this led him to reinterpret his own ideas as well. As we will now see in the next two sections, this new interpretation of both Jung's ideas *and* his own ideas would remain a constant feature of his thinking throughout the final two decades of his life.

6.1.2 Relevant sources from the 1970s

In this section I will deal with the following categories of sources from the 1970s:

- Books written by Campbell
- Essays written by Campbell
- Interviews
- Lectures

Books

About this category we can be relatively short, as Campbell published only two books in the 1970s: *Myths to live by* (1972)[21] and *The mythic image* (1974).[22] Of these two books only one is relevant here: *The mythic image. Myths to live by* is a collection which contains transcriptions of lectures given by Campbell, and I will therefore deal with it in the subsection on lectures from the 1970s below.

The mythic image is a very different book from *Masks: creative.* It seems that Campbell didn't really write it with a scholarly audience in mind, as he writes far less argumentatively in it. He is mostly pointing out similarities between myths rather than dealing with theories to explain these similarities. The book, therefore, isn't really relevant at all for our discussion here: it neither confirms nor disconfirms my hypothesis that Campbell's positive attitude to Jung remained constant throughout the rest of his career. Campbell certainly quotes Jung a lot (as opposed to Freud, who isn't quoted at all), but he doesn't deal with the technicalities of Jung's concept of the archetype at all. He never refers to the concept of the IRM either, and for that reason I feel that it isn't necessary to offer an analysis of the content of the book. One thing which I do want to point out is that many of the quotes from Jung's work which Campbell used in the section in *Masks: creative* which I dealt with in the previous section make an appearance in *The mythic image* as well, although Campbell never really analyses them. It seems, then, that even though Campbell chose not to make his new Jungian viewpoint more apparent in *The mythic image*, he was still convinced of the relevance of the material on which he drew in *Masks: creative.*

Essays

I am aware of only two essays by Campbell from the 1970s: 'Mythological themes in creative literature and art' (1970), and 'Erotic irony and mythic forms in the art of Thomas Mann' (1973), both published in the collection of essays *The mythic dimension.*[23] The essay about Mann isn't really relevant: even though Jung's ideas do make an appearance (Mann was heavily influenced by Jung), Campbell never makes it obvious whether he agrees with Mann's interpretation of Jung. In the second essay, however, Campbell does reveal more about his own take on Jung. Campbell explains that Jung made a distinction between the personal unconscious and the collective unconscious, and stresses that one therefore has to interpret visions which rise from these two spheres in differing ways. He continues:

> When the imagery of the warning visions rises from the Personal Unconscious, its sense can be interpreted through personal associations, recollections, and reflections; when, however, it stems from the Collective, the signals cannot be decoded in this way. They will be of the order, rather, of myth; in many cases even identical with the imagery of myths of which the visionary or dreamer will never have heard. (*The evidence for this in the literature of psychiatry seems to me now to be beyond question* [my italics].)[24]

The passage above makes it obvious not only that Campbell feels that Jung's ideas about psychology are correct ('the evidence . . . seems to me now to be beyond question') but also that Campbell feels that Jung's hypothesis of the collective unconscious adequately explains the similarities found in mythological traditions: '[the signals from the collective unconscious] will be of the order, rather, of myth.' In short, Campbell says basically the same here as he did in *Masks: creative.* This essay, however, is from 1970, and even though the statement above is one of the boldest endorsements of Jung's ideas on Campbell's part I've encountered, it therefore does not do much to confirm my claim that Campbell's positive evaluation remained *constant* throughout the 1970s. For that kind of evidence we must turn to other sources. As I will show below, both the interviews and lectures that I have found from the 1970s do in fact confirm this claim.

Interviews

I have found only three interviews from the 1970s in which Campbell explicitly endorses Jung: these are from 1971, 1976 and 1979 respectively. I will keep my discussion of these interviews here relatively short, as a complete overview of everything Campbell said in them is far beyond the purpose of the present discussion. As usual, Campbell talks about a wide variety of subjects: from shamanism to Jesus, from Dante to the symbolic significance of the Empire State Building. I will here quote only those passages in which Campbell explicitly endorses Jung and his core ideas. As these interviews were held throughout the 1970s, they show that Campbell's new positive evaluation of Jung – the 'Jungian turn', as I am calling it – remained constant. I will deal with them in chronological order.

The interview from 1971 was held by Sam Keen for the magazine *Psychology today*. He begins the interview by asking Campbell whether he thinks myth still serves some function or purpose in modern society. Campbell answers that he does not think that a modern myth will be a reality anytime soon: our society has become too fragmented and pluralistic for that. The discussion continues as follows:

> *Campbell*: But if we cannot reinstate such a mythology we can, at least, return to the source from which mythology springs – the creative imagination.
>
> *Keen*: In other words, a journey into the unconscious is now necessary to find the meanings and comforts that myths once gave us?
>
> *Campbell*: Yes. After all, the myths originally came out of the individual's own dream consciousness. Within each person there is what Jung called a collective unconscious. We are not only individuals with our unconscious intentions related to a specific social environment. We are also representatives of the species homo sapiens. And that universality is in us whether we know it or not. We penetrate to this level by getting in touch with dreams, fantasies and traditional myths; by using active imagination.[25]

This is the only instance I have come across where Campbell openly says that he believes that the collective unconscious exists; usually he offers support for Jung's core notion in a much more roundabout way. It is interesting to notice that in *Masks: primitive* Campbell said mostly the same things as he does in the passage above: there, too, he stressed that human beings are not just socially conditioned but are first and foremost members of the species *homo sapiens*. Now, however, Campbell confirms that he sees Jung's theory of the collective unconscious as compatible with this basic 'Campbellian' *leitmotiv*.

The next interview in which Campbell endorses Jung's ideas is from 1976. Campbell here goes into even less detail about why he likes Jung so much; he just says that he does, and then goes on to discuss other things. For that reason I will just quote the passage in which he mentions Jung, and then move on to the next interview. The passage in question is the following:

> [There] has to be something . . . to help the individual make modern sense of [mythic traditions] for his modern, individual search. And there, I think, the writings of C.G. Jung on individuation are about as sound and helpful as anything we've got. They don't represent a tradition, but they do represent the insights of a very grounded psyche: C.G. Jung's. I don't know of anybody else who I could give that much credit to as a guide.[26]

In the final interview from the 1970s which I would like to deal with here Campbell says basically the same thing: here, too, he doesn't really go into the technical details of why he thinks Jung's theories are valid; he just explains that Jung is the thinker which he feels most inspired by. I will let the passage in question (which I already quoted in Chapter 5) speak for itself:

> When I wrote *The Hero With A Thousand Faces* in the early '40s, these two men were sort of equal in my thinking. But then in the years following, Jung became more and more eloquent to me. My feeling is that Freud tells us what myths mean to neurotics, and Jung gives us a clue how to let the myth talk to us in its own terms without putting a formula on it. Jung is not the final word at all – I don't think there is a final word. But he opened me up to new prospects and vistas.[27]

Interestingly enough, this passage confirms the development in Campbell's thought which I am attempting to sketch through my model of the three phases: a move away from Freud, as well as a heightened interest in Jung, as the years progressed. Notice, however, that Campbell is here already far less 'dramatic' in his support for Jung. Whereas in the early 1970s he blatantly says things like 'there is in all of us a collective unconscious', or 'the evidence [for Jung's theories] seems to me now to be beyond question]', he now relativizes his endorsement of Jung by adding the claim that 'Jung is not the final word at all.' Further on in the interview Campbell also stresses that he himself is not a Jungian: 'I myself am not a Jungian, although as far as interpreting myths goes, Jung gives me the best clues I've got. But I am much more interested in diffusion and relationships historically than Jung was, very, very much so.'[28] In the same interview he also stresses the importance of Heinrich Zimmer, who he claims we should think of as his 'final guru'.[29] Perhaps by this time Campbell was beginning to realize that too much affinity for Jung was bad for his reputation. In all likelihood, he desperately wanted to be thought of as his own man, not merely someone who applied ideas that another thinker had already worked out in advance. Nevertheless, the interview still shows that Jung by that time remained of prime importance to Campbell.

Lectures

As I pointed out in the introduction to this chapter, Campbell retired from Sarah Lawrence College in 1971. From that moment on the number of lectures he gave rose exponentially. Not many transcriptions of those lectures have been published, however. *Myths to live by* contains four lectures from the 1970s; *Pathways to bliss* contains five of them; and *The mythic dimension* only one. Many of these talks aren't relevant for our discussion, as most of them deal with specific mythic traditions and not with theoretical explanations of the origins and functions of myth. Before I go on to deal with what I think is the most important talk (as it is the only one in which Campbell explicitly sheds light on his own theoretical framework and its relationship to Jung), I would like to draw attention to a talk from 1971, 'Schizophrenia: the inward journey' (chapter 10 in *Myths to live by*), in which Campbell states the following:

> The psychologist who has best dealt with these [mythic images], best described and best interpreted them, is Carl G. Jung, who terms them 'archetypes of the collective un-conscious', as pertaining to those structures of the psyche that are not the products of merely individual experience but are common to all mankind. In his view the basal depth or

> layer of the psyche is an expression of the instinct system of our species, grounded in the human body, its nervous system and wonderful brain.[30]

Also, I would like to draw attention to a talk published as part of *Pathways to bliss*: 'The self as hero' (1973, chapter six). In this talk Campbell relates the hero's journey explicitly to Jung, something which he never did in *The hero with a thousand faces*:

> I would like now to review the archetypal myth of the hero's journey as I dealt with it in *The Hero with a Thousand Faces*. This is what Joyce called the monomyth: an archetypal story that springs from the collective unconscious. Its motifs can appear not only in myth and literature, but, if you are sensitive to it, in the working out of the plot of your own life.[31]

In both of these talks, however, Jung receives only a passing mention. As such, the talks do not offer any new information regarding Campbell's evaluation of Jung in the 1970s. They only show that Campbell becomes strikingly positive about Jung after 1969, which is something I have already established above by dealing with the essays and interviews from the 1970s. There is one talk, however, in which Campbell talks explicitly about the relationship between Jung's ideas and his own theoretical framework. This talk is published as chapter five in *Pathways to bliss*, which is called 'Personal myth'. As I discovered during my visit to the Campbell Archive in early 2007, Campbell started giving this same talk over and over again, from the early 1970s onwards. The archive has in storage all the notes Campbell made to prepare for his lectures, and as I went through these notes, one thing struck me immediately: that the basic structure of the talk published in *Pathways to bliss* appears again and again in Campbell's lecture notes, starting in the early 1970s and continuing well into the 1980s (when the number of lectures, perhaps because of Campbell's old age, began to dwindle). Campbell usually called this talk 'Living your personal myth', or in some cases 'The vitality of myth'. In it, he explained what for him the essence of myth was, and what it means to live by your own 'personal myth'. As his lecture notes reveal, Campbell based this talk almost entirely on Jung's life and theories. He began by telling the story of how Jung came to build his famous tower in Bollingen on the shores of lake Zurich; he then used Jung's theory of the collective unconscious (as well as his notion of 'big dreams' and 'little dreams') to explain what, according to him (Campbell, not Jung) the origins and functions of mythology are. The fact that Campbell kept giving this talk until well into the 1980s confirms that Jung became the thinker he relied on most of all when he wanted to explain what the bedrock of his own theoretical framework was – not only right after 1969 (the beginning of the Jungian turn) but throughout the final two decades of his life. Luckily enough, the Joseph Campbell Foundation decided to publish a transcription of one version of this talk in *Pathways to bliss*, which means that I can give a brief overview of it here. I will keep my discussion of this talk short, as it contains some overlap with the discussion above in the section about *Masks: creative*. I will only focus on what would probably have been the first half of the talk, as it is here that Campbell makes the connection between his own ideas and Jung's.

Campbell begins his talk by telling a story from Jung's personal life, which he bases on Jung's autobiography *MDF*. The part of Jung's life which Campbell talks about here is described in chapter six, 'Confrontation with the unconscious'. In this chapter Jung writes that after he had published *Wandlungen und symbole der libido* he entered a period in his life of tremendous emotional turmoil. The second part of *Wandlungen* had led to the break with Freud, and after this event he found himself not only utterly isolated but also confronted by inner demons. In *MDF* Jung writes that in the midst of this highly chaotic period he had a moment of unusual clarity, during which he realized 'what it means to live with a myth, and what it means to live without one'.[32] It occurred to him to ask himself by what myth he himself was living, but he was forced to conclude that he didn't have a clue what this 'personal myth' was. Again, in Jung's own words: 'So, in the most natural way, I took it upon myself to get to know my myth, and this I regarded as my task of tasks.'[33] Jung's method of discovering his 'personal myth' was basically what he would later come to call 'active imagination'. He began to pay close attention to every impulse he had, and he made drawings by relying solely on his intuition, with no preformed plan worked out beforehand whatsoever. He also went back to an activity that he had enjoyed as a boy: making castles out of stones. After having played with small stones for a while, Jung decided that he would take the game a little more seriously and that he would build himself a retreat on the shore of Lake Zürich. This would become the famous 'tower' at Bollingen, where Jung did a lot of his reading and writing in his old age, and which the Jung family now uses as a summerhouse. Campbell has this to say about Jung's chosen method to discover his personal myth:

> So he said, Why, I'm a big man now, so I'll play with big stones. He bought himself a piece of property in a beautiful place on the lake opposite the

> city of Zurich. He began planning and building a house in this lovely place, Ascona [*sic* – Bollingen], and as he worked with his hands, he activated his imagination.
>
> Now, that's the big thing, to activate your imagination somehow. You can't do this by taking suggestions from somebody else. You must find that which your own unconscious wants to meditate on. With his imagination activated, Jung found all kinds of new fantasies coming, dreams of all kinds. He began making records of what he had dreamed and then amplifying it by all kinds of associations. By doing this he began to work out his personal myth.[34]

Campbell then states that a careful study of these dreams led Jung to the conclusion that they fell into two categories: so-called little dreams and big dreams.[35] This distinction is related to Jung's distinction between the personal unconscious and the collective unconscious in the sense that little dreams stem from the personal unconscious, whereas big dreams stem from the collective unconscious. Little dreams are basically autobiographical, whereas big dreams deal with problems that are not specific to one's personal life but to what Campbell calls 'the great problems of man'.[36] It is here that Campbell makes the connection to mythology: 'As it happens, the great mythologies deal with these problems also.'[37] Campbell then relates these two concepts (little dreams and big dreams) to Bastian's distinction between ethnic ideas and elementary ideas. He stresses that although the archetypal images of myth represent universal themes (the elementary ideas), the images themselves 'occur with different historical inflections'[38] (the ethnic ideas). Campbell then brings in a new topic into this already familiar discussion: the Indian concepts of *mãrga* and *desi*, which he puts forward as synonyms of Bastian's dichotomy:

> I find that in India the same two aspects are recognized. There they are called mãrga and desi, respectively. Mãrga comes from a root that has to do with an animal trail; it means 'the path'. By this, Indians mean the path by which the particular aspect of a symbol leads you to personal illumination; it is the path to enlightenment. Desi means 'of the province'. All mythological symbols, therefore, work in two directions: in the direction of mãrga and in the direction of desi. The desi, or local, aspect links the individual to the culture. . . . The mãrga or Elementargedanken [elementary ideas] provide a patch back to the heart of the issue.[39]

This then, is the basic outline of what would have been roughly the first half of the talk which Campbell would give again and again throughout the 1970s. He began by telling the story of how Jung came to build the tower at Bollingen, and then used this to introduce Jung's distinction between big dreams and little dreams. He would then bring up Bastian's dichotomy, and link this to the concepts of mãrga and desi. Again and again, he would stress that this was what he believed to be the essence of a mythic image: an elementary idea which has received a specific cultural stamp or 'inflection'. At the root of Campbell's talk, then, lies the distinction which he already developed in *Masks: primitive* between elementary ideas and ethnic ideas, which, as we have seen, Campbell thought of as the equivalent of the open IRM on the one hand and the imprints of experience on the other hand. Campbell now stresses that the concepts of mãrga and desi are also synonyms of this dichotomy as well. The fact that he now puts this dichotomy forward as part of a discussion which is almost solely based on a discussion of Jung's life as well as his core ideas shows quite clearly that by the early 1970s Campbell had no problem with explaining the essence of myth in strictly Jungian terms. Little dreams come from the personal unconscious; big dreams – as well as myths – come from the collective unconscious. The collective unconscious, in turn, should not be thought of as producing strictly predetermined 'inherited images': on the contrary, the elementary idea or archetype always has a local inflection; it is 'imprinted' by stimuli from the local environment and culture. The list of equivalent dichotomies which I offered in my discussion of *Masks: creative*, then, still holds. It should even be extended, so that it includes the concepts of mãrga and desi as well:

Elementary idea	–	*ethnic idea*
Mãrga	–	*desi*
Open IRM	–	*imprint*
Archetype-as-such	–	*archetypal image*

If Campbell had decided to use the material outlined above for just one talk then this would not have been of that much significance, as most of the topics he discusses are not that new. What gives this talk its significance, however, is that the lecture notes stored by the Joseph Campbell Archive show that the material outlined above became a kind of blueprint on which Campbell based countless lectures. Apparently, Campbell felt that the story of Jung's quest for his personal myth, as well as his distinction between little dreams and big dreams, illustrated his own intuitions about the exact nature of myth so well that he used it again and again. During the 1970s Campbell's main intellectual activity was lecturing, not the writing of books, and the fact that Jung played such a prominent a role in these lectures lends strong support to the hypothesis which I am trying to back up here: that Campbell saw his own theoretical framework as entirely compatible with Jung's concept of the archetype from 1969 onwards. As Campbell's lecture notes have obviously not been published, I must refer the reader to the Joseph Campbell Archive, where they can be found in boxes 107 and 108. Even a quick scan of the contents of the notes from the 1970s should be enough to confirm that the topics found in the talk discussed above return over and over again, thus confirming that from the early 1970s onwards the following statement made by Campbell in the 1980s was already true: '[As] far as the psychological interpretation of mythology and elucidation and evaluation go, I find Jung the base.'[40]

6.1.3 Relevant sources from the 1980s

In order not to become too repetitive I have decided to focus only on a limited amount of sources from the 1980s in this section: one book (the first volume of the *Historical atlas of world mythology* series) and two interviews. Before I begin, I will briefly explain the reasons for the choices I have made about what to include and what not.

Campbell did not write a great many essays during the 1980s. The essays that have been published in Campbell 'collections' (one in *The mythic dimension* and one in *Pathways to bliss*) do not offer anything new, and for that reason I have decided not to deal with them in this section. Campbell did write a significant number of books in the 1980s: five parts of the *Historical atlas of world mythology* series (from hereon abbreviated as *Atlas* followed by volume and part number[41]), as well as *The inner reaches of outer space*. Of all these books, the first part of volume 1 of the *Atlas* series is the only book in which Campbell discusses the topic of the IRMs of the human nervous system. As the concept of the IRM plays an important role in the arguments I am making in this book, I've decided to focus on this work alone. Jung is mentioned a few times in *Inner reaches*, but I do not feel that the way Campbell uses Jung in that book is in any way different to what has so far been discussed. The same goes for the four other parts in the *Atlas* series. Regarding the interviews Campbell gave in the 1980s: of these there are a great many. The 1980s was the time when Campbell became a well-known figure, particularly after the *Star wars* movies had come out and George Lucas started to mention that he had used Campbell's work to find inspiration. The majority of these interviews, however, deal with topics that are irrelevant here. I have also decided not to mention every little quote in which Campbell says something positive about Jung, as I feel that the evidence from the 1970s is already enough to back up my claim that Campbell became more positive about Jung as his career progressed. I have included here quotes from three interviews in which Campbell talks about the relationship between his ideas and Jung's, as I feel that they are particularly revealing about how one should see this relationship.

Atlas: volume 1, part 1

Atlas was the last project Campbell worked on before he died. As I already mentioned in Chapter 4, he had originally envisioned a four-volume series, but his death in 1988 meant that he never got to finish the project. We currently have available to us only the first two volumes: *The way of the animal powers* and *The way of the seeded earth.* These deal, respectively, with the mythology of the primitive hunter-gatherers (volume 1) and the mythology of the first planting people. The third volume would have dealt with the mythology of the first city-states, and the final volume with the myths and philosophical ideas of what the philosopher Karl Jaspers has called 'the axial age', which he claims began around 800 BC (Campbell uses 500 BC – see quote below) and which is the time of the Buddha, Confucius and Pythagoras. In an interview from 1984, Campbell explains how he came up with this division:

> Well, I had written what is now the first volume plus about two-thirds of what's going to be in the second volume. These were to have been one volume. And then we realized it was too heavy a volume, and so we cut it to where it is now. It's now going to start on what was to have been the second half of the first volume, namely 'the planting people'. As soon as we cut it – now this was only about three weeks before the whole thing went to press – soon as we cut it, I saw the four volumes, and their titles came through like that. I had thought of it as 'The Nonliterate People' and 'The Literate'. When you split it in half, each of these splits into an organic unit: the first, hunting/gathering people; the second, the planting people; third, the high culture/mythological periods; and then, from 500 B.C. – which is the dateline of the Buddha, Confucius, Aeschylus, Pythagoras – where mythology moves into gnosis, the primeal philosophy.[42]

In another interview (this one from 1983) Campbell reflects on the way this division differs from the division he used to structure the *Masks* series (*Primitive, Oriental, Occidental* and *Creative*):

> [Interviewer] How will the structure of the four volumes of the *Historical Atlas of World Mythology* differ from the structure of your four volumes of *The Masks of God?*
>
> [Campbell] I did *The Masks of God* in the 50s and I used a standard division: Primitive, Oriental and Occidental. The fourth volume, Creative Mythology, was an innovation. What has happened in my mind since is a division in terms of what might be called stages of mythological development. It's a totally different perspective and an immediately clarifying one, at least for one who is involved in the whole range of mythological material.[43]

Even though the organization of the *Atlas* series is different from the one he chose for the *Masks* series, the main topic is once again the same: not the theoretical explanation of what myth is and does, but the different historical inflections which the 'elementary ideas' have taken on throughout history. Once again, Campbell focuses a lot on the diffusion of mythic ideas as well, so that the book at first glance may not give a very Jungian impression. As I have already argued in the previous chapter, however, focusing on diffusion isn't incompatible with Jung's ideas at all; it is just that Jung didn't have much interest in writing about the diffusion of mythic ideas. Campbell, of course, did have such an interest; so much so that the psychological dimension of myths is very much in the background in the *Atlas* series. Nevertheless, it is discussed, even though Campbell only devotes three pages to it (this in contrast to *Masks: primitive,* where he devotes more than a hundred pages to the topic). Even though the passage in question is very short, it is still very valuable to our discussion here, as apart from the first two chapters of *Masks: primitive* it is the only passage from the 1980s of which I'm aware in which Campbell elaborates in detail on his ideas about the IRMs of the human nervous system. In the section on *Masks: creative* above, I drew the conclusion that Campbell's ideas about IRMs did not change as phase three began, but that his interpretation of Jung did. I based this conclusion on Campbell's claim in *Masks: creative* that '[the concept of the archetype is the equivalent of] those formative powers of the psyche that have been discussed at length in the first chapters of the opening volume of this study: *Primitive Mythology*',[44] which seems to confirm that Campbell still endorsed the view espoused in that book. However, as

Campbell never talks about the details of his ideas about IRMs in *Masks: creative* (nor in any of the sources from the 1970s I have discussed above), the reader might be inclined to think that this conclusion is a touch too hasty. If Campbell changed his mind about Jung's ideas, then surely he might have changed his ideas about this important aspect of his theoretical framework as well. The first part of the first volume of the *Atlas* series, however (from now on abbreviated as *Atlas: 1.1)*, confirms that Campbell's basic ideas about this topic remained the same. More importantly, it also confirms that Campbell still associated these ideas with the ideas of Jung. For this reason it is important that we spent some time looking at this text. Again, I will keep my discussion here short, as a lot of these ideas have already been dealt with at length. The purpose of the present discussion is merely to confirm that these ideas remained constant and that Campbell continued to associate them with Jung.

Campbell starts his discussion about what exactly an IRM is in *Atlas: 1.1* by giving an example of a 'closed' IRM. He again uses an example from the animal world which Anthony Stevens also uses in his book *Archetypes*: that of the zigzag dance of the stickleback fish.[45] Campbell quotes the following passage from Niko Tinbergen's work to illustrate this specific kind of courtship behaviour:

> The courting behaviour of a male stickleback before a pregnant female is dependent on at least two sign stimuli: the swollen abdomen and the special posturing movement of the female. . . . The female's reaction to the courting male is released by two sign stimuli: the red belly and the male's special movements, the 'zigzag dance'.[46]

After having offered a few more quotes from Tinbergen's work in which the latter connects the zigzag dance to his concept of the IRM, Campbell then asks the following question: are there any such IRMs in the human nervous system? Unsurprisingly, Campbell answers his own question with a resounding 'yes, of course!' However, he then takes his line of reasoning one step further, just as he did in *Masks: primitive*: he stresses that IRMs are of two orders – open and closed. Again, he stresses that most of the IRMs to be found in humans must be thought of as open:

> Most of the IRMs of the human species are of this kind, 'open', open to imprinting; and the imprintings are, of course, culture-bound, specific to the time and place of the individual's birth, earliest impressions, and development. They would not be the same for an American Indian

> born on the Kansan buffalo plains and the child of a Polynesian fisherman watching for sharks. They would be different again for the son of a Hasidic rabbi in the Bronx. Yet, in spite of the very great differences of the sign stimuli thus offered in the various theatres of human life, the innate energies to be released remain the same throughout the species. They are not of the culture, but of nature: innate, transpersonal, pre-rational, and when alerted, compulsive.[47]

Even though Campbell does not say so explicitly, it is obvious from the quote above that these imprintings are the equivalent of Bastian's ethnic ideas; the transpersonal and innate component of the IRM the equivalent of the elementary ideas. This becomes especially obvious if we compare the quote above to the following quote from *Masks: creative*:

> [It] is clear that the actual images and emphases of any mythological or dream system must be derived from local experience, while the 'archetypes', the 'elementary ideas', the 'roles' that the local images serve, must be of an order antecedent to experience; of a plot, so to say, a destiny or wyrd, inherent in the psychosomatic structure of the human species.[48]

So far, this is exactly the same as what Campbell said in *Masks: primitive.* However, whereas in that work Campbell stressed that this approach to mythology is *not* compatible with Jung's, he now makes no such claim at all. In fact, as is to be expected after what we have seen in this chapter thus far, Campbell now associates Jung with his ideas about the IRMs of the human nervous system. Even though he doesn't mention Jung in the text itself, the chapter from which the quotes above have been taken opens with the following quote, taken from Jung's *Psychological Types*:

> I term collective all psychic contents that belong not to one individual but to many, i.e., to a society; a people, or to mankind in general. The antithesis of collective is individual.[49]

It is obvious that the fact that Campbell chose this quote to open his chapter about IRMs means that he saw Jung's collective substratum of the psyche as the equivalent to what he calls 'the innate energies of the species', which are 'not of the culture, but of nature: innate, transpersonal, pre-rational, and when alerted, compulsive'.[50] In short, then, this passage from *Atlas: 1.1* confirms exactly what I have been claiming throughout this chapter: that Campbell's ideas about the IRMs of the human nervous system remained the same as the ideas expressed in *Masks: primitive*, but that he changed his mind regarding the compatibility of this point of view with Jung's ideas. As we will see below, the interviews from the 1980s confirm exactly the same thing.

Interviews

When Campbell mentions Jung in interviews from the 1980s it is generally in the same way as in the 1970s: he sings Jung's praises, and stresses that as far as the psychological interpretation of myth is concerned, he thinks that Jung is the most important thinker he knows. Thus, we find him saying the following in an interview from 1985:

> [Jung] was devoted to the psychological understanding of myth, and I think that he has gone further along that line than anyone in the field. He would himself not have said that he had completely explained mythology, or that his point of view is the only one from which myths can be interpreted; nor even that he had fully interpreted any single myth. From his point of view, each myth must be interpreted in its own right, as saying something different from any other, though using the same language. For my part, Jung has taught me more about the psychology of myth than anyone else, chiefly by opening individual psychology to mythic psychology.[51]

As we have seen, Campbell was already starting to become much less hyperbolic in his praise for Jung by the end of the 1970s, for example, when he said that 'Jung is not the final word at all – I don't think there is a final word. But he opened me up to new prospects and vistas.'[52] In the quote above Campbell says basically the same thing, this time by stressing that he felt that Jung himself did not think of his own theories as 'the final word'. In another interview from 1985 Campbell is even openly critical of Jung, something which he did not do since his critique of Jung in *Masks: primitive*:

> Hearing Zimmer's lectures and the way in which these myths came out, not as curiosities over there somewhere, but as models for understanding your own life – this is what I had felt myths to be all this time. Of course, Jung had it, but not the way Zimmer did. Zimmer was much more in

myth than Jung was. Jung tends to put forms on the myths with those archetypes; the Jungians kind of cookie-molded the thing.[53]

That said, however, the interviews from the 1980s do confirm that Campbell still thought that the hypothesis of the collective unconscious was valid, and that it was his theory of choice to turn to whenever he was asked to explain the similarities found in myths. To avoid repetition, I will here give only one example of an interview that confirms this, although I could quote several more. I have chosen the following passage, taken from the book *An open life* (a collection of interviews with Campbell by Michael Toms):

> What are you going to do with the fact that the same motifs appear everywhere? There's a constellation of motifs that are fundamental. How do you explain it? Myths come from the same zone as dreams, so that individual dreams won't be alike. But here we come to a level of what might be called racial dreams – the myths – and they match, they match, they match. The term 'collective unconscious', or general unconscious, is used in recognition of the fact that there is a common humanity built into our nervous system out of which our imagination works. The appeal of these constants is very deep.
>
> Now, the explanation that is often given in Freudian circles of individual experiences being the source of dream biography, and different racial histories being the source of their myth, is inadequate. That won't explain it! It doesn't fit. It may say something about a certain inflection or aspect of this mythology as compared with that one. Why does this group see themselves as the special people, though a group over there doesn't think that way – their deities have to do with the world of nature? What is it that gives those different pitches to the different culture systems – not special history and biography – but what about the general humanity? You can recognize a human being no matter where you see him. He must have the same kind of basic nervous system, therefore his imagination must work out of a comparable base. What's so damn mystical about all that? That seems to me to be obvious. And that's what the term 'collective unconscious' covers.[54]

Jung, then, remained very much at the centre of Campbell's theoretical framework, where, as I have argued, he had been ever since *Masks: creative*. What I have not dealt with up until now, however, is the question as to what may have caused Campbell to change his interpretation of Jung. It is to this question, then, that we will now turn to in the next section.

6.2 Reasons for the Jungian turn

The first possible reason for the fact that Campbell changed his interpretation of Jung that I would like to put forward is the fact that he edited *The portable Jung* for Viking press, published in 1971. Campbell wrote a lengthy introduction to the book and selected the texts from Jung's *Collected works* which were to be included in the volume. To prepare for this mammoth task, Campbell reread most of Jung's works, as his biographer Stephen Larssen claims.[55] If the book was published in 1971, it seems highly likely that Campbell would have started to prepare long in advance, as this 'reading project' would have taken up considerable time. Reasoning in this way, we are forced to draw the conclusion that Campbell was reading Jung intensively by the time he was working on *Masks: creative*, if not earlier. Looking at this period of Campbell's life this way, the fact that *Masks: creative* is suddenly strikingly Jungian in tone begins to make sense. However, a simple re-reading of the work of a scholar with whom one is already familiar does not necessarily lead to a change of opinion regarding his core ideas. Although we can, of course, explain the fact that Campbell changed his mind about Jung because he had simply gained an extended knowledge of his work, it seems likely that another influencing factor was involved.

As Larsen also claims, Campbell had read most of Jung's works for the first time by the time he was in his early thirties,[56] which would have been around 1935. By the time Campbell began his project of working his way through Jung's works for the second time, however, a lot more texts by Jung had become available. Jung wrote some of his most important works well after 1935: as we have seen, he only wrote *On the nature of the psyche* (in which he put forward the distinction between the archetype-as-such and the archetypal image) in 1946; the book about synchronicity was only published in 1951, and his biography *MDF* was only published in English in 1961. Most importantly, however, by the early 1960s the first volumes of the collected works had begun to be published in an English translation. By 1968, which seems a likely date for the start of Campbell's 'reading project', almost all of the volumes had been published. As we have seen in the previous chapter, Campbell owns first editions of almost all the volumes, which makes it likely that he would have owned almost the entire *Collected works* at that time. As I have pointed out several times, Jung was very much in the habit of rewriting his own work, sometimes up to five or six different times. For the *Collected works* he took considerable effort to add or rewrite passages in order to help clear up common misunderstandings about his work, and it is this encounter by Campbell with an 'enhanced' version of Jung's most important texts which I would also like to put forward as a reason for the Jungian turn. I believe that it is highly likely that these clarifications helped Campbell to see Jung's work in a different light, as I will now illustrate with the following example.

One of the oldest books by Jung that Campbell owned is a book called *The integration of the personality*.[57] It was published in 1939, and it is a collection of speeches delivered by Jung at the Eranos conference. Almost all of the passages from Jung's work which Campbell quotes in *Hero* are from texts collected in this book (in a later, revised edition of *Hero* Campbell updated his quotes so that they refer to the *Collected works* version of the same texts). As we have seen in the previous chapter, the book contains an early version of an essay called 'Archetypes of the collective unconscious', which Jung first presented as a lecture at the Eranos conference of 1934. The essay in Campbell's copy of the book is heavily underlined, which proves that Campbell studied it and was aware of its contents. The same essay later found its way into the *Collected works*, where it can be found as the very first text in volume 9 part one, under the same title. If we compare the two versions of the essay, however, it soon becomes obvious that Jung rewrote and added a few key passages which are likely to have made Campbell aware that Jung's notion of the archetype can be read as compatible with his own ideas. To illustrate this, I will focus on paragraph six, in which Jung explains what the relationship is between myth and the concept of the archetype (for the complete passage from both the 1939 edition and the *CW* edition I refer the reader to Appendix). The 1939 version opens as follows:

> Another well-known expression of the archetype is myth and fable. But here also we are dealing with conscious and specifically moulded forms that have been handed on relatively unchanged, through long periods of time.[58]

In the *Collected works* version, however, the same sentence is phrased differently:

> Another well-known expression of the archetypes is myth and fairytale. But here too we are dealing with forms that have received a specific stamp and have been handed down through long periods of time.[59]

The second version of the sentence is, to my mind, much clearer: 'specifically moulded forms' is rather abstruse; 'forms that have received a specific stamp', however, is much easier to understand. It also comes awfully close to Campbell's assertion that myths always receive a historical 'inflection', and it seems to me that this sentence would have certainly drawn Campbell's attention. This does seem to have been the case, as the sentence is underlined in Campbell's copy of *CW 9 part 1*.

Of course, this difference between the two versions of the text may not have been Jung's doing at all: it may have arisen simply because both texts were translated by different people.[60] There is another difference between the two texts, however, which does rather obviously show Jung's influence. When one compares the two versions of the paragraph in question, it becomes obvious that Jung added an extra sentence at the end of the *Collected works* version. The sentence reads as follows:

> The archetype is essentially an unconscious content that is altered by becoming conscious and by being perceived, and it takes its colour from the individual consciousness in which it happens to appear.[61]

He also added a footnote to this sentence, which reads as follows:

> One must, for the sake of accuracy, distinguish between 'archetype' and 'archetypal ideas'. The archetype-as-such is a hypothetical and irrepresentable model, something like the 'pattern of behaviour' in biology. Cf. 'On the nature of the psyche', sec. 7.

Campbell, in his copy of *CW 9 part 1*, has drawn brackets around this extra sentence. He has also written the word 'definition' next to it. It seems, then, that he certainly thought that the sentence was important. It represents Jung's attempt to correct what he saw as a common misunderstanding: that an archetype is already filled out with content. In another text from *CW 9 part 1*, he writes: 'Again and again I encounter the mistaken notion that an archetype is determined in regard to its content, in other words that it is a kind of unconscious idea (if such an expression if permissible).'[62] As we have seen, Campbell himself once drew this conclusion as well (in *Masks: primitive*, where he concluded that an archetype is an 'inherited image', the equivalent of a 'closed' IRM). Even though he had read 'On the nature of the psyche' – in which Jung tried once and for all to put an end to this misunderstanding by making the distinction between the archetype-as-such and the archetypal image or idea – by the time he wrote *Masks: primitive*,[63] it seems that the importance of this distinction did not really sink in at that time. I think that it is likely that it is passages such as the one we have just looked at from *CW 9 part 1* that made Campbell abandon this interpretation of Jung. As we have seen, one of Campbell's core ideas from *Masks: primitive* onwards was that the elementary ideas of mythology always appear in a specific historical inflection: the ethnic ideas. Jung, by stressing that the archetype 'takes its colour from the individual consciousness in which it happens to appear', seems to be saying exactly the same thing. Although it is certainly not a hundred percent clear that Jung is indeed saying the same thing, it seems to me that it is rather obvious that Campbell came to believe that he was. It is impossible to verify with certainty that the passage we have discussed above is one of the reasons which led Campbell to this reinterpretation of Jung's ideas; however, it seems to me very likely that it did have an influence. I am not claiming here that this passage was the most important influence, or that it was only this passage which led to Campbell's Jungian turn. I have used it here as an example: I merely want to point out that the *Collected works* contain rewritten texts of certain key essays and lectures which Campbell was already familiar with, and that this may have led him to change his mind about Jung.

Finally, there is a third possible reason which I feel we should consider when trying to explain why Campbell changed his interpretation of Jung: the increased popularity of Jung with Campbell's core audience from the middle of the 1960s onwards. As Campbell often explained, the 1960s were a critical period as far as the reception of his own work was concerned. This was the decade during which Campbell suddenly found himself becoming a lot more successful, as his ideas were beginning to find favour with the same audience which was increasingly drawn to Eastern mysticism, meditation and yoga, among other things. Campbell had this to say about this period in an interview from 1975:

> Before 1964 my work was regarded by those on the faculty where I taught as elitist, esoteric, and, in general, way off in the woods. They thought that they were on the great line with their Freud and Marx. Of course, I did have an audience; I knew that my work had significance for some people; and fortunately, they were the kind of people I really happened to care for. But then something happened during the 1960's. In one year, my royalties went up ten times, and since then they have stayed up. Now I could be lecturing every day of every week of every year.[64]

The 1960s was also the period when Jung began to become more and more popular with the same generation. By the time the 1970s had arrived,

Jung had become a household name, as Campbell explained in an interview from 1975: 'And I find, on campuses when I go to lecture here there and elsewhere – Jung.'[65] (In the same interview, Campbell says that in his perception, this increased popularity of Jung started around 1965.) One way this popularity may have influenced the Jungian turn is in the following way: Campbell realized that his audience liked Jung's ideas, and came to the conclusion that relating his own ideas to Jung's was simply a smart 'marketing move'. Given Campbell's apparent disinterest in making money, however, I don't think that this is a very likely scenario. After all, Campbell urged his audience not to work for money, but for love: to 'follow their bliss', as he himself would have put it. In all probability, this is a philosophy of life that he not only preached but also practised. There is, however, also a less cynical way to connect Jung's popularity to the Jungian turn. Perhaps Campbell realized that because his audience could be expected to know Jung's work well, referring to Jung's theories when explaining how he interpreted mythology was simply an easy way to make himself understood: it meant he had to explain far less than if he relied on the highly technical language of the ethologists, as he did in *Masks: primitive*. However, although I do think that the popularity of Jung among his audience is likely to have had some influence on the topics Campbell talked about in his lectures, I don't think that this alone is enough to explain why Campbell changed his mind regarding his interpretation of Jung. I think it is certainly highly likely that the reason why Campbell designed what was one of his most delivered talks ('Living your personal myth' – see section 6.1.2 above) the way that he did was because of Jung's popularity. His audience enjoyed hearing about Jung's quest for his personal mythology: this was simply a topic 'that went down well', which explains why Campbell talked about it again and again. However, I don't think that Campbell connected Jung to his core ideas *only* because he felt that this was an easy way to make himself understood, without any critical reflection on whether this was actually a theoretically justified match. The amount of underlining in Campbell's copies of Jung's books shows that he took his job of reading Jung's work seriously. Also, the answers he gave in interviews when he was asked about the relationship between Jung's work and his own clearly show that he had given the matter a great deal of thought. Therefore, while I do think that Jung's popularity may serve as an explanation for the large number of times Campbell delivered his 'personal myth' talk (in which Jung's life and ideas played a key role), I don't think that the latter's popularity is enough to explain why Campbell changed his mind about how to interpret Jung's work. The first two reasons given above – of simply re-reading most of Jung's work as preparation for *The portable Jung*, and of having revised texts at hand because the *Collected works* had come out – remain to my mind the best possible explanations for the Jungian turn.

6.3 The metaphysical theme in phase three

As we have seen in the previous chapter, from the very start of his career Campbell interpreted myth not only psychologically but also metaphysically. The way he interpreted myth metaphysically, however, changed as his career progressed. In *Hero*, for example, he claimed that mythic symbols have a metaphysical connotation because myths have been created consciously. The shamans and mystics who created the myths arrived at certain 'ontological intuitions' and then used the picture language of myth to communicate these intuitions. The symbols themselves stem from the psyche; their meaning, however, is metaphysical. In that work he had the following to say about this metaphysical meaning of myths:

> [Mythic symbols] are not only symptoms of the unconscious . . . but also controlled and intended statements of certain spiritual principles which have remained as constant throughout the course of human history as the form and nervous structure of the human physique itself. Briefly formulated, the universal doctrine teaches that all the visible structures of the world – all things and beings – are the effects of a ubiquitous power out of which they rise, which supports and fills them during the period of their manifestation, and back into which they must ultimately dissolve.
>
> . . .
>
> Myth is but the penultimate; the ultimate is openness – that void, or being, beyond the categories – into which the mind must plunge alone and be dissolved.[66]

In the second phase of Campbell's career, however, Campbell's ideas about what I have so far called the metaphysical theme of his theoretical framework changed somewhat. First of all, in *Masks: oriental* he suddenly aligned himself with the ideas of Rudolf Otto. The experience of the numinous, or in Otto's terms the *mysterium tremendum et fascinans*, is the experience which, as Campbell now suddenly claims, lies at the root of all religion and mythology. As I argued in section 5.3.1, this new concept of the numinous should be seen as a direct equivalent of what he called in

Hero 'a ubiquitous power' (see quote above). As I also pointed out in that section, however, the notion that the numinous lies at the root of *all* mythic symbols (as Campbell claimed in *Masks: oriental*) is in direct conflict with the place he assigns the experience of the numinous in *Masks: primitive.* In that work Campbell related the experience of the numinous to the IRMs of the human nervous system. As we also saw in section 5.3.1, Campbell stressed in *Masks: primitive* that the human nervous system consists of open IRMs which are imprinted by the experiences of the individual who inherits them. One of the most important imprints, Campbell claimed, is the experience of the numinous. However, as I have argued, making mystical experience one of the common imprints of the IRMs of humanity means that only some symbols point to the numinous. Other IRMs have been imprinted by different experiences, and thus give rise to symbols with an entirely different connotation. This, obviously, is a direct contradiction of his claim in *Masks: oriental* that *all* mythic symbols point to the numinous (or metaphysical).

It seems, then, that Campbell didn't really succeed in putting together a coherent theoretical framework on which to base the first three books of the *Masks* series. Not only did he draw conclusions about Jung that he later came to recall, he also failed to put forward ideas about the metaphysical theme that did not 'clash' with his ideas about the psychological theme. Just as Campbell came to different conclusions regarding the psychological theme in *Masks: creative* (concluding that his own ideas about IRMs were compatible with Jung after all), however, he also came to different conclusions in that book regarding the place of the metaphysical theme in his theoretical framework, as we will now see.

In *Masks: creative* Campbell once again claims that *all* symbols point to the metaphysical (or numinous), which he now frequently refers to as a 'ground of being':

> [Myth is] the revelatory factor by which the incidents of the daylight world are discovered linked to that ground which is the ground of all and gives to everything its life.[67]

He is also still endorsing Rudolf Otto's concept of the numinous, which he relates to this 'ground of being'.[68] Where he differs from the earlier works of the *Masks* series, however, is that he now manages to connect the metaphysical theme to the psychological theme in a way that is no longer contradictory, as he has stopped claiming that the numinous is one of the 'imprints' of experience. In the same section in which he claims that his ideas about IRMs are compatible with Jung's concept of the archetype after all (see section 6.1.1), Campbell puts forward his new theory about the role of the numinous: that this metaphysical 'ground' is not only what one breaks through to if one goes down deep enough into the unconscious, but also where the energies which penetrate the archetypes of the collective unconscious arise from. Myths, therefore, are both psychologically *and* metaphysically inspired. Campbell uses the analysis of the mystical syllable AUM put forward in the Mandayuka Upanishad to clarify this new idea. According to Campbell, this analysis 'supplies a touchstone for the classification of symbols',[69] and he therefore uses it to clarify his new theory about the relationship between the psychological and the metaphysical.

According to this ancient text the letters of the word AUM each correspond to a layer of consciousness. The letter A corresponds to waking consciousness, or in psychoanalytical terms, the ego. Campbell's analysis of this state is of no importance here, so I will move on straight away to the next layer: dream consciousness, which corresponds to the letter U.

It is in his discussion of this state that Campbell makes the claim that Jung's concept of the archetype is compatible with the ideas expressed in *Masks: primitive* after all. He begins by mentioning Freud, but quickly moves on to his discussion of Jung, whose ideas (as we have seen above) he now embraces. Dream consciousness, as Campbell claims, is the unconscious, but, as should by now have become obvious, the unconscious is for Campbell now an essentially Jungian unconscious. This layer, therefore, contains both a personal and a collective layer. It is in this collective layer where the archetypes and the instincts reside, and Campbell relates it both to Nietzsche's concept of the Dionysian and Schopenhauer's concept of the will. This is the layer in the unconscious which is governed by the forces of nature and biology. It links human beings to the outside world, as it is governed by the same rules which govern the world of nature *outside*. To this effect, Campbell would often say: 'nature is not only outside but also inside.'

Beyond the layer of dream consciousness, however, lies a third and final layer. In the Mandayuka Upanishad this layer is called 'deep dreamless sleep', and it is associated with the letter M. 'Here', states the Upanishad, 'a sleeper neither desires anything desirable nor beholds any dream. Undivided, he is an undifferentiated, homogeneous lump or mass of consciousness, consisting of bliss and feeding on bliss, his only mouth being spirit. He is here "The Knower": the Lord of All, the Omniscient, the Indwelling Controller, the Source or Generative Womb of All: the

Beginning and End of beings.'[70] It is this layer which Campbell connects to his 'ground of being':

> [The state of deep dreamless sleep] is, as we have read [in the Mandayuka Upanishad] 'the Source . . . of All: the Beginning and End of beings'. Here the world is created, not in the way of an act at the beginning of time, but continuously forever, as the ground of being; for there was never a beginning of time, there will never be an end, the creative moment is now.[71]

This, in a nutshell, is what Campbell's new 'hierarchical model' of the nature of symbols is all about. Summing up, the hierarchy which he puts forward is the following:

Ego
Unconscious (or 'dream consciousness' in the Upanishads)
Ground of being (or 'deep dreamless sleep' in the Upanishads)

What I think is important to realize is that Campbell felt that when one goes deeply enough into the unconscious one begins to make contact with layers that are truly transpersonal, that connect one to more than just the individual psyche. This is already true for dream consciousness, which contains the collective unconscious: this layer is transpersonal in the sense that it is the same in all of us, and because it is instinctual also connects us to the world of nature. The layer of deep dreamless sleep, however, is even more transpersonal, as it is a layer of which it is no longer possible to say whether it is inside of us or outside of us: as a 'ground of being' it lies at the root of both matter and psyche. Dreams and myths arise from it, and by getting in touch with dreams and myths we connect to this source.

> The value of [dreams and mythic images] to our waking consciousness will be to alert us to an unknown aspect of ourselves, which if we are to 'know ourselves', and so realize our destiny, our *wyrd*, will have to be recognized. Dream Consciousness, then, to summarize and terminate, is the channel or medium of communication between the spheres of M, Deep Dreamless Sleep, and A, Waking Consciousness.[72]

The symbols themselves exist on the level of dream consciousness; however, because they themselves are ultimately the product of a yet deeper layer (a layer which is truly metaphysical) they also connect the psyche to this 'ground of being' from which they arise. This, then, is how Campbell now sees the nature of mythic symbols. It is no longer the case that only *some* symbols point to the ground of being, as he implied in phase two of his career; by stressing that this ground is contained within a psychological and ontological hierarchy which leads from waking consciousness to deep dreamless sleep – to use the terminology of the Mandayuka Upanishad – he now makes it obvious that for him *all* symbols point to the metaphysical. As far as I have been able to trace it, this new hierarchical model remained constant throughout the rest of Campbell's career. I have never come across any sources from phase three in which he puts forward the position he took up in *Masks: primitive:* that mystical experience is simply one of the imprints of experience. The idea of a hierarchy, however, is something which he came back to again and again, and in my opinion his ideas about this topic remained constant after *Masks: creative.* It is not my intention to offer the same amount of proof for my claim that this idea remained constant as I offered in section 6.1 for my claim that Campbell's positive attitude to Jung remained constant in phase three. Instead I would like to offer an example of Campbell talking about this idea in the 1980s, and show that it is still basically the same idea as the one he put forward in *Masks: creative.* I have chosen a talk he gave from 1981, in which he bases his exposition of this idea not on the Mandayuka Upanishad but on the Taittiriya Upanishad. This talk was published as the introductory chapter to the book *Pathways to bliss.* Because this book isn't as widely available in libraries and bookshops as *Masks: creative* is, I've decided to quote here the entire passage in which Campbell discusses this topic.

> There is a doctrine that comes out of the Vedantic tradition that has helped me to understand the nature of the energy that flows through myths. The Taittiriya Upanishad speaks of five sheaths that enclose the atman, which is the spiritual ground or germ of the individual.
>
> The first sheath is called annamaya-kosa, the food sheath. That is your body, which is made out of food and which will become food when you die. The worms, the vultures, the hyenas, or the flame will consume it. This is the sheath of our physical body: the food sheath.
>
> The second sheath is called the sheath of breath, pranamaya-kosa. The breath oxidizes the food; the breath turns it into life. That's this thing, this body: food on fire.
>
> The next sheath is called the mental sheath, manomaya-kosa. This is the consciousness of the body, and it coordinates the senses with the you that thinks it is you. Then there is a big gap.

And the next sheath is called the wisdom sheath, vijnanamaya-kosa. This is the sheath of the wisdom of the transcendent pouring in. This is the wisdom that brought you to form in the mother womb, that digests your dinners, that knows how to do it. This is the wisdom that, when you cut yourself, knows how to heal the wound. The cut bleeds, and then a scab comes along; finally a scar forms, and this is the wisdom sheath going to work.

You go for a walk in the woods. Somebody has built a barbed-wire fence. It leans right into the tree. The tree incorporates that barbed wire. The tree has it, the wisdom sheath. *This is the level of your nature wisdom that you share with the hills, with the trees, with the fish, with the animals. The power of myth is to put the mental sheath in touch with this wisdom sheath, which is the one that speaks of the transcendent* [my italics].[73]

And the sheath inward of the wisdom sheath is the sheath of bliss, anandamaya-kosa, which is a kernel of that transcendence in and of itself. Life is a manifestation of bliss. But manomaya-kosa, the mental sheath, is attached to the sufferings and pleasures of the food sheath. And so it thinks, Is life worth living? Or, as Joyce asks in Finnegans Wake, 'Was life worth leaving?'[74]

The first two sheaths aren't of any importance to this discussion; it is only with the third sheath that establishing a link to Campbell's discussion of the mystical syllable AUM becomes possible. The mental sheath, at least in Campbell's interpretation of it, is obviously what he calls in that exposition 'waking consciousness': it is the ego, the consciousness through which we deal with the demands of the ordinary world. Then comes the wisdom sheath, which is, in Campbell's words, 'the level of your nature wisdom that you share with the hills, with the trees, with the fish, with the animals'. This description is very similar to what Campbell had to say about the level of 'dream consciousness' in his analysis of the Mandayuka Upanishad in *Masks: creative.* About that level he claimed that it is the layer of the psyche that contains the 'nature wisdom' of the collective unconscious: the instinctual, biological part of ourselves that we share with the animals and the world of nature as a whole. As we have seen, Campbell felt that this layer is what is somehow ontologically closest to the 'ground of being' (as he calls it in *Masks: creative*) or the 'transcendent' (as he calls it in the quote above), as 'dream consciousness' lies right above this layer in his hierarchical model (which, using the terminology of the Mandayuka Upanishad, is called 'deep dreamless sleep'). So, too, in this discussion: the wisdom sheath is followed by the sheath of bliss, 'which is a kernel of that transcendence in and of itself'. The layer of 'deep dreamless sleep', too, was characterized by an experience of bliss. It seems obvious that the two are the same, for the relationship they have with the layer which lies right above it is exactly the same too. The layer of 'deep dreamless sleep' is the layer out of which the symbols of 'dream consciousness' arise, and the wisdom sheath is the sheath 'which speaks of the transcendent'; it is able to function as it does because it has 'the wisdom of the transcendent pouring in'.

The way Campbell describes the function of myth is also exactly the same in *Masks: creative* and the talk about the five sheaths. In *Masks: creative* Campbell said that one of the functions of myth is to form a bridge between 'waking consciousness' and the ground of being represented by the layer of 'deep dreamless sleep'. Here he says exactly the same: 'The power of myth is to put the mental sheath in touch with this wisdom sheath, which is the one that speaks of the transcendent.' Mythic symbols, then, have *two* connotations: a psychological one *and* a metaphysical one. In an interview he gave in the 1980s Campbell expressed this idea with great clarity:

> [A mythic image is] a metaphor, and the metaphor points to two ends: one is psychological – that's why the dream is metaphoric; the other is metaphysical. Now, dream is metaphoric of the structures in the psyche, and your dream will correspond to the level of psychological realization that you are operating on. The metaphysical, on the other hand, points past all conceptualizations, all things, to the ultimate depth. And when the two come together, when psyche and metaphysics meet, then you have a real myth.[75]

So how do we relate all of this to Jung's ideas? To begin with, it should be noted that Jung developed a hierarchical model that is strikingly similar to Campbell's. Of course, there is his hierarchical model of the psyche, which is characterized by the levels of ego consciousness, personal unconscious and collective unconscious. In his synchronicity phase, however, Jung added another layer to this hierarchy: the *unus mundus*, which, as he argued, is not only what one bumps into if one goes down deep enough into the unconscious but also what the findings of quantum-mechanics are pointing towards:

> Microphysics is feeling its way into the unknown side of matter, just as complex psychology is pushing forward into the unknown side of the psyche. . . . But this much we do know beyond all doubt, that empirical

reality has a transcendental background. The common background of microphysics and depth psychology is as much physical as psychic and therefore neither, but rather a third thing, a neutral nature which can at most be grasped in hints since its essence is transcendental.[76]

The *unus mundus*, then, lies not only at the root of the psyche but at the root of matter as well. The similarity to Campbell's ideas is obvious. His 'ground of being' or 'transcendent', after all, is also something which lies 'beyond' both matter and psyche. Like Jung, Campbell related this ground to the findings of microphysics as well. He doesn't do this in *Masks: creative,* but throughout phase three he continuously said things like this:

MOYERS: One of the intriguing points of your scholarship is that you do not believe science and mythology conflict.

CAMPBELL: No, they don't conflict. Science is breaking through now into the mystery dimensions. It's pushed itself into the sphere the myth is talking about. It's come to the edge.

MOYERS: The edge being –

CAMPBELL: – the edge, the interface between what can be known and what is never to be discovered because it is a mystery that transcends all human research. The source of life – what is it? No one knows. We don't even know what an atom is, whether it is a wave or a particle – it is both. We don't have any idea of what these things are.

That's the reason we speak of the divine. There's a transcendent energy source. When the physicist observes subatomic particles, he's seeing a trace on a screen. These traces come and go, come and go, and we come and go, and all of life comes and goes. That energy is the informing energy of all things. Mythic worship is addressed to that.[77]

To make the similarities even more apparent, Campbell also claimed that his transcendent ground was what depth psychology was beginning to make contact with as well. In quotes like the following, Campbell is indeed beginning to sound remarkably similar to Jung in his synchronicity phase:

[In the past,] all of the basic mythology revolved around that which put the society in accord with the world of nature, and then the individual, who was also a product of nature, was put in accord with nature – his own nature – through participation in those rites. Well, now that's blown

> apart. We don't have the idea of micro-macrocosm – the little cosmos of man, the big cosmos of nature, and then the middle cosmos of society which shows the laws that govern them all. We don't have that same unity anymore. Physics and psychology really are not the same science anymore, although in their outermost reaches they're beginning to bump into the same mysteries.[78]

Of course, the similarity between Jung's ideas about the *unus mundus* and Campbell's transcendent could be no more than a coincidence. Maybe Campbell simply put forward ideas that happened to sound vaguely Jungian, while in reality he meant something completely different. Does Campbell's 'transcendent' really represent the same level of unity and oneness as Jung's *unus mundus*? To answer this question with absolute certainty is decidedly impossible, as comparing the ideas of two thinkers always involves an act of interpretation. What we can compare are *interpretations* of the ideas of Jung and Campbell – not the ideas themselves. As we can never be a hundred percent sure that our interpretations of their ideas are accurate, comparing them is a tricky business indeed. That said, there is way to deal with this problem. While ascertaining that Campbell and Jung thought exactly the same thing is ultimately impossible, we can answer another, altogether more practical question: did Campbell *himself* think that his ideas about this topic were the same as Jung's? Although he almost never related Jung's ideas to his notion of the transcendent (he mostly talks about Jung when discussing the psychological dimension of this theoretical framework), I have found one source in which he openly connects his ideas about this topic to Jung. This source is an unpublished interview by Cate Miodini with Campbell, held in 1980 and now owned by the Campbell Archive. It seems to me to prove beyond reasonable doubt that at least Campbell himself thought that he and Jung were talking about the same thing.

In his answer to Miodini's first question Campbell talks briefly about quantum-mechanics. He stresses that he feels that the physicists have broken through into a realm of 'mystery':

> I think that what we're experiencing through science today is a breakthrough, you might say, into mysteries of nature beyond what formerly had been our rationally constructed notion of the universe. The physicists have broken through to sub-atomic particles and they don't know what they are. They seem to be at once particles and waves; but these are .just the ways in which we experience them. Actually the very act of experiencing them affects the experience in some way. So that we've

> broken through to a real mystery in the realms of the primary nature sciences.[79]

The realm of 'mystery' which Campbell is talking about here is of course what he also referred to as the 'transcendent'. Campbell often referred to the transcendent in these terms; I have quoted him above, for example, as giving the following description of the 'transcendent': 'Science is breaking through now into the mystery dimensions. It's pushed itself into the sphere the myth is talking about. It's come to the edge.'[80] After the passage in which he refers to the transcendent as a 'realm of mystery', Campbell then goes on to claim something which I have never found him saying in any other interview: that this realm is also a part of Jung's theoretical framework.

> And then in psychology, the old rational systems of the Eighteenth Century, already exploded by the Romantics of the Nineteenth, have been left still further behind through the works of Freud and particularly of Jung. . . . His term, 'collective unconscious', refers to the inward experience of the body itself and the body is a child of nature. And so, in listening to the unconscious, we're actually listening to wisdom from the nature forces that built the human race, that built the world of nature. And this is what's important, it seems to me, in the new findings in the realms of psychology. When you add this to the new findings in physics, you have a double breakthrough into the same mystery – which is really wonderful.[81]

Even though Campbell doesn't mention the concept of the *unus mundus* by name in the Miodini interview, it is obvious that this is indeed the aspect of Jung's theoretical framework that he is referring to when he says that in Jung's work one finds 'a double breakthrough into the same mystery'. The logical conclusion is therefore that Campbell did indeed feel that his ideas about the metaphysical theme were compatible with Jung. The problem, however, is that Miodini interview is from 1980. All we can say with confidence, therefore, is that Campbell saw Jung's metaphysical ideas as compatible with his own ideas in 1980; what he thought about this topic before that time is hard to argue. Nevertheless, I have attempted to show above that Campbell's statements about the metaphysical theme become strikingly similar to Jung's ideas about metaphysics (which revolve around the *unus mundus*) from the beginning of phase three onwards. Given that the passages about the *unus mundus* are heavily underlined in Campbell's copies of the *Collected works*, as well as the fact that Campbell probably read most of these passages around or just before 1968 (see section 6.2 for my argument about this) I do think that it is highly likely that Campbell saw his ideas about the metaphysical theme as compatible with Jung's ideas throughout the whole of phase three, not just from 1980 onwards. Although I think that the Jungian turn was brought about primarily because Campbell concluded that his ideas about the psychological theme were compatible with Jung's ideas (as I have argued in section 6.1), this realization may have influenced it as well.

The metaphysical theme in phase three and the ideas of Anthony Stevens

Although the *Miodini* interview by itself already represents rather strong evidence that connecting Jung's *unus mundus* to Campbell's ideas about the metaphysical theme is justified, I would like to offer one more final layer of proof to strengthen this supposition. The work of Anthony Stevens has been the lens through which we have looked at Campbell's ideas about the psychological theme, and for consistency's sake I feel that it is his work we should turn to as well to deal with the metaphysical theme. Only then can we really come to a conclusion about the question which lies at the root of this section: should we think of Campbell's treatment of the metaphysical theme in phase three as an essentially Jungian position? I am arguing here that it is: not only because Campbell himself thought so – as the *Miodini* interview proves – but also because of the fact that Stevens' interpretation of the *unus mundus* bears an even more striking resemblance to Campbell's ideas than Jung's own treatment of this concept, as I will now show.

The reason why Stevens' work makes it more obvious that we can compare Campbell's transcendent to Jung's *unus mundus* is because he explicitly links it to religion. This is something which Jung himself doesn't really do: he mainly brings up this concept in texts where he is discussing his concept of synchronicity, and uses it to explain this phenomenon – not religion.[82] If there were no link between religion and the *unus mundus* then my argument that we can think of Campbell's treatment of the metaphysical theme in phase three as a Jungian position would break down immediately, as Campbell rather obviously links the transcendent to mythology and religion. Such a link, however, does exist in the form of Stevens' interpretation of this important concept. We have already discussed this interpretation at length in section 3.2. As we have seen, Stevens' primarily discusses it in his article 'Thoughts on the psychobiology of religion and the neurobiology of archetypal experience',[83] written for the academic journal *Zygon*. The main point Stevens tries to make in that article is that a Jungian interpretation of religion does not reduce religion to 'nothing but' archetypes. This is because he feels that Jung's concept of the *unus mundus* makes it obvious that 'the archetypes which order our perceptions and ideas are themselves the product of an objective order which transcends both the human mind and the external world.'[84] A Jungian theory of religion, therefore, does not 'psychologize' religion:

> There is good reason to suppose that religious belief and ritual are manifestations of the archetypal blueprint for human existence encoded in the genetic structure of our species. As a consequence, religion has become a focus of study for psychobiologists and neuroscientists. However, scientific explanations of religious experience do not 'explain away' such experience nor are they substitutes for the experience itself. On the contrary, scientific discoveries may be seen as corroboration of religious insights into the *unus mundus*, . . . which links human nature with the nature of the cosmos.[85]

Another aspect of Stevens' interpretation of the *unus mundus* is that he does not think of it merely as an abstract metaphysical layer; instead, he feels that it is something of which one can also have an *experience*:

> The Self, Jung believed, not only constitutes the evolutionary history of our species (what he sometimes referred to as the two-million-year-old human being within us) but lies at the heart of all religious intimations as to the essential oneness of life – the *unus mundus*, the *satori* experience of Zen Buddhism.[86]

He characterizes this kind of experience as a *mystical* experience, writing that the concept represents the outcome of Jung's attempt 'to penetrate that unitary reality which he, like the mystics of many religious traditions, believed to underlie all manifest phenomena'.[87] He calls the outlook which such an experience leads to 'the sacred view', and stresses that 'all religions teach this'.[88] 'At this supreme point', he writes, 'physical science, psychology and theology all coalesce'.[89]

All of this means that Stevens' interpretation of the *unus mundus* is highly similar to Campbell's ideas about the transcendent in phase three. For example, Campbell frequently related his 'transcendent' to mystical experience as well. Take, for example, this quote, from an interview in

1982. When the interviewer asks Campbell where an experience of the transcendent can be found, he has this to say:

> You find it in mysticism and get in touch with mystics who read these symbolic forms symbolically. Mystics are people who are not theologians; theologians are people who interpret the vocabulary of scripture as if it were referring to supernatural facts. There are plenty of mystics in the Christian tradition, only we don't hear much about them. But now and again you run into it. Meister Eckhart is such a person. Thomas Merton had it. Dante had it. Dionysus the Areopagyte had it. John of the Cross breaks through every now and again and then comes slopping back again. He flashes back and forth.[90]

But there are more similarities between Stevens and Campbell than just a focus on mystical experience: both are also in agreement about the connotation of religious (or mythological) symbols. As we have seen, Campbell drew the conclusion that all religious or mythic symbols point towards the transcendent, and Stevens – by stressing that all religions teach the 'sacred view' – says basically the same thing. For both, therefore, symbols are not only a reflection of the collective unconscious but of a 'ground of being' as well.

Because of the reasons mentioned above I feel that we can truly conclude that Stevens' interpretation of the *unus mundus* is highly similar to Campbell's ideas about the metaphysical theme (in phase three). The logical conclusion, therefore, is that Campbell is not just in accord with Stevens as far as the *psychological* theme is concerned (something which I argued in section 6.1) but also as far as the *metaphysical* theme is concerned. As far as the *origins* of myth and religion are concerned, then, Campbell is in perfect agreement with Stevens. In the next section I will point out that Campbell and Stevens are also in agreement about the *functions* of myth and religion.

6.4 Stevens and Campbell: the final verdict

Stevens work plays an important role in this book. First of all, I am arguing that his interpretation of Jung is highly similar to the interpretation of Jung that Campbell arrived at in phase three of his career (something that has become apparent throughout this chapter). More importantly, however, I am also arguing that his ideas are highly similar to the *theoretical framework* that Campbell arrived at in phase three of his career. In this section I will back up this claim by showing that Stevens and Campbell (in phase three of his career) give identical accounts of both the origins and functions of myth and religion. To enhance the readability of this section, I have decided to omit the phrase 'in phase three' from hereon when referring to Campbell's ideas, even though it will be this particular phase that I will be referring to throughout this section.

The origins and functions of myth and religion

That there are similarities between Stevens's ideas and Campbell's theoretical framework has been a central theme throughout this chapter. In section 6.1, we have seen that Campbell's ideas about the *psychological theme* are basically the same as Stevens' ideas: both think of the human nervous system as consisting of IRMs; both claim that these IRMs are 'open', not 'closed'; furthermore, both associate these ideas with Jung's concept of the archetype. We have also seen that Campbell's ideas about the *metaphysical theme* are highly similar to Stevens' ideas: both claim that the archetypes (or IRMs) found in the human psyche are not just products of our evolutionary history but of a transcendent 'ground of being' as well; both claim that we can have an experience of this 'ground of being'; finally, both also claim that it is this 'ground of being' that we should be concerned with if we want to understand the meaning of religious symbols. As far as the *origins* of myth and religion are concerned, then, Campbell and Stevens both make exactly the same claims. For both, religious experience stems from two sources: a psychological one and a metaphysical one. Religion comes through the psyche and therefore bears the imprints of the psyche; because it is also related to a transcendent 'ground', however, it cannot be thought of as 'nothing but' psychology.

But the similarities between Campbell and Stevens don't end there. As far as the *functions* of religion are concerned, Campbell and Stevens are even more obviously in accord, as both put forward the exact same four functions of mythology and religion. Campbell usually called these functions the metaphysical function, the cosmological function, the moral function and the psychological function. He first writes about them in 1968 in *Masks: creative*,[91] and from that date on mentions them in almost every single book, article, lecture or interview. In an interview from 1971 he described them as follows:

> In the past, the mythological system of any tribe or culture has served four functions.

> First, the mystical or metaphysical function of linking up regular waking consciousness with the vast mystery and wonder of the universe. Any part can be a symbol for the whole. For instance, for Dante, Beatrice's beauty leads to the realization of divine love as the moving power of the universe.
>
> Second, the cosmological function of presenting some intelligible image or picture of nature. In primitive cultures the relationship between man and woman is frequently seen as a mirror of nature: the universe is created by a union of Father Sky and Mother Earth.
>
> Third, the sociological function of validating and enforcing a specific social and moral order. The example that comes to mind is the Ten Commandments and the Deuteronomic Law which were believed to have been revealed directly to Moses by God.
>
> And, finally, the psychological function of providing a marked pathway to carry the individual through the stages of life: the dependency of childhood, the responsibility of adulthood, the wisdom of old age, and the ultimate crisis of death. Every culture has rites of passage and related myths that serve this need.[92]

Anthony Stevens, on the other hand, describes the functions of religion as follows in his *Zygon* article:

> If religions are indeed psychobiological entities, what functions do they perform and why did they evolve in the first place? The following are what I take to be their essential functions.
>
> *Mythological/explanatory function.* Religion provides believers with a coherent story-explanation as to how things began and how a special relationship came to be formed between the community and its gods.
>
> *Sanctification of the ethical code.* Religion ensures group cohesion by granting absolute validity to the moral code on which society is based and by inducing individuals to sacrifice their narrow self-interest to the wider interests of the community as a whole. As long as a religion is able to perform this function it promotes the survival of the group which adheres to it.
>
> *Ritual function.* By prescribing rites of passage to mark crucial stages in the life cycle of each member of the community . . . religious rituals linked the individual to the group and the group to the individual, ensured group participation in the great events of the individual's life, heightened consciousness of the transformation the individual was undergoing, and gave the courage to move on to the next stage ordained for the individual.

> *The spiritual function.* In the most advanced cultures, this has been regarded as the most exalted function of religion – the perception of a transcendent meaning, the sense of participating in a higher purpose soaring far above the mundane preoccupations of the purely personal ego. The experience of the numinosum, the feeling of awe and wonder, and participation mystique in the order of nature and the great dance of the universe.[93]

If we compare these two quotes it is immediately obvious that both Campbell and Stevens acknowledge the same three 'profane' functions: Campbell's cosmological function, sociological function and psychological function are completely identical with, respectively, Stevens' mythological/explanatory function, sanctification of the ethical code and ritual function. Furthermore, both also put forward one 'sacred' function: Campbell calls this the metaphysical function and Stevens the spiritual function. Here, however, whether both mean exactly the same thing is not directly obvious. Campbell's description of his metaphysical function in the quote above is rather short, and although there are definitely some similarities with Stevens' description of his spiritual function, whether both men are talking about exactly the same thing is not a hundred percent clear. However, if we compare Stevens' description of this function (as quoted above) to the following description of the metaphysical function by Campbell from *Masks: creative*, the similarity is much more obvious:

> The first function of a living mythology, the properly religious function, in the sense of Rudolf Otto's definition in The Idea of the Holy, is to waken and maintain in the individual an experience of awe, humility, and respect, in recognition of that ultimate mystery, transcending names and forms, 'from which', as we read in the Upanishads, 'words turn back'.[94]

Whether Stevens developed these ideas about the functions of religion in a dialogue with Campbell's work (which he may well have done, even though he never mentions Campbell in this context) is not the issue at stake here; neither is it important to deal with the question whether Stevens is *correct* in claiming that a Jungian theory of myth would acknowledge the four functions that he mentions.[95] What I am pointing out is that Stevens' account of the Jungian functions of myth and religion is exactly the same as Campbell's treatment of the functions of myth and religion; Campbell, therefore, is not just in accord with Stevens as far as the *origins* of myth and religion are concerned, but also as far as the *functions* are concerned. In the next chapter I will draw on this conclusion to deal with the question which this entire book has been designed to answer: should Campbell's work be seen as Jungian or not?

Notes

1 My own rough estimation based on the amount of lecture notes owned by the Campbell Archive.
2 Sam Keen, 'Man and myth: a conversation with Joseph Campbell', *Psychology today*, July 1971 (Campbell Archive: box 107, folder I11), p. 35.
3 Joseph Campbell, *An open life – Joseph Campbell in conversation with Michael Toms*, ed. John M. Maher and Dennie Briggs (New York: Harper & Row, 1990), p. 50.
4 Joseph Campbell, *Masks: creative*, p. 653.
5 D. J. R. Bruckner, 'Joseph Campbell: 70 years of making connections', *New York times book review*, 18 December 1983 (Campbell Archive: box 107, folder I6).
6 Campbell, *Masks: creative*, p. 65.
7 Ibid., p. 85.
8 Ibid., p. 391.
9 Ibid., p. 652.
10 Jung, *CW 8*, par. 589.
11 Ibid.
12 Ibid.
13 Jung, *CW 9 part 1*, par. 155. Quoted in Campbell, *Masks: creative*, p. 655.
14 Campbell, *Masks: creative*, p. 653.
15 Joseph Campbell, *Pathways to bliss – mythology and personal transformation*, ed. David Kudler, The collected works of Joseph Campbell (Novato: New World Library, 2004), p. 48.
16 Joseph Campbell, *Masks: primitive*, p. 48.
17 Jung, *CW 9 part 1*, par. 155.
18 Campbell, *Masks: creative*, p. 655.
19 Ibid., p. 653.
20 Ibid.
21 Joseph Campbell, *Myths to live by* (New York: Bantam Books, 1972).
22 Joseph Campbell, *The mythic image* (New York: MJF Books, 1974).
23 Joseph Campbell, *The mythic dimension – selected essays 1959–1987*, ed. Antony van Couvering, The collected works of Joseph Campbell (New York: Harper Collins, 1997).
24 Ibid., p. 200.
25 Keen, 'Man and myth: a conversation with Joseph Campbell', p. 35.
26 Lorraine Kisly, 'Living myths: a conversation with Joseph Campbell', *Parabola* 1, no. 2, 1976 (Campbell Archive: box 107, folder I13), p. 76.
27 Michael Toms, 'Interview with Joseph Campbell', *Sunrise*, August–September 1979 (Campbell Archive: box 113, folder A1), p. 329.

[28] Ibid.
[29] Ibid.
[30] Campbell, *Myths to live by*, p. 216.
[31] Campbell, *Pathways to bliss*, p. 113.
[32] Quoted in ibid., p. 86.
[33] Ibid.
[34] Ibid., p. 94.
[35] Ibid., p. 95.
[36] Ibid., p. 96.
[37] Ibid.
[38] Ibid.
[39] Ibid.
[40] Campbell, *An open life*, p. 50.
[41] There are two volumes, both of which have been published in separate 'parts': part one and two together make up volume 1; the remaining three parts make up volume 2.
[42] Derrick Jensen Joe Nigg, 'An interview with the master of mythology Joseph Campbell', Bloomsbury review, April/May 1984 (Campbell Archive: box 107, folder I25).
[43] John Lobell, 'Interview with Joseph Campbell', *New age book review* 1983 (Campbell Archive: box 107, folder I16).
[44] Campbell, *Masks: creative*, p. 653.
[45] Anthony Stevens, *Archetype revisited – an updated natural history of the self*, second edn (London: Brunner-Routledge, 2002), p. 17.
[46] Joseph Campbell, *Atlas volume 1 part 1*, p. 47.
[47] Ibid., p. 46.
[48] Campbell, *Masks: creative*, p. 654.
[49] Campbell, *Atlas volume 1 part 1*, p. 47.
[50] Ibid., p. 46.
[51] Costis Ballas, 'Unpublished interview with Joseph Campbell', 1985 (Campbell Archive: box 107, folder I2).
[52] Toms, 'Interview with Joseph Campbell', p. 329.
[53] Michael McKnight, 'Elders and guides: a conversation with Joseph Campbell', *Parabola* V, no. 1, 1980 (Campbell Archive: box 107), p. 59.
[54] Campbell, *An open life*, p. 123.
[55] Stephen Larsen, 'Freud, Jung and Campbell', in *Uses of comparative mythology: essays on the work of Joseph Campbell*, ed. Kenneth L. Golden (New York/London: Garland publishing, 1992), p. 33. (Larsen also claims that, having already read most of Jung's work in English, Campbell now read them in the original German. This seems unlikely, however, as Campbell owned hardly any books by Jung in German.)
[56] Ibid., p. 22.
[57] Carl G. Jung, *The integration of the personality*, trans. Stanley M. Dell (New York: Farrar & Rinehart, 1939).
[58] Ibid., p. 54.
[59] Jung, *CW 9 part 1*, par. 6.
[60] The 1939 version was translated by Stanley Dell; the *CW* version by R. F. C. Hull.

[61] Jung, *CW 9 part 1*, par. 6.
[62] Ibid., par. 155.
[63] See Chapter 5 for my argument about this.
[64] Gerald McDermott, 'Interview with Joseph Campbell', *New Boston Review* 1, no. 2, 1975 (Campbell Archive: box 107, folder I18).
[65] Joseph Campbell, *The lost teachings of Joseph Campbell volume 2* (Redmond: Zygon International), [Audiotape]. [This section is on the beginning of tape 1a.]
[66] Joseph Campbell, *Hero*, pp. 256, 257, 258.
[67] Campbell, *Masks: creative*, p. 373.
[68] Ibid., pp. 352–353, 609.
[69] Ibid., p. 647.
[70] Quoted in ibid., p. 656.
[71] Ibid., p. 665.
[72] Ibid., p. 668.
[73] Campbell, *Pathways to bliss*, pp. xx, xxi.
[74] Ibid., pp. xx–xxi.
[75] Campbell, *An open life*, pp 21, 22.
[76] Jung, *CW 14*, par. 767–769.
[77] Joseph Campbell, *The power of myth*, ed. Betty Sue Flowers (New York: Doubleday, 1988), p. 132.
[78] Kisly, 'Living myths: a conversation with Joseph Campbell', p. 74.
[79] C. Miodini, 'Unpublished interview with Joseph Campbell', 1980 (Campbell Archive: box 107, folder I83).
[80] Campbell, *The power of myth*, p. 132.
[81] Miodini, 'Unpublished interview with Joseph Campbell.'
[82] Jung did link the *unus mundus* to his concept of the self, which means that there exists an indirect connection (as Jung did link the self to religion again and again). In *MDF*, for example, he writes: 'For Buddha, the self stands above all gods, a *unus mundus* which represents the essence of human existence and of the world as a whole' (p. 279). What precisely Jung means by this somewhat vague passage, however, never really becomes clear.
[83] Anthony Stevens, 'Thoughts on the psychobiology of religion and the neurobiology of archetypal experience', *Zygon* 21 (March 1986).
[84] Anthony Stevens, 'The archetypes', in *The handbook of Jungian psychology*, ed. Renos K. Papadopoulos (New York/London: Routledge, 2006), p. 88.
[85] Stevens, 'Thoughts on the psychobiology of religion and the neurobiology of archetypal experience', p. 9.
[86] Ibid., p. 24.
[87] Anthony Stevens, *Jung – a very short introduction* (Oxford: Oxford University Press, 2001), p. 57.
[88] Stevens, 'Thoughts on the psychobiology of religion and the neurobiology of archetypal experience', p. 23.
[89] Stevens, *Jung – a very short introduction*, p. 57.
[90] Tom Collins, 'Unpublished interview with Joseph Campbell', 1985 (Campbell Archive: box 107, folder I9).
[91] Campbell, *Masks: creative*, p. 609.
[92] Keen, 'Man and myth: a conversation with Joseph Campbell.'

93 Stevens, 'Thoughts on the psychobiology of religion and the neurobiology of archetypal experience', p. 14.

94 Campbell, *Masks: creative*, p. 609.

95 As I will point out in the next chapter it is certainly possible to cast doubt on this, as several Jung scholars have put forward completely different 'Jungian' functions of myth and religion.

Chapter 7

Conclusion

In this chapter I will offer both an overview of the exact conclusions that I have drawn in this book and some reflections on the potential benefit of these conclusions for other scholars. I will start by giving a brief summary of my model of the three phases of Campbell's career in section 7.1. I will then give a presentation of what I feel are the most important claims that I am making in this book (section 7.2), followed by an analysis of the question which lies at the root of this entire book: should Campbell be seen as a Jungian or not (section 7.3)? Finally, in section 7.4, I will offer my thoughts on the potential use of my findings for the following three areas of investigation: the academic study of Campbell's ideas, the field of Jungian scholarship and the field of Religious Studies as a whole.

7.1 The model of the three phases: a summary

At the root of the chapters that deal with Campbell's ideas lies my model of the three phases of Campbell's career. In a nutshell, it can be summed up as given in the following table:

Name of phase	Dates	Key works
Phase one	1943–1959	*The hero with a thousand faces*
Phase two	1959–1968	*Masks* volumes 1 to 3; most of the essays in *Flight of the wild gander*
Phase three	1968–1988	*Masks: creative*; the *Atlas* series

I will now give a detailed summary of Campbell's key ideas in each of these three phases.

Ideas in phase one

As far as the psychological theme is concerned, the keywords Campbell uses in this phase are mostly related to psychoanalysis. He frequently states that myth is of the order of dream, and he explains the fact that common motifs can be found in myths from all over the world by referring to several different psychoanalytical theories of the unconscious, without openly choosing sides. In an interview given in phase three he said that at this point in his career he still thought that Jung and Freud were equal;[1] however, as I argued in section 5.1 (and Robert Segal did before me in his *Introduction*), Campbell definitely leans more towards Jung than towards Freud in this period. Like Jung, he thinks of the unconscious in a much more positive way than Freud did: he views it as a source of creativity and vitality, and also states that one of the functions of myth has always been 'to carry the human spirit forward' – something which Freud never would have said. At the end of *Hero,* however, he takes a decidedly un-Jungian stance when he claims that myth is not a spontaneously generated product of the psyche but should be seen as a collection of conscious and controlled statements, created with the intent to teach a metaphysical truth. The building blocks of myths – what he himself would later sometimes call the 'mythic images' – are products of the unconscious; the *meaning* of myth, however, is metaphysical. Campbell adopts this position in other writings from this period as well. In his commentary to the Pantheon edition of *Grimm's fairy-tales* (1944), for example, he writes the following:

> The 'monstrous, irrational, and unnatural' motifs in folktale and myth are derived from the reservoirs of dream and vision. On the dream level such images represent the total state of the individual dreaming psyche. But clarified of personal distortions and propounded by poets, prophets, and visionaries, they become symbolic of the spiritual norm for Man the Microcosm. They are thus phrases from an image-language, expressive of metaphysical, psychological, and sociological truth.[2]

This, then, is what Campbell has to say in this phase as far as the metaphysical theme is concerned. Myth, seen this way, is much closer to a philosophy than it is to an irrational product of the unconscious or a divine revelation. 'The old teachers knew what they were saying',[3] Campbell wrote in his foreword to *Hero,* and this seems indeed to be the logical implication: myth now becomes something of which the creators knew that it was only a 'picture language'. The masses might have believed that it was all true and that the reference of the symbols was to real gods and goddesses, but the enlightened few who created the myths were conscious of its true point of reference: the divine or sacred 'ground of being'.

Ideas in phase two

This phase begins with the publication of *Masks: primitive*, in which Campbell uses a rather different theoretical framework than he did in *Hero*. Where in *Hero* he draws mostly on the findings of psychoanalysis to present his views about the psychological theme, in *Masks: primitive* he bases his treatment of the psychological theme mostly on the findings of ethologists like Niko Tinbergen and Konrad Lorenz. He now uses the ethological concept of the IRM to explain the common motifs found in myths from different cultures. He distinguishes between the closed IRM and the open IRM, stressing that the IRMs that are to be found in the human nervous system should all be thought of as open. A closed IRM is the kind of instinctual structure that can be found mostly in animals: an example Campbell gives is the observation that newborn chicks will screech and cower when the wooden model of a hawk is pulled over their hatch, a 'pattern of behaviour' which involves no learning whatsoever. An open IRM, on the other hand, isn't fixed and completely innate like the closed IRM; rather, it is open to 'imprinting' by stimuli from the environment. Jung's concept of the archetype, Campbell claims, is the equivalent of a closed IRM, and for this reason he dismisses it as an inadequate approach to explain the origins of myth. In this phase, then, Campbell still sees Jung's archetype as a 'closed', wholly innate structure, and because of his own emphasis on the more flexible open IRM he draws the conclusion that his own ideas are not in line with Jung's.

As far as the metaphysical theme is concerned, Campbell's ideas are distinctly contradictory in phase two. On the one hand he claims that *all* mythic symbols point to what he now calls the 'numinous' (the 'ground of being' which he would later call the transcendent); on the other hand he also writes at the beginning of *Masks: primitive* that the experience of the numinous is only one of the many imprints which humans have been exposed to throughout history, thus implying that only *some* symbols point towards the numinous (i.e. those related to an open IRM that has been imprinted by an experience of it). Unlike in phase one, where he did mention Jung when discussing the metaphysical theme,[4] Campbell never mentions Jung in relation to the metaphysical theme in phase two.

Ideas in phase three

Phase three begins with the publication of *Masks: creative*, in which Campbell makes the following statement:

> Dr. Jung used the terms 'archetype' and 'primordial image' interchangeably, to designate those formative powers of the psyche that have been

discussed at length in the first chapters of the opening volume of this study: *Primitive Mythology*, Chapter I, 'The Enigma of the Inherited Image', and II, 'The Imprints of Experience'.[5]

As Campbell actually dismissed Jung as incompatible with his own approach (based on the concept of the open IRM) in *Masks: primitive*, this statement is surprising to say the least. As I have argued in Chapter 6, Campbell makes this statement because he has now come to reinterpret Jung's ideas. He no longer sees the concept of the archetype as the equivalent of a closed IRM, but has come to the conclusion that it is much more akin to an open IRM. He is therefore forced to admit that Jung is compatible with his core ideas after all, which indeed he does. As far as the psychological theme is concerned, then, Campbell sees his own ideas as perfectly compatible with Jung's in this phase of his career.

Campbell's ideas about the metaphysical theme in phase three are an extension of his ideas in phase two, but with one crucial difference: they are no longer contradictory. He no longer claims that the numinous – or transcendent as he now mostly calls it – is but one of the many 'imprints' of human experience; instead he now consistently claims that all mythic images arise from, and therefore point towards, the transcendent. Closely resembling the ideas which Jung put forward when discussing his concept of the *unus mundus*, Campbell frequently claims that the transcendent lies not only at the root of the psyche but at the root of the material world as well. He also associates his concept of the transcendent with the findings of quantum-mechanics, something which Jung did with his concept of the *unus mundus* as well. Although Campbell never mentions the *unus mundus*, he did have the following to say in an interview from 1980 which implies that he felt that his concept of the transcendent was compatible with Jung's ideas:

> I think that what we're experiencing through science today is a breakthrough, you might say, into mysteries of nature beyond what formerly had been our rationally constructed notion of the universe. The physicists have broken through to sub-atomic particles and they don't know what they are. They seem to be at once particles and waves; but these are .just the ways in which we experience them. Actually the very act of experiencing them affects the experience in some way. So that we've broken through to a real mystery in the realms of the primary nature sciences.[6]
>
> And then in psychology, the old rational systems of the Eighteenth Century, already exploded by the Romantics of the Nineteenth, have been left still further behind through the works of Freud and particularly of Jung. . . . His term, 'collective unconscious', refers to the inward experience

> of the body itself and the body is a child of nature. And so, in listening to the unconscious, we're actually listening to wisdom from the nature forces that built the human race, that built the world of nature. And this is what's important, it seems to me, in the new findings in the realms of psychology. When you add this to the new findings in physics, you have a double breakthrough into the same mystery – which is really wonderful.[7]

In phase three of his career, then, Campbell arrived at the conclusion that his own ideas were in accord with Jung's ideas both as far as the metaphysical and the psychological theme are concerned. As I have shown in Chapters 2 and 6, the fact that Campbell's ideas can be seen as compatible with Jung's ideas becomes even more obvious when we compare the former's ideas to the work of Anthony Stevens. Stevens puts forward an interpretation of Jung which is almost completely identical to Campbell's theoretical framework in phase three, and for that reason I feel that we may justifiably draw the conclusion that Campbell made Jung part of the very backbone of his theoretical framework in phase three.

7.2 Overview and close analysis of my most important arguments

Even though I feel that my model of the three phases of Campbell's career offers an important contribution in the sense that it helps us to clearly see the development of Campbell's ideas, not everything related to it represents a new insight on my part. That Campbell's ideas change radically from phase one to phase two, for example, is something that other scholars have picked up on as well. Robert Segal's *Introduction* is a case in point. Segal does an excellent job mapping the differences between *Hero* and the first three volumes of the *Masks: Series*, thus acknowledging quite clearly the transition from phase one to phase two. He does not, however, emphasize that there are important differences between phase two and phase three (what I have been calling the 'Jungian turn'). This transition (from phase two to phase three) is something which, to the best of my knowledge, has never been acknowledged by other scholars. It is in this area, therefore, that I feel that I am making my most important contribution. The arguments that I have made about this transition can be summed up as follows:

1. Campbell's *attitude* to Jung changes at the beginning of phase three.
2. Campbell's *interpretation* of Jung changes at the beginning of phase three.

3. The core of Campbell's theoretical framework in phase three is the same as Anthony Stevens' interpretation of Jung.

I will now give an overview of each of these statements.

Argument 1: Campbell's attitude to Jung changes at the beginning of phase three

That Campbell's attitude to Jung changed over time is something that he himself – somewhat covertly – acknowledged. In Chapter 6 I already quoted the following passage from an interview published in 1979:

> When I wrote *The Hero With A Thousand Faces* in the early '40s, these two men were sort of equal in my thinking. But then in the years following, Jung became more and more eloquent to me. My feeling is that Freud tells us what myths mean to neurotics, and Jung gives us a clue how to let the myth talk to us in its own terms without putting a formula on it. Jung is not the final word at all – I don't think there is a final word. But he opened me up to new prospects and vistas.[8]

This interview was held by Michael Toms, and eventually found its way into the book *An open life.*[9] Most scholars who have undertaken serious research into Campbell's ideas will have read this book, and we might therefore expect other scholars to pick up on this notion of a development in Campbell's attitude to Jung as well. As far as I am aware, however, this is a topic that remains strangely undiscussed. Robert Segal does offer the quote at the beginning of chapter 12 of his *Introduction,* but does not use it to illustrate that Campbell's attitude to Jung changed over time. Instead, he uses it to highlight the fact that Campbell is generally much more positive about Jung than about Freud, which indeed the quote illustrates as well. After having quoted the passage, Segal claims that Campbell himself sometimes denied being a Jungian, but did frequently praise Jung. As Segal puts it himself: 'Campbell praises Jung rather than defers to him.'[10] Although I do not object to this statement as such, my position differs from Segal's in that I don't hold that Campbell *always* showered such praise on Jung. As I have shown in Chapter 5, Campbell didn't have a positive attitude to Jung's core ideas in phase two of his career at all. I have given a great many examples of Campbell making highly positive remarks about Jung in interviews, books and lectures;

however, as I have shown in Chapter 6, all of these examples are from after 1968.

Although I believe that a change of *interpretation* of Jung's ideas on Campbell's part lies at the root of this sea change (which is indeed my second argument; see below), the current argument refers merely to a shift in *attitude*. I have made a division between these two arguments here because the first argument (that Campbell's attitude to Jung changed) requires much less deduction and 'reading between the lines'; instead, it relies solely on what are in my opinion established facts.

These facts are represented first of all by the many quotes in which Campbell expressed his admiration for Jung. I have given many, many examples of them in the previous chapter, and to deny their existence is simply an untenable position. Second of all, I am also arguing that there exists a fact of a higher order, a 'meta-fact' for want of a better word: that all of these quotes are from after 1968, and never from before that date. This is an inductive observation that can't really be verified, only falsified. In theory, it is possible that a critical reader of my work might produce a quote from before 1968 of which I am not aware in which Campbell says something exceedingly positive about Jung, or a quote from after 1968 in which he says something radically negative about Jung. Such a quote would immediately falsify my 'meta-fact' that Campbell only became extremely positive about Jung after 1968. After having examined all the evidence of which I am aware, however, I have become convinced that such a quote does not exist. Finally, the argument or theory which I am basing on these facts can be summed up by the following statement: the *reason* why we can only find quotes in which Campbell showers excessive praise on Jung from after 1968 is because Campbell's *attitude* to Jung changed significantly around that time. Of course, it could just be a random coincidence that Campbell only started praising Jung after 1968. One can come up with other reasons than an attitude shift to explain this fact: maybe no one bothered to ask Campbell what he thought about Jung in interviews before 1968; maybe Campbell was under the impression that praising Jung would hurt his career up until 1968. If we really want to be confident about the fact that Campbell's attitude to Jung changed, then, we would also need to find a plausible hypothesis as to what may have caused his shift in attitude to Jung. It is my opinion that such a cause exists: Campbell's *interpretation* of Jung's work changed from 1968 onwards. It is to this second, related argument that we will now turn in the next section.

Argument 2: Campbell's interpretation of Jung changes at the beginning of phase three

The first indication that Campbell had arrived at a new interpretation of Jung occurs in *Masks: creative* (1968), in which he writes the following:

> Dr. Jung used the terms 'archetype' and 'primordial image' interchangeably, to designate those formative powers of the psyche that have been discussed at length in the first chapters of the opening volume of this study: *Primitive Mythology*, Chapter I, 'The Enigma of the Inherited Image', and II, 'The Imprints of Experience'.[11]

If we bear in mind that Campbell actually dismissed the concept of the archetype as incompatible with his own approach in these two chapters,[12] this passage seems to establish quite clearly that Campbell now feels that his own ideas (which revolve around the concept of the open IRM) are compatible with Jung's concept of the archetype after all. Even though, in a nutshell, this is the actual conclusion which I have drawn in Chapter 6, I would like to stress here first of all that the analysis which I have used to back up this conclusion involves much more 'leaps of interpretation' than argument one. Campbell, for reasons which elude me, never wrote much about the concept of the IRM after *Masks: primitive*. As he also never openly acknowledged that his ideas about the compatibility of his ideas about this topic with Jung's concept of the archetype had changed drastically, it is therefore difficult to pinpoint exactly how his ideas changed regarding this important aspect of his theoretical framework. That said, I have nevertheless attempted to draw some conclusions about this change, which can be summarized as follows. Campbell's ideas about the IRMs of the human nervous system remained the same in phase two and phase three: this is established by the fact that his treatment of this topic is exactly the same in *Atlas: 1.1* (1988) as it is in *Masks: primitive* (1959). His interpretation of Jung, however, changed: from 1968 onwards he came to believe that Jung's concept of the archetype can be seen as the equivalent of an 'open' IRM. A careful analysis of both *Masks: creative* and *Atlas: 1.1* lends strong support to this conclusion, which is what I have attempted to show in section 6.1.1 and section 6.1.3. Campbell, then, came to see Jung's most important concept in a completely different light around 1968. Even though he himself never acknowledged this change, I still think that I have offered enough evidence to support this conclusion. I also think that it is this change of interpretation which caused Campbell to become so positive about Jung after 1968 (argument one). Argument two, therefore, can be used as 'circumstantial evidence' to lend support for argument one. As for the reasons behind the change in interpretation of Jung, I have given some suggestions for what these may have been in section 6.2.

The change of interpretation outlined so far, however, has to do solely with what I have been calling the *psychological* theme in Campbell's work. As I have continuously stressed throughout this book, there is also a *metaphysical* theme running through Campbell's work. In section 6.3, I have attempted to show that in phase three of his career Campbell's ideas about this metaphysical theme are highly similar to Jung's ideas about the *unus mundus*. In that section I also showed that a quote exists from phase three in which Campbell himself acknowledged these similarities, thus implying that he saw his ideas about the metaphysical theme as compatible with Jung's ideas in phase three. This quote, in which Campbell implies that he felt that his ideas about the 'transcendent' are the same as Jung's ideas about the *unus mundus*, is from 1980. I am aware of only one passage in which Campbell *dismisses* Jung for not dealing adequately with the metaphysical theme: this is the section at the end of *Hero* in which he claims that myths are reflected on, and contain a metaphysical message because they have been consciously created to have this message (see the summary of phase one for more about this).[13] As this passage is from 1949, that means there are 31 years between this section and the quote from 1980. Obviously, this isn't enough to claim that at the beginning of phase three, Campbell went from negative to positive regarding the notion that Jung's metaphysical ideas are compatible with his own ideas, just like he did with his ideas about the psychological theme. All we can say with confidence is that Campbell saw Jung's metaphysical ideas in a positive light in 1980; what he thought about this topic before that time is hard to argue. Nevertheless, I have attempted to show in section 6.3 that Campbell's statements about the metaphysical theme become strikingly similar to Jung's ideas about metaphysics (which revolve around the *unus mundus*) from the beginning of phase three onwards. Given that the passages about the *unus mundus* are heavily underlined in Campbell's copies of the *Collected works*, as well as the fact that Campbell probably read most of these passages around 1968 (see section 6.2 for my argument about this) I do think that it is highly likely that Campbell saw his ideas about the metaphysical theme as compatible with Jung's ideas throughout the whole of phase three, not just from 1980 onwards. Although I think that the shift in attitude to Jung (argument one) was brought about primarily because Campbell realized his ideas about the psychological theme were compatible with Jung's ideas, this realization may have influenced it as well.

Argument 3: The core of Campbell's theoretical framework in phase three is the same as Anthony Stevens' interpretation of Jung

As far as the psychological theme is concerned, the bedrock of Campbell's ideas in both phases two and three is the concept of the open IRM. As I have pointed out throughout Chapters 5 and 6, Campbell's ideas about this concept are exactly the same as the ideas put forward by Anthony Stevens in his book *Archetype*. Both Campbell and Stevens claim that the human psyche is innately equipped with a host of preformed psychological structures; both agree that in contrast to the structures found in animals, these structures are open to imprinting; finally, both connect this idea to the ethological concept of the 'open' IRM, made famous by Tinbergen and Lorenz. Campbell concluded in phase two that this approach is un-Jungian; in phase three, however, he concluded the exact opposite and arrived at the conclusion that this approach is compatible with Jung's ideas. As his basic ideas about the concept of the IRM itself stay the same, however, we can draw the conclusion that Campbell's ideas related to the psychological theme are fully in line with Stevens' ideas in both phase two and phase three.

As far as the metaphysical theme is concerned my argument is slightly different. Unlike the psychological theme, Campbell's treatment of the metaphysical theme did *not* stay the same in phases two and three. In phase three Campbell consistently says that the connotation of *all* mythic symbols is metaphysical, whereas in phase two he implies in one crucial passage that only some mythic symbols point towards the transcendent (see section 5.2.1 or the summary of phase two above). Stevens, however, consistently says that *all* symbols are inherently metaphysical. This is because he relates the concept of the archetype not only to the innate structures of the psyche but also to Jung's concept of the *unus mundus*. This is a concept that not many Jung scholars draw attention to. Stevens, however, attaches primary importance to it, stressing that archetypes are not just a product of our evolutionary history but also 'the product of an objective order which transcends both the human mind and the external world'[14] – the *unus mundus*. As I have argued in section 6.3, this is basically the same theoretical outlook which Campbell arrived at in phase three of his career. He, too, came to hold that mythic symbols should not just be related to psychological structures; rather, they are also an expression of what he called, using a slightly different term, the 'transcendent'. I do not wish to repeat the analysis that I have used to back up this point here. Instead, I merely want to point out that this means that even though Campbell's ideas about the psychological theme are compatible with Stevens' ideas in both phases two and three, Campbell's ideas about the metaphysical theme only become compatible with Stevens in phase three.

As far as the *origins* of religion are concerned, then, Campbell is in complete agreement with Stevens in phase three. In that phase, like Stevens, he relates these origins not only to the open IRM (the psychological theme), but also to a transcendent dimension which underlies both the psyche and the material world (the metaphysical theme). As far as the *functions* of religion are concerned, however, one might expect there to be differences between Campbell and Stevens. Several scholars have identified Jungian functions of myth that are distinctly different from the four functions that Campbell puts forward. Robert Segal, for example, writes in his *Introduction* that 'Jung would consider Campbell's four functions as a whole askew to his own.'[15] Another example is Steven Walker, who also identifies different Jungian functions of mythology than the ones that Campbell puts forward in his book *Jung and the Jungians on myth and mythology*.[16] Stevens, however, has a somewhat idiosyncratic take on the Jungian functions of myth and religion. He claims that a Jungian theory of myth and religion would acknowledge the following four functions: the spiritual function, the explanatory function, sanctification of the ethical code and the ritual function. As I pointed out in section 6.4, these are the exact same four functions that Campbell puts forward (despite the fact that Stevens uses slightly different names). Whether Stevens is justified in identifying these four functions as Jungian or not, the logical conclusion is that Campbell, in phase three of his career, agrees with Stevens not only about the psychological theme and the metaphysical theme, but also about both the origins *and* functions of myth and religion. The core of Campbell's theoretical framework in phase three, then, is exactly the same as Anthony Stevens' interpretation of Jung: this, in a nutshell, is my third main argument. I will now draw on it to deal with the question which this entire book has been designed to answer: should Campbell's work be seen as Jungian or not?

7.3 Campbell as a post-Jungian

As I have stressed throughout this book, Jung's writings are often highly ambiguous. This means that making an argument about Jung's ideas depends very much on the interpretation of his work that one subscribes to. The way one answers the question 'is Campbell a Jungian or not', then, depends on the specific interpretation of Jung that one subscribes to. As the interpretation that I have used in this book to enable a comparison between Jung and Campbell is the one put forward by the scholar Anthony Stevens, making a judgement about Campbell's status as a Jungian depends – in the context of this book, at least – on whether Campbell's ideas are in agreement with Stevens' interpretation of Jung. My main argument about the relationship Stevens-Campbell is that Campbell's ideas are fully in accord with Stevens' interpretation of Jung in phase three of his career (argument three; see outline above). Given this argument, it follows logically that Campbell can therefore be seen as Jungian in phase three of his career.

Before I go on to assess the implications of this conclusion, I would like to point out first of all that I am not claiming that Stevens' interpretation of Jung is right. The scholarly merit of Stevens' work is a discussion all its own, and represents a subject that I do not wish to deal with here. Although the reader certainly has every right to doubt the accuracy of Steven's ideas about Jung, there is one thing about which there can be no doubt: the fact that his work is Jungian in nature. Unlike Campbell, Stevens is an actual Jungian analyst, and his ideas (again, unlike Campbell's) are put forward in books and articles that have as their explicit goal to clarify and analyse Jung's ideas. Right or wrong, Stevens' ideas would certainly be classified as Jungian in nature by the vast majority of his readers. If one therefore accepts my argument that the core of Campbell's theoretical framework in phase three is in direct agreement with Stevens' ideas, then the logical conclusion would indeed seem to be that Campbell should be seen as Jungian as well.

With the slight exception that I prefer the term post-Jungian to Jungian (about which more below), this is the conclusion that I will be defending in this section. As with any argument, however, there are several possible counterarguments to this claim. A first counterargument, for example, might be that Campbell himself sometimes denied being a Jungian. I have already quoted him in Chapter 6 as saying the following:

> I myself am not a Jungian, although as far as interpreting myths goes, Jung gives me the best clues I've got. But I am much more interested in diffusion and relationships historically than Jung was, very, very much so.[17]

The reason which Campbell offers in this quote for not thinking of himself as a Jungian is that he is interested in diffusion. What Campbell *doesn't* say, however, is that Jung had no interest in diffusion, nor that Jung thought that his ideas were radically opposed to theories of diffusion; instead, he merely says that Jung was less interested in it than he himself is. I already pointed out in Chapter 5 that Jung didn't claim that theories of diffusion should not be used to explain the similarities in myths. In that chapter I quoted the following passage from Jung's *Collected works*, which does indeed establish this with great clarity:

> The first investigator in the field of ethnology to draw attention to the widespread occurrence of certain 'elementary ideas' was Adolf Bastian. Two later investigators, Hubert and Mauss, followers of Durkheim, speak of 'categories' of the imagination. And it was no less an authority than Hermann Usener who first recognized unconscious preformation under the guise of 'unconscious thinking'. If I have any share in these discoveries, it consists in my having shown that archetypes are not disseminated only by tradition, language, and migration, but that they can rearise spontaneously, at any time, at any place, and without any outside influence.[18]

Stevens, too, stresses that diffusion is not incompatible with a Jungian approach to the study of myths. In Chapter 5 I quoted the following passage from *Archetype*:

> Jung was not so naïve as to deny that this universal parallelism of motifs, ideas and images could be brought about by the combined operation of tradition and migration, but he argued that some form of transmission through heredity must also occur since he was able to discover numerous instances where such motifs arose spontaneously, without any previous encounter with them on the part of the subject. Jung, therefore, concluded that they must correspond to 'typical dispositions', 'dominants' or 'nodal points' within the structure of the psyche itself.[19]

Although Campbell was definitely right in saying that he was far more interested in diffusion than Jung was, stressing that an interest in diffusion disqualifies him as being Jungian is misleading in my opinion. Jung did not oppose theories of diffusion, and for that reason Campbell's argument that he is not a Jungian because of his interest in them is simply not valid. If one is looking for reasons to argue that Campbell's theories are un-Jungian, therefore, then there are more suitable areas of Campbell's theoretical framework to look at than his interest in diffusion.

I am not claiming here that no such reasons exist. Where in Campbell's work, one might ask, is the fascination with the problem of evil and the 'dark side of God', so prominent in late works by Jung like *Answer to Job*? Where is the obsession with trinities and quaternities, or the belief that UFOs are projections of the self? A second possible counterargument to my claim that Campbell can be seen as Jungian in phase three, therefore, could be that regardless of the similarities to Stevens' interpretation of Jung, there remain a great deal of differences between Jung and Campbell. My response to this counterargument would be to point out that none of these topics play any role in Stevens' work. Jung might have thought that these subjects mattered; however, as they play no role in Stevens' reception of Jung, it does not matter these topics cannot be found in Campbell's work. If we accept that Stevens' work is Jungian, as well as my argument that Campbell's ideas closely match Stevens' ideas, then it still follows that Campbell's work (at least in phase three) can be seen as Jungian as well.

The question, then, is not really 'is Campbell a Jungian?' but 'is *Stevens* a Jungian?' A final possible counterargument, therefore, could be that it simply isn't appropriate to see Stevens' work in this way. There is indeed some ground to argue this, as there are many ways in which Stevens goes 'beyond' Jung. First of all, Stevens' suggestion that the concept of the archetype should be seen as the direct equivalent of the concept of the open IRM is a major innovation. Jung never used the term 'IRM' in any of his writings, and even though it was developed during his lifetime, it is likely that he wasn't even aware of its existence. Second of all, Stevens can be seen as going beyond Jung when he stresses that the concept of the *unus mundus* is central to a Jungian theory of religion. Jung, to the best of my knowledge, never made an explicit connection between the *unus mundus* and religion; instead, he used it to explain the synchronicity phenomena that he became so interested in towards the end of his life. Stevens' claim, then, that such a connection should be made represents somewhat of an innovation as well. Finally, Stevens goes beyond Jung when he stresses that the functions of religion can be adequately described by the four functions he puts forward in his *Zygon* article (which, as we have seen, are the same as Campbell's four functions). Jung never explicitly stated that these are the four functions of religion which he discerns, and several other Jung scholars have put forward Jungian functions of myth and religion that are decidedly different than the ones that Stevens puts forward.

Despite these innovations, however, I still think that arguing that Stevens' work should not be seen as Jungian misses the mark. Stevens' work is rooted firmly in Jung's ideas, and I think that he himself would certainly object if one suggested that we see his ideas instead as 'Stevensian' (for want of a better word). At the same time, I do think that the areas where Stevens goes beyond Jung are too significant to simply dismiss. My suggestion, therefore, is that we don't classify Stevens as a Jungian but as a post-Jungian. This is the Jung scholar Andrew Samuels' term for a thinker who in some ways has parted ways with what Jung himself would have claimed, but whose work should still be seen as an extension of his work. Samuels gives the following description of the term:

> It was in 1985 . . . that I coined the tag 'post-Jungian'. This was prompted mainly by my own confusion in a field that seemed utterly chaotic and without any maps or aids as the various groups and individuals fell out, split, and in some cases split again. I intended to indicate some connection to Jung and the traditions of thought and practice that had grown up around his name and also some distance or differentiation. In order to delineate post-Jungian analytical psychology, I adopt a pluralistic methodology in which dispute rather than consensus is permitted to define the field. The field is defined by the debates and arguments that threaten to destroy it and not by the core of commonly agreed ideas. A post-Jungian is someone who can plug into, be interested and energized by, and participate in post-Jungian debates whether on the basis of clinical interests, or intellectual exploration, or a combination of these.[20]

Given this definition, one would not expect a post-Jungian scholar to agree with every single word Jung ever wrote; nevertheless, one would expect there to be a substantial amount of continuity between their work and Jung's. In Samuels words, we would look for 'some connection to Jung and the traditions of thought and practice that [have] grown up around his name and also some distance or differentiation' in order to justify the label post-Jungian. It is my opinion that such a connection clearly exists between Stevens' work and Jung's, and that I am therefore justified in labelling Stevens a post-Jungian. If the reader accepts my argument that Campbell's ideas in phase three are virtually indistinguishable from Stevens' ideas, then it follows logically that Campbell (at least in phase three) should be seen as post-Jungian as well.

Samuels distinguishes three different 'schools' within the overall field of post-Jungian scholarship: the classical school, the developmental school and the archetypal school. Samuels gives the following description of the archetypal school:

> The archetypal school is perhaps no longer strictly a clinical group. Its principal writers valorize Jung's key concept of the archetype, using it as a base from which to explore and engage with the depth dimensions of all kinds of imaginal experience, whether dream or waking fantasy.[21]

As Stevens attaches such primary importance to the concept of the archetype, it is my opinion that we should see him as a post-Jungian of the archetypal school. Again, the logical conclusion is that we should therefore see Campbell's work in phase three as an example of the archetypal school as well. By this conclusion I don't mean to imply that Campbell was an active member of a certain type of social network that held common 'archetypal' ideas in phase three of his career. Campbell seems to have been a rather solitary figure, and although he frequently lectured at Jung centres throughout the United States, he certainly wasn't an active member of any Jungian organizations or clubs. In fact, in a letter written on 12 March 1980 (written in response to someone who had asked whether Campbell could recommend any good Jung scholars for an upcoming book with articles about Jung's ideas) Campbell even said that he had lost touch with the Jungian crowd, and that the scholars who he thought most highly of were all dead.[22] My conclusion that we should link Campbell to Samuel's 'archetypal school', then, does not imply that he was a member of a certain kind of social circle; it merely means that this school represents most accurately the kind of ideas that Campbell held. Both Stevens and Campbell attach primary importance to the concept of the archetype, and for this reason I believe that – given Samuels definitions as outlined above – both can be labelled post-Jungians of the archetypal school.

7.4 Reflections on the potential benefits of my findings

I will now offer my thoughts on the potential benefits of my arguments for other scholars, with a specific focus on the following three areas of investigation:

1. The academic study of Campbell's ideas (section 7.4.1)
2. The field of Jungian scholarship (section 7.4.2)
3. The field of Religious Studies (section 7.4.3)

7.4.1 Benefit to the academic study of Campbell's ideas

The first potential benefit of my book to this area that I would like to mention is that it shows how drastically Campbell's ideas changed over time. In my opinion, this fact has not been adequately acknowledged up until now. With the exception of Robert Segal, most scholars seem to assume that Campbell's theoretical outlook is roughly the same in all of his works, and readily combine quotes from books sometimes written 20 years apart to sketch a picture off Campbell's ideas about a certain topic. An example of this approach can be found in the book *Pathways to bliss*,[23] edited by David Kudler. In this book Kudler has selected for publication several transcriptions of lectures by Campbell which have been hard to find up until now, which is certainly an admirable endeavour. What Kudler has done, however, is to piece together the various chapters from several different lectures, often given in different years. What at first glance appears to be a single lecture upon examination often turns out to be a combination of sections from different lectures, sometimes given as many as ten years apart. In chapter three, for example ('Society and symbol'), Campbell – among other things – talks about how he feels Jung's concept of the archetype should be related to the concept of the IRM. As we have seen, Campbell's ideas about this topic were not the same in phase two and phase three. In this chapter, however, Kudler has combined texts written in phase two (1962) with texts written ten years later (1972 and 1973), when phase three was already well on its way. It seems to me that my book has shown that this is a highly inadequate way of dealing with Campbell's ideas, and certainly hope that it will contribute to rectifying such mistakes in the future.

A second, perhaps more important, contribution my arguments in this book might make to the academic study of Campbell's ideas is to help other scholars to understand Campbell's theoretical framework better. I believe it is absolutely crucial to realize the exact nature of Jung's influence on Campbell if one wants to have a clear picture of the 'essence' of the latter's core ideas. Campbell, as I have shown, made Jung a part of the very backbone of his theoretical framework in phase three, not only as far as the psychological theme is concerned but also as far as the metaphysical theme is concerned. Jung's work, then, is of vital importance if one wants to understand what Campbell's ultimate theoretical position was. It is to this understanding that I hope my book will make a contribution.

7.4.2 Benefit to the field of Jungian scholarship

Acknowledging the continuity between Campbell and Jung certainly has implications for the field of Jungian scholarship as well, as stressing this continuity makes it clear that Campbell is probably one of the most important popularizers of Jung's ideas. His work represents a kind of 'sanitized' version of Jung: there are no references to obscure alchemical texts which almost no one has heard of, no allusions to astrology, ghosts or other parapsychological phenomena, and no mention of the 'dark side of God' or UFOs either. Instead, Campbell relies mostly on the findings of modern science to explain his ideas: he uses the language of the ethologists (who are certainly more 'salonfähig' at present than Jung) to explain his ideas about the innate structures of the mind, and he uses the findings of quantum-mechanics when explaining his metaphysical ideas. In this way, Campbell has done a lot to make Jungian ideas more acceptable to what is certainly a very large audience indeed. Up until now, however, Jung scholars have not really acknowledged Jung's connection to Campbell at all. Steven Walker, for example, does not write more than two lines about Campbell in his otherwise excellent book *Jung and the Jungians on myth and mythology*.[24] Where he would have been justified, in my opinion, in devoting an entire chapter to Campbell, he writes only that Campbell seems to have drawn different conclusions about myth than Jung did.[25] Such an approach not only gives people the wrong impression of Campbell, it also gives people an inadequate impression of who the key players are in the post-Jungian 'ball-game'. Walker quite rightly mentions a host of important post-Jungian scholars, the most important ones being Marie-Louise von Franz and James Hillman. Omitting Campbell from this list seems to me a grave mistake, as his popularity has much to say about the resonance Jung's ideas still have with a very large audience. Von Franz and Hillman are certainly important in their own right, but neither of them ever had the rapport that Campbell had with such a large group of people from all across the globe.

7.4.3 Benefit to Religious Studies

I believe my arguments in this book have implications for the field of Religious Studies as well. First and foremost this is the case because 'Campbellian scholarship' (for want of a better word) is primarily a subfield of Religious Studies: most of the scholars writing about Campbell today work in Religious Studies, and for that reason a book which sheds new light on his ideas can be said to be relevant to the field. In my opinion, however, there are other areas of research within Religious Studies apart from 'Campbellian scholarship' to which my book contributes. I will now give my thoughts on what I consider to be the two most important ones.

Research into New Age practices and beliefs

In Religious Studies considerable interest exists in so-called New Age beliefs and practices. One of the foremost authorities on this topic is the

Dutch scholar Wouter Hanegraaff, who stresses that the primary difference between New Age religion and traditional, institutional forms of religion is that whereas the latter places emphasis on the authority of divine revelation, the former relies more on what he refers to as *gnosis*: 'the authority of personal spiritual experience or inner enlightenment'.[26] He also stresses that New Age beliefs and practices are a modern offshoot of what he labels 'Western esotericism', a historical tradition he describes as 'a distinct current of "alternative" religion and religious philosophy, the history of which can be traced from the Renaissance through the succeeding centuries, and indeed up to the New Age movement.'[27] According to Hanegraaff, Western esotericism can be characterized by the following four characteristics:

> [A] belief in invisible and noncausal 'correspondences' between all visible and invisible dimensions of the cosmos, a perception of nature as permeated and animated by a divine presence or life force, a concentration on the religious imagination as a power that provides access to worlds and levels of reality intermediate between the material world and God, and the belief in a process of spiritual transmutation by which the inner man is regenerated and reconnected with the divine.[28]

With the possible exception of a belief in 'worlds and levels of reality intermediate between the material world and God', all of these characteristics can be readily identified in Jung's work. The belief in noncausal 'correspondences' would undoubtedly be represented by Jung's concept of synchronicity (which he himself even called an 'a-causal' connecting principle), the 'divine presence' or 'life force' thought to be inherent in the cosmos could be seen as an equivalent of Jung's concept of the *unus mundus*, and finally the belief in a divine 'inner man' could be seen as similar to Jung's concept of the Self, which he often related to what he called the 'God-image' or *imago dei.*

Given these similarities, it should come as no surprise that Jung's ideas have been identified by a host of scholars as highly relevant to the study of Western esotericism in general, and the study of New Age beliefs and practices in particular. Scholars who have written about Jung in the context of New Age spirituality are Hanegraaff himself,[29] Tacey,[30] Segal,[31] Heelas[32] and Hammer.[33] It is to this field of investigation that I feel my book makes a contribution. Campbell's work is in many ways even more closely related to the New Age than Jung's work is. To begin with, Campbell is much more upfront and honest about his belief in a sacred dimension which is truly transcendent (as opposed to psychological or immanent), thus making his work even more appealing to a New Age audience. He also has a much more obvious connection to popular culture, which is relevant in the sense that the New Age movement has most of its adherents among non-academics as well. It could be argued, therefore, that Campbell has done more than anyone to spread Jung's ideas among the group of people who are most receptive to New Age ideas. This was already the case when he went on the lecture circuit after his retirement from Sarah Lawrence College (when he lectured primarily at 'human potential' centres on the North American west coast), but it is specifically the case when his ideas exploded into the mainstream through his appearance on PBS with Bill Moyers. By acknowledging the continuity between Jung and Campbell it becomes obvious that the 'Joseph Campbell phenomenon' is in many ways a 'Jung' phenomenon as well. An interesting topic for further research might be the extent to which Campbell has contributed to the spread of Jungian ideas among the popular culture, a topic that without a doubt would be of great interest to New Age scholars as well.

Recent 'evolutionary' approaches to the study of religion

In the introduction to his book *The blank slate* (which I already referred to in Chapter 3) the psychologist Steven Pinker writes the following:

> [Every society] must operate with a theory of human nature, and our intellectual mainstream is committed to [a highly specific one]. The theory is seldom articulated or overtly embraced, but it lies at the heart of a vast number of beliefs and policies. Bertrand Russel wrote, 'Every man, wherever he goes, is encompassed by a cloud of comforting convictions, which move with him like flies on a summer day.' For intellectuals today, many of those convictions are about psychology and social relations. I will refer to those convictions as the blank slate: the idea that the human mind has no inherent structure and can be inscribed at will by society or ourselves.[34]

This argument – that the notion of an infinitely malleable psyche is one of the most dominant paradigms among academics nowadays – has been argued by other scholars as well. Lida Cosmides and John Tooby, for example, even go as far as to call the blank slate paradigm the 'Standard Social Sciences Model' (SSSM),[35] indicating that the idea is particularly widespread among academics working in the social sciences.

Anthony Stevens makes a similar argument in his book *Archetype revisited*, in which he refers several times to the SSSM term coined by Cosmides and Tooby. As we have seen in Chapter 3, Stevens identifies several areas of scientific discovery that are currently challenging the blank slate or SSSM paradigm, the most important ones being ethology, evolutionary psychology and evolutionary psychiatry.[36] Both Pinker and Cosmides and Tooby make similar claims, although they identify slightly different fields. Pinker mentions cognitive science, neuroscience, behavioral genetics and evolutionary psychology;[37] Cosmides and Tooby mention evolutionary biology, cognitive science, behavioral ecology, hunter-gatherer studies, social anthropology, biological anthropology, primatology and neurobiology.[38] What Pinker, Stevens and Cosmides and Tooby have in common, though, is that all of them stress that the move away from the blank slate paradigm has only relatively recently begun to pick up pace. This is an observation that I agree with. Rather than being infinitely malleable, the human mind is increasingly being described by scholars in a host of different fields as equipped with a large number of innate functions and modules. The keyword in this development seems to be evolution. What all of the fields of investigation mentioned by Pinker, Stevens and Cosmides and Tooby have in common is that the scientists working in them all link their findings in some way or other to speculations about evolutionary processes. Even though the respective scientists may – and will – disagree about the details, most of them seem to agree as far as the big picture is concerned: that the mind's innate structures have all been shaped by mankind's common evolutionary history in some way or other. In Religious Studies, this 'evolutionary mindset' is commonplace among scholars who take a so-called cognitive theory approach. Again, the respective scholars disagree about the details, for example, about the question as to whether religion arose as a useful 'adaption' to our prehistoric environment (the so-called adaptionist viewpoint) or as a by-product of some other adaptive trait (the so-called spandrelist viewpoint, which is the one that Richard Dawkins endorses in *The god delusion*[39]).[40] As far as the big picture is concerned, however, the cognitive theory scholars all seem to be in agreement: religion can, and should be, related to the mind's cognitive structures, which in turn are seen as a product of our evolutionary history.

As Anthony Stevens points out in several of his books and articles, Jung's ideas have much in common with many of the above-named scientific theories that are currently challenging the blank slate model. In his book *Jung – a very short introduction*, for example, he offers the following quote from the French molecular biologist (and Nobel Laureate) Jacques Monod to illustrate this point:

> Everything comes from experience, yet not from actual experience, reiterated by each individual with each generation, but instead from experience accumulated by the entire ancestry of the species in the course of its evolution.[41]

If we compare this quote to the following quote from Jung's work, we can see that Stevens most definitely has a point:

> All those factors, therefore, that were essential to our near and remote ancestors will also be essential to us, for they are embedded in the inherited organic system.[42]

Given Campbell's debt to Jung, we would expect him to say similar things, which indeed he does:

> And who that has knowledge of the numerous vestigial structures of our anatomy, surviving from the days when we were beasts (for example, the muscles of the caudal vertebrae that once wagged our tail), would doubt that in the central nervous system comparable vestiges must remain . . . ?[43]

In Religious Studies, however, these similarities seem to have been completely overlooked up until now. I am aware of not a single scholar in Religious Studies writing about evolutionary psychology or cognitive theory who has made any connection to either Jung or Campbell whatsoever. This is somewhat odd, as outside of Religious Studies this connection has certainly been recognized. Even though their number is small, a select group of scholars has linked the ideas of Jung (and in a few cases also Campbell) to the scientific developments sketched above. I have already mentioned Stevens and the neurobiologists Newberg and D'Aquili[44] (see Chapter 1); here I would also like to draw attention to Gray,[45] Card,[46] Walters[47] and McDowell.[48] Yet I believe that my work in this book shows that the ideas of both Jung and Campbell are highly relevant to the current debate about the relationship between religion and evolutionary processes taking place among cognitive theory scholars working in Religious Studies. If anything, both Jung and Campbell should at the very least be recognized as important precursors who have explored this field in the past; however, I also believe that their ideas might have an inherent theoretical (as opposed to merely historical) relevance as well. Along with Stevens' book *Archetype revisited* (which I feel would be a particularly good place to start for cognitive theory scholars of religion to start their exploration of Jung's ideas), I believe that Campbell's discussion of the relationship between mythology and the concept of the IRM in the first two chapters of *Masks: primitive* (as well as, to a lesser extent, his discussion of the same topic in *Atlas: 1.1)* is also particularly relevant.

By claming this relevance for the ideas of Campbell and Jung, however, I do not mean to imply that their ideas should be thought of as true in the absolute sense. It is by no means my intention here to persuade the reader of becoming a staunch Jungian or 'Campbellian'; rather, I am merely pointing out that certain aspects of their theoretical frameworks can be said to be *useful*. Religious Studies, to my mind, remains a field where no truth with a Capital T can be established. Despite claims to the opposite by scholars like Wiebe,[49] I am of the opinion that one cannot claim 'hard' scientific validity for theories in the field of Religious Studies; rather, they can be said to be useful in the sense that they help to provide *insight*. To that effect, I agree with the anthropologist Victor Turner, who in his essay 'Social dramas and ritual metaphor' (1974) had the following to say about the way the merit of a thinker's theoretical framework should be evaluated:

> In moving from experience of social life to conceptualization and intellectual history, I follow the path of anthropologists almost everywhere. Although we take theories into the field with us, these become relevant only if and when they illuminate social reality. Moreover, we tend to find very frequently that it is not a theorist's whole system which so illuminates, but his scattered ideas, his flashes of insight taken out of systemic context and applied to scattered data. Such ideas have a virtue of their own and may generate new hypotheses. They even show how scattered facts may be systematically connected! Randomly distributed through some monstrous logical system, they resemble nourishing raisins in a cellular mass of inedible dough. The intuitions, not the tissue of logic connecting them, are what tend to survive in the field experience.[50]

I strongly believe that it is in this context that we should assess the merit of the ideas of Jung and Campbell as well. Is studying their ideas useful?

Despite the fact that we might object to some aspects of their theoretical framework, are there nevertheless some 'nourishing raisings' which might provide us with flashes of insight? I certainly hope that I have shown in this book that both Campbell and Jung had many such intuitions and ideas, and remain convinced that one of the most important fields of investigation within Religious Studies to which these ideas may be of use is the current cognitive theory approach.

Notes

1 Michael Toms, 'Interview with Joseph Campbell', *Sunrise*, August–September 1979 (Campbell Archive: box 113, folder A1), p. 329.
2 Published as chapter one of Joseph Campbell, *Gander*, p. 34.
3 Joseph Campbell, *Hero*, p. vii.
4 He does this when putting forward the theory that myths are consciously created (and teach a metaphysical message) at the end of *Hero* (part two, chapter one, section one). Here he states that this idea opposes the ideas of Jung and all other thinkers in the psychoanalytical 'school'.
5 Joseph Campbell, *Masks: creative*, p. 653.
6 C. Miodini, 'Unpublished interview with Joseph Campbell', 1980 (Campbell Archive: box 107, folder I83).
7 Ibid.
8 Toms, 'Interview with Joseph Campbell', p. 329.
9 Joseph Campbell, *An open life – Joseph Campbell in conversation with Michael Toms*, ed. John M. Maher and Dennie Briggs (New York: Harper & Row, 1990), p. 121.
10 Robert Segal, *Introduction*, p. 245.
11 Campbell, *Masks: creative*, p. 653.
12 Joseph Campbell, *Masks: primitive*, p. 48.
13 Campbell, *Hero*, p. 255.
14 Anthony Stevens, *Jung – a very short introduction* (Oxford: Oxford University Press, 2001), 57.
15 Segal, *Introduction*, p. 259.
16 Steven Walker, *Jung and the Jungians on myth and mythology: an introduction* (New York/London: Routledge, 2002).
17 Toms, 'Interview with Joseph Campbell', p. 329.
18 Jung, *CW 9 part 1*, p. 79.
19 Anthony Stevens, *Archetype revisited – an updated natural history of the self*, second edn (London: Brunner-Routledge, 2002), p. 46.
20 Polly Young-Eisendrath et al., eds., *The Cambridge companion to Jung* (Cambridge: Cambridge University Press, 1997), p. 7.
21 Ibid., p. 8.
22 Joseph Campbell, 'Letter to Vernon Gras', 12 March 1980 (Campbell Archive: box 125, folder 'Levi Straus [455]').

[23] Joseph Campbell, *Pathways to bliss – mythology and personal transformation*, ed. David Kudler, The collected works of Joseph Campbell (Novato: New World Library, 2004).

[24] Walker, *Jung and the Jungians on myth and mythology*.

[25] Ibid., p. 4.

[26] Wouter J. Hanegraaff, 'New Age religion', in *Religions in the modern world*, ed. Linda Woodhead, Paul Fletcher, Hiroko Kawanami and David Smith (Abingdon: Routledge, 2005 [2002]), p. 254.

[27] Ibid., p. 256.

[28] Ibid.

[29] Wouter J. Hanegraaff, *New Age religion and Western culture: esotericism in the mirror of secular thought* (Leiden: Brill, 1996).

[30] David Tacey, *Jung and the new age* (Hove: Brunner-Routledge, 2001).

[31] Robert Segal, 'Jung's psychologising of religion', in *Beyond New Age: exploring alternative spirituality*, ed. Steven Sutcliffe and Marion Bowman (Edinburgh: Edinburgh University Press, 2000).

[32] Paul Heelas, *The New Age movement: the celebration of the self and the sacralization of modernity* (Oxford: Blackwell, 1996).

[33] Olav Hammer, *Claiming knowledge: strategies of epistemology from theosophy to the New Age* (Leiden: Brill, 2001).

[34] Steven Pinker, *The blank slate: the modern denial of human nature* (London: Allen Lane, 2002), p. 2.

[35] Leda Cosmides et al., 'The psychological foundations of culture', in *The adapted mind: evolutionary psychology and the generation of culture*, ed. Jerome Barkow, Leda Cosmides and John Tooby (New York/Oxford: Oxford University Press, 1992), p. 23.

[36] Stevens, *Archetype revisited*.

[37] Steven Pinker, *The blank slate, the noble savage, and the ghost in the machine* [online] (Talk given at Yale University, 20–21 April 1999, accessed 15 April 2008); available from http://tinyurl.com/4h8bt3

[38] Cosmides et al., 'The psychological foundations of culture', p. 23.

[39] Richard Dawkins, *The god delusion* (London: Bantam Press, 2006).

[40] For a good overview of the differences between these two 'schools' see: Joseph Bulbulia, 'Area review: The cognitive and evolutionary psychology of religion', *Biology and philosophy* 19 (2004).

[41] Stevens, *Jung – a very short introduction*, p. 54.

[42] Jung, *CW 8*, par. 717.

[43] Campbell, *Masks: primitive*, p. 34.

[44] Andrew Newberg et al., *Why God won't go away: brain science and the biology of belief* (New York: Ballantine Books, 2001).

[45] Richard M. Gray, *Archetypal explorations: an integrative approach to human behaviour* (London: Routledge, 1996).

[46] Charles R. Card, 'The emergence of archetypes in present-day science and its significance for a contemporary philosophy of nature', in *Mind in time*, ed. B. Goertzel, A. Coombs and M. Germine (Creskill: Hampton Press, 2000).

[47] Sally Walters, 'Algorithms and archetypes: evolutionary psychology and Carl Jung's theory of the collective unconscious', *Journal of social and evolutionary systems* 17, no. 3 (1994).

[48] Maxson J. McDowell, 'Principle of organization: a dynamic-systems view of the archetype-as-such', *Journal of analytical psychology* 46, no. 4 (2001).

[49] Donald Wiebe, 'Appropriating religion: understanding religion as an object of science', in *Approaching religion (part one)*, ed. T. Ahlback (Stockholm: Almqvist & Wiksell International, 1999). Quoted in Veikko Anttonen, 'Identifying the generative mechanisms of religion: the issue of origin revisited', in *Current approaches in the cognitive science of religion*, ed. Ilkka Pyysiainen and Veikko Anttonen (London: Continuum, 2002).

[50] Victor Turner, 'Social dramas and ritual metaphors', in *Ritual, play, and performance: readings in the social sciences/theatre*, ed. R. Schechner and M. Schuman (New York: Seabury, 1976).

Appendix

Paragraph from *The integration of the personality*

Another well-known expression of the archetype is myth and fable. But here also we are dealing with conscious and specifically moulded forms that have been handed on, relatively unchanged, through long periods of time. It is thus only indirectly that the concept of the archetype fits the representations collectives, for it properly designates the psychic content that has as yet been subjected to no conscious treatment and so represents an immediate psychic actuality. There is a considerable difference between such an archetype and the formula that has become historic or has been elaborated. Especially on the higher levels of esoteric teaching, the archetypes appear in a form that usually reveals in an unmistakable way the elements of judgement and valuation introduced by conscious elaboration. On the other hand their immediate manifestation, as it confronts us in dreams and visions, is much more natural, less understandable: or more naïve than in the myth for example. In this respect the fairy tale is, no doubt, much truer to nature.[1]

Paragraph from *Collected works 9 part 1*

Another well-known expression of the archetypes is myth and fairytale. But here too we are dealing with forms that have received a specific stamp and have been handed down through long periods of time. The term "archetype" thus applies only indirectly to the "representations collectives," since it designates only those psychic contents which have not yet been submitted to conscious elaboration and are therefore an immediate datum of psychic experience. In this sense there is a considerable difference between the archetype and the historical formula that has evolved. Especially on the higher levels of esoteric teaching the archetypes appear in a form that reveals quite unmistakably the critical and evaluating influence of conscious elaboration. Their immediate manifestation, as we encounter it in dreams and visions, is much more individual, less understandable, and more naïve than in myths, for example. The archetype is essentially an unconscious content that is altered by becoming conscious and by being perceived, and it takes its colour from the individual consciousness in which it happens to appear [footnote].

[footnote]
'One must, for the sake of accuracy, distinguish between "archetype" and "archetypal ideas." The archetype as such is a hypothetical and irrepresentable model, something like the "pattern of behaviour" in biology. Cf. "On the Nature of the Psyche," sec. 7.'[2]

Notes

[1] Carl G. Jung, *The integration of the personality*, trans. Stanley M. Dell (New York: Farrar & Rinehart, 1939), p. 54.
[2] Jung, *CW 9 part 1*, par. 6.

Bibliography

Anttonen, Veikko. 'Identifying the generative mechanisms of religion: the issue of origin revisited.' In *Current approaches in the cognitive science of religion*, ed. Ilkka Pyysiainen and Veikko Anttonen, pp. 14–37. London: Continuum, 2002.

Badcock, Christopher. *Evolutionary psychology: a critical introduction*. Cambridge, UK: Polity Press, 2000.

Ballas, Costis. 'Unpublished interview with Joseph Campbell.' 1985 (Campbell Archive: box 107, folder I2).

Berger, Joseph. 'A teacher of legends becomes one himself.' *New York times*, 10 December 1988 (Campbell Archive: box 106, folder AA18).

Bruckner, D. J. R. 'Joseph Campbell: 70 years of making connections.' *New York times book review*, 18 December 1983 (Campbell Archive: box 107, folder I6).

Bulbulia, Joseph. 'Area review: The cognitive and evolutionary psychology of religion.' *Biology and philosophy* 19 (2004): 655–686.

Campbell, Joseph. 'Strictly platonic.' *Liberty magazine* 1933 (Campbell Archive: box 107, folder F12).

—. *Oriental mythology*. Vol. 2. 4 vols. *The masks of God*. New York: Viking Press, 1962.

—. *Primitive mythology*. Vol. 1. 4 vols. *The masks of God*. New York: Viking Press, 1965 [1959].

—. *Creative mythology*. Vol. 4. 4 vols. *The masks of God*. New York: Penguin Books, 1968.

—. *Myths to live by*. New York: Bantam Books, 1972.

—. *The mythic image*. New York: MJF Books, 1974.

—. *The power of myth*, ed. Betty Sue Flowers. New York: Doubleday, 1988.

—. *The way of the animal powers – mythologies of the primitive hunters and gatherers*. Vol. 1, part 1. 5 vols. Historical atlas of world mythology. New York: Harper & Row, 1988.

—. *The flight of the wild gander – explorations in the mythological dimensions of fairy tales, legends and symbols*. New York: Harper Perennial, 1990.

—. *The hero's journey: Joseph Campbell on his life and work*, ed. Phil Cousineau. San Francisco/London: Harper & Row, 1990.

—. *An open life – Joseph Campbell in conversation with Michael Toms*, ed. John M. Maher and Dennie Briggs. New York: Harper & Row, 1990.

—. *A Joseph Campbell companion – reflections on the art of living*, ed. Diane K. Osbon. New York: HarperCollins, 1991.

—. *The lost teachings of Joseph Campbell volume 2*. [Audiotape]. Redmond: Zygon International, 1993.

—. *The hero with a thousand faces*. London: Fontana Press, 1993 [1949].

—. *The mythic dimension – selected essays 1959–1987.* The collected works of Joseph Campbell, ed. Antony van Couvering. New York: Harper Collins, 1997.

—. *Pathways to bliss – mythology and personal transformation.* The collected works of Joseph Campbell, ed. David Kudler. Novato: New World Library, 2004.

—. 'Letter to Pascal Covici.' 4 January 1957 (Campbell Archive: box 108, folder P1).

—. 'Letter to Vernon Gras.' 12 March 1980 (Campbell Archive: box 125, folder 'Levi Straus [455]').

Campbell, Joseph, Maud Oakes and Jeff King. *Where the two came to their father: a Navaho war memorial* Bollingen Series I. Richmond: Old Dominion Foundation, 1943.

Campbell, Joseph and Henry Morton Robinson. *A skeleton key to Finnegan's wake.* New York: Harcourt, Brace & Co., 1944.

Card, Charles R. 'The emergence of archetypes in present-day science and its significance for a contemporary philosophy of nature.' In *Mind in time,* ed. B. Goertzel, A. Coombs and M. Germine. Creskill: Hampton Press, 2000.

Clarke, J. J. *In search of Jung.* New York: Routledge, 1992.

Cole, K. C. 'Master of the myth.' *Newsweek,* 14 November 1988 (Campbell Archive: box 113, folder A92).

Collins, Tom. 'Unpublished interview with Joseph Campbell.' 1985 (Campbell Archive: box 107, folder I9).

—. 'Mythic reflections – an interview with Joseph Campbell.' *The new story* 12 (winter 1985).

Colum, Padraic, ed. *The complete Grimm's fairy tales.* New York/Toronto: Pantheon, 1944.

Cosmides, Leda and John Tooby. 'The psychological foundations of culture.' In *The adapted mind: Evolutionary psychology and the generation of culture,* ed. Jerome Barkow, Leda Cosmides and John Tooby. New York/Oxford: Oxford University Press, 1992.

Dawkins, Richard. *The god delusion.* London: Bantam Press, 2006.

Durkheim, Emile. *The rules of sociological method.* Translated by S. S. Solvay and J. H. Mueller. New York: Free Press, 1950 [1895].

The encyclopedia of religion. ed. Mircea Eliade. New York: Macmillan.

The Freud-Jung letters. Translated by R. F. C. Hull and Ralph Manheim, ed. William McGuire. London: Penguin Books, 1979.

Golden, Kenneth L., ed. *Uses of comparative mythology: essays on the work of Joseph Campbell.* New York/London: Garland Publishing, 1992.

Gray, Richard M. *Archetypal explorations: an integrative approach to human behaviour.* London: Routledge, 1996.

Hammer, Olav. *Claiming Knowledge: Strategies of Epistemology from Theosophy to the New Age.* Leiden: Brill, 2001.

Hanegraaff, Wouter J. *New Age religion and Western culture: esotericism in the mirror of secular thought.* Leiden: Brill, 1996.

—. 'New Age religion.' In *Religions in the modern world,* ed. Linda Woodhead, Paul Fletcher, Hiroko Kawanami and David Smith. Abingdon: Routledge, 2005 [2002].

Hauke, Christopher. 'The unconscious: personal and collective.' In *The handbook of Jungian psychology,* ed. Renos K. Papadopoulos. New York/London: Routledge, 2006.

Heelas, Paul. *The New Age movement: the celebration of the self and the sacralization of modernity*. Oxford: Blackwell, 1996.
Helgesen, Sally. 'Every day column.' *Harper's bookletter*, 14 February 1977 (Campbell Archive: box 113, folder A33).
Henderson, Mary. *Star wars: the magic of myth*. New York: Bantam, 1997.
Hinde, R. A. 'Ethological models and the concept of "drive".' *The British journal for the philosophy of science* 6, no. 24 (February 1956): pp. 321–331.
Homans, Peter. *Jung in context: modernity and the making of a psychology*. Chicago: University of Chicago Press, 1995 [1979].
Jacobi, Jolande. *Complex, archetype, symbol*. London: Routledge & Kegan Paul, 1959.
—. *The psychology of C.G. Jung*. London: Routledge, 1999 [1942].
Joseph Campbell Foundation update April 2007 [online] (21 April 2007, accessed 30 April 2007); available from http://tinyurl.com/5rqg37
Jung, Carl G. *The psychology of the unconscious*. Translated by Beatrice M. Hinkle. London: Kegan Paul, Trench, Trubner & Co. Ltd., 1922 [1912].
—. *Collected papers on analytical psychology*. Second edn, ed. Constance E. Long. London: Bailliére, Tindall and Cox, 1922 [1917].
—. *Psychological types*. London: Routledge & Kegan Paul, 1923 [1921].
—. *Wandlungen und symbole der libido*. Leipzig: F. Deuticke, 1925 [1912].
—. *Dream symbols of the individuation process*. New York: Private copyright, 1937.
—. *The integration of the personality*. Translated by Stanley M. Dell. New York: Farrar & Rinehart, 1939.
—. *Symbols of transformation*. Translated by R. F. C. Hull. Vol. 5. 20 vols. The collected works of C.G. Jung, ed. Herbert Read, Michael Fordham and Gerhard Adler. London: Routledge & Kegan Paul, 1956.
—. *Gegenwart und zukunft*. Zürich: Rascher-Verlag, 1957.
—. *Mysterium Coniunctionis*. Translated by R. F. C. Hull. Vol. 14. 20 vols. The collected works of C.G. Jung, ed. Herbert Read, Michael Fordham and Gerhard Adler. London: Routledge & Kegan Paul, 1963.
—. *Civilisation in transition*. Translated by R. F. C. Hull. Vol. 10. 20 vols. The collected works of C.G. Jung, ed. Herbert Read, Michael Fordham, Gerhard Adler and William McGuire. Princeton: Princeton University Press, 1964.
—. *Memories, dreams, reflections*. New York: Random House, 1965 [1961].
—. *Two essays on analytical psychology*. Translated by R. F. C. Hull. Vol. 7. 20 vols. Second edn. The collected works of C.G. Jung, ed. Herbert Read, Michael Fordham, Gerhard Adler and William McGuire. Princeton: Princeton University Press, 1966 [1953].
—. *Analytical psychology: its theory and practice; the Tavistock lectures*. New York: Pantheon Books, 1968.
—. *The archetypes and the collective unconscious*. Translated by R. F. C. Hull. Vol. 9, part 1. 20 vols. Second edn. The collected works of C.G. Jung, ed. Herbert Read, Michael Fordham, Gerhard Adler and William McGuire. London: Routledge & Kegan Paul, 1968 [1959].
—. *The structure and dynamics of the psyche*. Translated by R. F. C. Hull. Vol. 8. 20 vols. Second edn. The collected works of C.G. Jung, ed. Herbert Read, Michael Fordham, Gerhard Adler and William McGuire. Princeton: Princeton University Press, 1969 [1960].

—. *Psychological types.* Translated by R. F. C. Hull and H. G. Baynes. Vol. 6. 20 vols. The collected works of C.G. Jung, ed. Herbert Read, Michael Fordham, Gerhard Adler and William McGuire. Princeton: Princeton University Press, 1971.

—. *The visions seminars.* Zürich: Zürich Spring Publications, 1976.

—. *Flying saucers: a modern myth of things seen in the skies.* Princeton: Princeton University Press, 1978.

—. *Psychology and the East.* Princeton: Princeton University Press, 1978.

—. *The symbolic life.* Translated by R. F. C. Hull. Vol. 18. 20 vols. Second edn. The collected works of C.G. Jung, ed. Herbert Read, Michael Fordham, Gerhard Adler and William McGuire. Princeton: Princeton University Press, 1980 [1950].

—. 'Letter to Joseph Campbell.' 4 November 1953 (Campbell Archive: box 116, folder L694a).

Jung, Carl G., and C. Kerényi. *Essays on a science of mythology: the myth of the divine child and the mysteries of Eleusis.* New York: Pantheon Books, 1949.

Jung, Carl G., and W. Pauli. *The Interpretation of nature and the psyche.* New York: Pantheon Books, 1955.

Keen, Sam. 'Man and myth: a conversation with Joseph Campbell.' *Psychology today,* July 1971 (Campbell Archive: box 107, folder I11).

Kisly, Lorraine. 'Living myths: a conversation with Joseph Campbell.' *Parabola* 1, no. 2, 1976 (Campbell Archive: box 107, folder I13).

Larsen, Stephen. 'Freud, Jung and Campbell.' In *Uses of comparative mythology: essays on the work of Joseph Campbell,* ed. Kenneth L. Golden. New York/London: Garland publishing, 1992.

Larsen, Stephen, and Robin Larsen. *A fire in the mind – the life of Joseph Campbell.* New York: Doubleday, 1991.

Lobell, John. 'Interview with Joseph Campbell.' *New age book review* 1983 (Campbell Archive: box 107, folder I16).

—. *Joseph Campbell – the man & his ideas.* San Anselmo: Joseph Campbell Foundation, 1993.

McDermott, Gerald. 'Interview with Joseph Campbell.' *New Boston review* 1, no. 2, 1975 (Campbell Archive: box 107, folder I18).

McDowell, Maxson J. 'Principle of organization: a dynamic-systems view of the archetype-as-such.' *Journal of analytical psychology* 46, no. 4 (2001): pp. 637–654.

McKnight, Michael. 'Elders and guides: a conversation with Joseph Campbell.' *Parabola* V, no. 1, 1980 (Campbell Archive: box 107).

Main, Roderick, ed. *Jung on synchronicity and the paranormal.* London: Routledge, 1997.

Mead, Margaret. *Sex and temperament in three primitive societies.* New York: Harper Perennial, 2001 [1935].

Miodini, C. 'Unpublished interview with Joseph Campbell.' 1980 (Campbell Archive: box 107, folder I83).

Mishlove, Jeffrey. *Thinking allowed: conversations on the leading edge of knowledge and discovery.* Tulsa: Council Oak Books, 1995.

Moss, Linda. 'Myth to the money at doubleday.' *Crain's New York business,* 16 January 1989 (Campbell Archive: box 106, folder AA70).

Newberg, Andrew , Eugene D'Aquili and Vincent Rause. *Why God won't go away: brain science and the biology of belief.* New York: Ballantine Books, 2001.

Newlove, Donald. 'Interview with Joseph Campbell.' *Esquire* 88 (September 1977).

Nigg, Joe and Derrick Jensen. 'An interview with the master of mythology Joseph Campbell.' *Bloomsbury review*, April/May 1984 (Campbell Archive: box 107, folder I25).

Noel, D. C., ed. *Paths to the power of myth: Joseph Campbell and the study of religion*. New York: Crossroad, 1990.

Otto, Rudolf. *The idea of the holy*. London: Oxford University Press, 1925.

Palmer, Michael. *Freud and Jung on religion*. London: Routledge, 1997.

Pinker, Steven. *The blank slate: the modern denial of human nature*. London: Allen Lane, 2002.

—. *The blank slate, the noble savage, and the ghost in the machine* [online] (Talk given at Yale University, 20–21 April 1999, accessed 15 April 2008 online); available from http://tinyurl.com/4h8bt3

Plotkin, Henry. *Evolution in mind: an introduction to evolutionary psychology*. Cambridge, MA: Harvard University Press, 1998.

Radin, Paul. *The trickster: a study in American Indian mythology*. New York: Philosophical Library, 1956.

Rauch, Stephen. *Neil Gaiman's the Sandman and Joseph Campbell: in search of the modern myth*. Holicong: Wildside Press, 2003.

Reitman, Ivan. 'Ghost busters.' 105 min. United States: Columbia Tri-Star, 1984.

Segal, Robert. *Joseph Campbell – an introduction*. New York/London: Garland Publishing, 1987.

—. *Joseph Campbell – an introduction (revised edition)*. New York: Penguin Books (Mentor imprint), 1990.

—. 'Book review: "The transformation of consciousness in myth" by John W. Tigue.' *Zygon* 32.3 (1997).

—. 'Jung's psychologising of religion.' In *Beyond New Age: exploring alternative spirituality*, ed. Steven Sutcliffe and Marion Bowman. Edinburgh: Edinburgh University Press, 2000.

Semon, Richard. *The Mneme*. London: George Allen & Unwin, 1921.

Sharp, Daryl. *Jung lexicon – a primer of terms and concepts*. Toronto: Inner City Books, 1991.

Sharpe, E. J. *Comparative religion: a history*. London: Duckworth, 1975.

Smith, Will. *Press conference about the movie I am Legend* [online] (2007, accessed 12 June 2008); available from http://tinyurl.com/594gg2

Stevens, Anthony. *Archetype – a natural history of the self*. London: Routledge & Kegan Paul, 1982.

—. *Jung – a very short introduction*. Oxford: Oxford University Press, 2001.

—. *Archetype revisited – an updated natural history of the self*. Second edn. London: Brunner-Routledge, 2002.

—. 'The archetypes.' In *The handbook of Jungian psychology*, ed. Renos K. Papadopoulos. New York/London: Routledge, 2006.

—. 'Thoughts on the psychobiology of religion and the neurobiology of archetypal experience.' *Zygon* 21 (March 1986).

Stevens, Anthony and John Price. *Evolutionary psychology: a new beginning*. Second edn. London: Routledge, 2000.

Sureck, Nancy. 'In class with Joseph Campbell.' *Sarah Lawrence College magazine* 1986 (Campbell Archive: box 106, folder AA33), p. 4.

Suzuki, D. T. *Introduction to Zen Buddhism (with a foreword by C.G. Jung)*. New York: Philosophical Library, 1949 [1934].

Tacey, David. *Jung and the new age*. Hove: Brunner-Routledge, 2001.

Tigue, John W. *The transformation of consciousness in myth: integrating the thought of Jung and Campbell*. The reshaping of psychoanalysis series, vol. 4. New York: Peter Lang, 1994.

Toms, Michael. 'Interview with Joseph Campbell.' *Sunrise*, August–September 1979 (Campbell Archive: box 113, folder A1).

Turner, Victor. 'Social dramas and ritual metaphors.' In *Ritual, play, and performance: Readings in the social sciences/theatre*, ed. R. Schechner and M. Schuman. New York: Seabury, 1976.

Vogler, Christopher. *The writer's journey*. London: Pan Macmillan, 1999.

von Franz, Marie-Louise. *C.G. Jung – his myth in our time*. New York: Putnam, 1975.

Walker, Steven. *Jung and the Jungians on myth and mythology: an introduction*. New York/London: Routledge, 2002.

Walters, Sally. 'Algorithms and archetypes: evolutionary psychology and Carl Jung's theory of the collective unconscious.' *Journal of social and evolutionary systems* 17, no. 3 (1994): pp. 287–306.

Watson, J. B. *Behaviorism*. Second edn. New York: Norton, 1930.

Whitney, Mark. *Matter of heart*. [DVD]. USA: Kino Video, 2004 [1986].

Wiebe, Donald. 'Appropriating religion: understanding religion as an object of science.' In *Approaching religion (part one)*, ed. T. Ahlback. Stockholm: Almqvist & Wiksell International, 1999.

Young-Eisendrath, Polly and Terence Dawson, eds. *The Cambridge companion to Jung*. Cambridge: Cambridge University Press, 1997.

Index

www.ingramcontent.com/pod-product-compliance
Ingram Content Group UK Ltd.
Pitfield, Milton Keynes, MK11 3LW, UK
UKHW020810290926
15470UKWH00003B/1070

9 781441 151124